*Magic
Maker*

Magic Maker

THE ENCHANTED PATH TO CREATIVITY

Pam Grossman

HAY HOUSE

Carlsbad, California • New York City
London • Sydney • New Delhi

Published in the United Kingdom by:
Hay House UK Ltd, 1st Floor, Crawford Corner, 91–93 Baker Street, London W1U 6QQ
Tel: +44 (0)20 3927 7290; www.hayhouse.co.uk

Text © Pam Grossman, 2025

The moral rights of the authors have been asserted.

This edition published by arrangement with VIKING, an imprint and registered trademark of Penguin Random House LLC.

Grateful acknowledgment is made for permission to reprint the following:

Doreen Valiente, "The Spell of the Cord" from *Witchcraft for Tomorrow*. Published in 1978 by Robert Hale Ltd., London. Used with the consent of The Doreen Valiente Foundation.

Anne Waldman, excerpt from "Fast Speaking Woman" from *Fast Speaking Woman: Chants and Essays*. Copyright © 1975, 1978, 1996 by Anne Waldman. Reprinted with the permission of The Permissions Company, LLC on behalf of City Lights Books, www.citylights.com. All rights reserved.

Diane di Prima, excerpt from "Revolutionary Letter #68—Life Chant" from *Revolutionary Letters: Expanded Edition*. Copyright © 1971, 2020 by Diane di Prima. Reprinted with the permission of The Permissions Company, LLC on behalf of City Lights Books, www.citylights.com. All rights reserved.

June Jordan, excerpt from "Intifada Incantation: Poem #8 for b.b.L." from *Directed by Desire: The Complete Poems of June Jordan*, Copper Canyon Press. Copyright © Christopher D. Meyer, 2007. Reprinted by permission of the Frances Goldin Literary Agency.

Diane di Prima, excerpt from "Rant" from *Pieces of a Song: Selected Poems*. Copyright © 2014 by Diane di Prima. Reprinted with the permission of The Permissions Company, LLC on behalf of City Lights Books, citylights.com. All rights reserved.

Designed by Alexis Sulaimani

All rights reserved. No part of this book may be reproduced by any mechanical, photographic or electronic process, or in the form of a phonographic recording; nor may it be stored in a retrieval system, transmitted or otherwise be copied for public or private use, other than for 'fair use' as brief quotations embodied in articles and reviews, without prior written permission of the publisher.

The information given in this book should not be treated as a substitute for professional medical advice; always consult a medical practitioner. Any use of information in this book is at the reader's discretion and risk. Neither the authors nor the publisher can be held responsible for any loss, claim or damage arising out of the use, or misuse, of the suggestions made, the failure to take medical advice or for any material on third-party websites.

A catalogue record for this book is available from the British Library.

Tradepaper ISBN: 978-1-83782-272-0
E-book ISBN: 978-1-83782-273-7
Audiobook ISBN: 978-1-83782-274-4

10 9 8 7 6 5 4 3 2 1

This product uses responsibly sourced papers, including recycled materials and materials from other controlled sources. For more information, see www.hayhouse.co.uk

The authorized representative in the EU for product safety and compliance is Penguin Random House Ireland, Morrison Chambers, 32 Nassau Street, Dublin D02 YH68, Ireland. https://eu-contact.penguin.ie

Printed and bound by CPI Group (UK) Ltd, Croydon CR0 4YY

For my magical makers, Nina and Rich

The investigations of the magician and the
artist, when they *enchant the universe*, seem to me
guided by the feeling that is acquainted with freedom.

René Magritte, Enquiry response in *L'Art Magique*

You are creator and creation. Your life is craft, your
supple body molded by word, sculpted by desire, fired by
deed. You poise yourself between life and fate, the will of
men and the will of gods. In the beat of a heart, the suck of
breath, you are the universe. Making. Making. Making.

Normandi Ellis, *Awakening Osiris*

Contents

Introduction xiii

PART I
Initiation

In Defense of Magic ✴ 5

So What Is Magic Exactly? ✴ 14

The Artful Occult ✴ 19

Maker as Magician ✴ 28

Magic-Made ✴ 38

PART II
Supernatural Preparation

Cleansing/Clearing ✴ 47

Circling/Centering ✴ 57

Invocation/Altar-cation ✳ *67*

Anointment/Adornment ✳ *74*

Shape-Shifting/Name-Taking ✳ *85*

PART III

The Craft

INSPIRED INPUT ✳ *105*

Opening the Channel ✳ *109*

Spiritual Advisors ✳ *113*

Automatic for the People ✳ *119*

Gettin' 'Mancy ✳ *123*

Cartomancy ✳ *126*

Bibliomancy ✳ *132*

Other Wordy Oracles ✳ *136*

Handy Advice ✳ *142*

The Art of Augury ✳ *144*

Nocturnal Transmissions ✳ *150*

ENCHANTED OUTPUT ✳ *153*

Bewitching Intentions ✳ *159*

Entrancing Energy ✳ *165*

Musica Magica ✳ *169*

Word Witchery ✳ *178*

Magic Markers ✳ *186*

Numinous Numbers ✳ *192*

Magical Correspondences ✳ *200*

Raising the Dead ✳ *207*

PART IV

Keeping the Cauldron Lit

DEMON SLAYING ✳ *215*

The Demon of Self-Doubt ✳ *222*

The Demon of Distraction ✳ *225*

The Demon of Inertia ✳ *228*

The Demon of Scarcity ✳ *232*

The Demon of Perfectionism ✳ *238*

The Demon of Suffering ✳ *242*

The Demon of Judgment
(Demon of All Demons) ✳ *246*

MYSTIC GIFTS ✳ *251*

The Gift of Play ✳ *257*

The Gift of Collaboration ✳ *266*

The Gift of Divine Timing ✷ *271*

The Gift of Place ✷ *276*

The Gift of Handcraft ✷ *282*

The Gift of Eternity ✷ *287*

The Gift of Devotion ✷ *293*

PART V

Complete Magic

RITUALS FOR RELEASING ✷ *305*

Revel ✷ *309*

Request ✷ *311*

Respect ✷ *315*

Reveal ✷ *317*

Return ✷ *319*

Afterword: A Magician Imagines ✷ *323*

Acknowledgments ✷ *331*

Index ✷ *337*

About the Author ✷ *353*

INTRODUCTION

Writing a book about creativity and magic requires a strange sort of double consciousness.

Throughout the process of writing this book, I found myself turning again and again to many magical techniques to help bring it into being. The gods breathed its first spark of inspiration into my consciousness many years ago, and I've been ignited by the notion of the creator as magician—and magician as creator—ever since.

When it finally came time to put these ideas into words, I lit my candles, invited otherworldly intervention, and drew invisible forces down into my magic circle and onto each blank page. Day after day I worked at keeping the creative fires burning and demons at bay so that I might eventually (gods willing) finish it. I cast my spells and summoned supernatural support, welcoming whatever came through with curiosity and a hopeful heart.

Thankfully, my arcane RSVP did not go unanswered. Messages arrived. Occult casseroles were cooked. Beings turned up with party hats and surprising presents and plenty—and I mean *plenty*—to say. They gave me guidance and kept me company as I strove to catch their words in my net. I did my darndest to do them justice—attempting to translate their boundless, multidimensional ideas into a text that is organized, cogent, and imaginatively nutritive.

By the time you read this, I will have also employed magic to release

INTRODUCTION

this book into the world so that it may reach the readers it's meant to for whatever reasons Spirit has in store.

I'm so glad that it found you.

If you've read this far, I imagine you have some curiosity about magic, even if you don't consider yourself an all-in believer. Whether you take my words literally or metaphorically is entirely up to you and won't affect the efficacy of these techniques in the least. When I write of Spirit or spirits, you may replace those terms with whatever analogue feels right to you. Energy, entity, deity, daemon—it truly doesn't matter what you call Creative Force or any anthropomorphized originator of it. You just need to be open to the idea that this force is relational. That it can be connected with, communicated with, cooperated with, collaborated with. And that it's possible that it comes not only *from* you but also *to* you from somewhere or something else.

This book is for anyone who feels intrigued by the notion that creativity is an expression of the spirit as well as the intellect. It does *not* suggest that magic is a replacement for hard work. Would that I could wave a magic wand and have this book be written for me! But labor is an essential part of any creative process. Even if you engage in magical practice of some kind, you still have to get your butt in the seat, studio, or other incubation chamber of choice, day in and day out—and I would never suggest otherwise or trust anyone who does. Like any action of intentional enchantment, the creative act requires hard work and an energetic exchange. Many make the mistake of assuming that creativity is easy. That all one must do is show up (as if showing up is always so simple!) and let the ideas come. And while on the best days the creative process can absolutely feel like a faucet of inspiration from Elsewhere has been turned on, there are plenty of times when it feels like ice-skating on quicksand.

INTRODUCTION

There is no cheat code to generativity. Manifesting anything new is a devotional act. It requires our time, our attention, our resources, our commitment. At some moments these offerings can feel like a joy and at others, a loving sacrifice—or, let's be honest, a total fucking drag. And while I have real issues with the cliché of the struggling artist (more on that later), there are certainly times when the creative process is full of inner and outer obstacles that we must overcome in order to see our project through. The same is true of undergoing a magical initiation, casting a spell, or conducting a sacred ceremony. The efficacy of each is directly related to how much is poured into them. One must care about, and care for, their magic. And to do this well takes a specific sort of skill: the ability to let go while never fully letting up.

Engaging with magic won't immediately bring your projects to completion or help you master a new skill overnight. What using magical techniques *can* do is broaden the spectrum of what is possible for you to make and bring more inspiration, ease, and support to you in your making. And this is true whether you're a painter, a coder, a potter, or a composer. You might be an architect, an astrophysicist, or an entrepreneur. A stay-at-home dad who loves to doodle or the empress of a media empire. Creativity comes in countless forms, and magic is an ever-replenishing resource.

I've experienced this firsthand over decades as a writer, curator, and podcaster, as well as a lifelong student of various schools of esoteric thought, from witchcraft to alchemy to Jewish mysticism to Zen Buddhism. I've identified as a witch for much of my life, though that word doesn't encapsulate the full scope of my seeking (and what word does?). I do know this: my creativity and my spirituality have always felt profoundly linked.

INTRODUCTION

For our purposes I'll say I'm a Magic Maker, and since this book called you to it, I presume that you're one as well (even if you don't realize it yet). I believe that the creative impulse is inherently magical, and I believe that magical practice is the most potent when it's the most personal. In other words, creativity is the truest expression of our magic. And our magic is made more powerful when expressed with sincerity from our own unique point of view.

The path that led me to this conclusion is a weird and winding one, but the worthwhile paths always are, aren't they?

Or perhaps a truer telling of this tale is to say that all my life I've been on three paths at the same time: that of the artist, the researcher, and the witch. The mythologically infused poems and paintings I made throughout my formative years, my studies in anthropology and art history as an undergrad, and my identity as a magic-practicing Pagan that deepened during adulthood—all of this informed my search for meaning in different, albeit complementary, ways. Eventually, however, I realized that each of these paths took me to the same clearing. (Hecate, goddess of the crossroads, was no doubt pleased by this arrival.) It's been a lifetime of trying to reconcile these varying approaches and interests of mine, and I'm happy—relieved, really—that I have distilled it all enough within the alembic of myself to be able to share some of the resulting elixir here with you now.

So many of life's great lessons, I've found, require a spiraling back to what we intuitively knew as children. The Surrealist artist and esoteric scholar Kurt Seligmann wrote, "In every man there is a child that yearns to play, and the most attractive game is occultation, mystery." Gratefully, my own occulted inner child has never been fully hidden away from me, as I never stopped believing in magic. If seeking mystery is a game, then it's one I've been playing quite consistently, though the trappings keep changing.

INTRODUCTION

I first got some inkling about creativity and magic being interconnected when I was very small.

My earliest memory of writing from some other, deeper state took place in the temples of art. As a child, my parents would take me to museums and let me roam freely from painting to painting without any sort of agenda or instruction, following whatever called to me. I would drift through the galleries, notebook in hand, like a little beauty-hungry ghost. When I felt a pull toward a particular piece, I would stop in front of it and write whatever came to me. Usually these were poems about the work: how they looked, how they made me feel, what they made me think about. The experience of writing an ode to one of Morris Louis's prismatic *Unfurled* paintings left a particularly lasting impression on me. As I stood in front of his enormous, color-streaked canvas, the words came tumbling out of me with ease and ecstasy. It wasn't writing for any practical purpose, really. No one had assigned it, nor was it something I penned with the intention of showing anyone. I was doing it because I felt called to. I was doing it because I wanted to melt into something gorgeous and ineffable and grand, and writing let me be even closer to that wondrous Whatever It Was. To step inside it somehow, and swim in its swirling.

I later learned that this technique of writing about a work of art is called *ekphrasis*, from the Greek words for "out" and "speak." The phrase implies that the writer is speaking out about a piece—describing it and adding their own embellishments to it through their unique interpretation. But my later experiences with ekphrasis have made me wonder if something else is speaking out from the work and through us. It's as if an animating force fills the artist and infuses whatever they create, and that creation can then get amplified by another artist in a different medium. The whole experience feels holographic, and arguably might be considered

INTRODUCTION

a communion across time—or perhaps more romantically as an artistic séance of a sort. The force that compelled Morris Louis to make his art and the force that compelled me to write my poem about it formed a kind of circuit. Who was I speaking to when I wrote my poem? The specter of Louis? Some phantom presence that my words conjured from his canvas? Did my poem have its own propulsive energy or was it coming from the same source as Louis's polychrome lines?

Regardless of how it all actually worked, I know that ten-year-old me was having a magical experience. That I was open enough to feel Louis's painting reel me in, and that by writing about it—*with* it?—I was fully submerged in an ensorcelled sea.

Museums have continued to be spiritual sanctuaries for me. Whispering poetic devotions by way of H.D. to the winged, talon-footed *Queen of the Night* relief at the British Museum; making a pilgrimage to Mexico City's Museo de Arte Moderno to bask in the bewitching imaginings of Remedios Varo's paintings; periodically paying my respects to the Met's luminous moon goddess *Diana* not far from my home in New York City—these moments have felt far more sacred to me than attending my family's synagogue in suburban New Jersey ever did.

Same goes for the work of the musicians, writers, and filmmakers I've gravitated to over my four decades on this earth. Anger, Bowie, Carrington, di Prima . . . the alphabet of my mystical guides is full of seekers and creators who used their art to interface with something cosmic and otherwise uncontainable. Their work was born out of a desire to transmute mystery into materiality. Or as James Broughton writes in his 1992 filmmaking manifesto, *Making Light of It*, "Art is a way of seeing the unseen and the unnoticed, the unseeable and the unacknowledged." The

INTRODUCTION

imagination is the best tool we have for turning these twilight visions into reality. It enables us to partner with invisible forces and literally change the world.

If that's not magic, I don't know what is.

My relationship with these crafty witches and wizards evolved from one of a fantastically inclined fangirl to that of an ardent adept. By studying not only their music, artworks, films, and books but also the processes and influences involved in the making of them, my suspicions were confirmed: not only was their work often *about* magic, it was *created using magical means*. Divination. Invocation. Meditation. Manifestation. Whether or not the maker uses terminology like this to describe their way of creating, the truth remains: they collaborated with ethereal energies to generate something new.

And that's the primary intention of this book: to help you unlock your own creative magic and make whatever it is you're meant to in this lifetime. Together we'll delve into magical techniques that makers from a multitude of arts and industries have used for centuries to ideate, cultivate, and offer up their work to others—and Others.

Throughout, I'll also share my own experiences of engaging with the divine as I've navigated my journey of writing and other witchery. Blurring the line between my spirituality and my artistry, or better yet, giving myself permission to erase that line entirely, has been one of the most freeing developments of my life. The anxiety around my input, output, and shoutput surrounding each project has lessened, as I'm now able to tap into something beyond my own perceived restrictions and trust that it will work with and through me.

In addition to what I've learned in my personal practice, many of these

INTRODUCTION

ideas have been confirmed or further developed from years of researching and writing my prior books on witchcraft and culture, as well as getting to interview some of the most magical creators on the planet via my podcast, *The Witch Wave*. Curating exhibitions of spiritually derived art and co-organizing the biennial Occult Humanities Conference at New York University with my frequent coconspirator Jesse Bransford also taught me that there is a wide audience of people who are hungry for more on this subject matter. My 2016 art survey, *Language of the Birds: Occult and Art at NYU's 80WSE Gallery*, had lines around Washington Square Park and broke attendance records. And our occult conference at NYU has sold out every year since our first one in 2013. Though esoteric topics may still be considered taboo in certain circumstances, the appetite for them has grown immensely since the turn of the twenty-first century.

Giving lectures and teaching workshops on the relationship between creativity and magic to thousands of people around the world has further affirmed my belief that there are many others like me who have a desire for a creative practice that is infused with enchantment. Classes like Writing Ritual, which I have been teaching with the occult poet Janaka Stucky, have also proven popular—and effective. We each get notes from students recounting the ways in which their creative output exploded after being encouraged to meld it with magic, and it's been a pleasure teaching them ways to do so. I've also consulted with filmmakers to weave their projects with real movie magic, and worked one-on-one with artists and witches alike to help them more deeply connect with their purpose and supernal power.

In addition to guiding others, I am a perennial student, and I know I will never stop learning how to work with magic in new and exhilarating ways. This very book has been one giant exercise in "practicing what I priestess." It's required me to put my magic where my mouth is, and to

INTRODUCTION

use the techniques I write about in order to see this undertaking through to the end.

Anthropologically speaking, I might be considered a participant-observer, for I've been experiencing the very thing I'm studying as I'm studying it. Or, to use the language of science, I'm my own test subject, experimenting on myself as I go. This has also made me rather curious about other authors of creativity books—surely they had to word-wrangle at times, or be reminded that their endeavor was part of something bigger than themselves. A book about creativity is inherently self-reflexive for its writer, which can be a blessing or a hex.

The wonder of this peculiar exercise of meta-making is that every moment working on this book could be considered somehow useful. The struggles I had along the way revealed themselves to be reminders and abettors: though it feels vulnerable to share the doubts I had as I wrote, I feel certain that they were instructive. I know I am far from the first person to feel cowed by the creative process at times or to question if my efforts would end up being worthwhile. Exploring those shadowy corners became as illuminating for me as the parts that flowed more easily. I hope they shed some light for you as well.

One thing you'll notice is that this book is chock-full of concepts and illustrative examples but not prescriptive step-by-step exercises. *Magic Maker* is intended as a buffet of ideas, and not a formal sit-down dinner. In other words, you're encouraged to take what resonates and discard what doesn't. To sample some tantalizing new flavors as you wish, and to go back for seconds on the parts that you find specifically delicious (and of course avoid anything you're allergic to). There may be techniques you choose to incorporate regularly, and others that you cycle through or switch up as needed. My favorite methods might not click with you,

INTRODUCTION

which is why I've included anecdotes about so many other creative people. Every Magic Maker is different, and each of us must be allowed to experiment and evolve as we venture forth into new inventive terrain.

The book is organized into five parts. You can read it in the order presented, but you are also welcome to approach it in whatever order compels you.

Part I: Initiation provides further context for the relationship between creativity and magic, and it explores the archetype of the Magician as a creative conduit.

Part II: Supernatural Preparation focuses on ways to prepare to do magically devised work. It covers both physical methods and spiritual ones to help shift you into a more receptive state of being.

Part III: The Craft is about the dual aspects of *doing* the work. It covers methods to help you receive inspiration and to express your creative magic with intention. It explores various ways you can collaborate with external forces, whether you are in the throes of working on a project or simply trying to come up with exciting ideas for something new.

Part IV: Keeping the Cauldron Lit is all about maintaining creative energy once you've gotten a project started. So often our focus or confidence flags when we are creating, or unexpected things come up that make it challenging to bring something to completion. This section covers ways to keep goblins from sabotaging the process—whether they are self-inflicted or circumstantial. It also highlights boons and beneficent helpers that can keep you on track.

Part V: Complete Magic is about letting go of a project once you've brought it to fruition. Whether you choose to share it with a wider audience or are simply ready to bring it to a close and move on to something else, this section focuses on sending your work forth with good energy and grace.

INTRODUCTION

Pulling the lines of this book from the imaginal realm of Spirit into the material world has been a long process of sustained enchantment, and I'm overjoyed to share this offering with you now. I hope it stirs your own creativity, whether it's been dormant for a while or just needs a bit of divine direction.

May this creation beget more creations. Here's to the magic you'll make.

PART I

Initiation

We're here to discuss the mystical art of creating.

That may sound rather exclusionary and aggrandizing, I realize. In fact, the Secret Order of Making Stuff is open to all. It's a sect we're each born into, and only when we get older can we lose our way and stumble out of its sumptuous, curtained alcove. Discouragement comes from all sides as we mature, with external influences saying that we're wasting our talents and internal voices telling us we're wasting our time. But these stifling messages are learned, societally imposed, and have nothing to do with our intrinsic tendencies to imagine, puzzle, produce, embellish, and transform.

We each have the ability to reconnect to that original impulse to conjure something out of nothing. To reclaim our creative magic. To be born-again wonder-workers.

As a young person, I did most of my making in my bedroom. My pastel-floral wallpaper got plastered over with images of the stars in my own personal firmament: postcards of favorite pieces by fantastical artists like Remedios Varo and Kiki Smith, photocopied illustrations of mythic creatures and celestial comic book characters, and posters of my musical holy trinity: Tori Amos, PJ Harvey, and Björk. I would light dozens of candles (bless my parents for putting up with this recurrent fire hazard!), put on a mixtape or a few carefully curated CDs in my five-disc carousel, and then lie on my pink-carpeted floor, surrounded by the tools of whatever project I was working on that night. An eight-track recorder; a sketchbook and colored pencils; canvases and brushes and pots of acrylic paint; doll parts, hot glue guns, X-ACTO knives, and old magazines; pens and poetry books and reams of blank paper. No matter the medium, this was my ritual.

I would also do more obvious rituals here as a burgeoning teen witch. Spell books and skeleton keys and bottles of dried flowers covered my dresser and spilled from my shelves. I collected precious stones and dead insects and depictions of Artemis, the Greek goddess of the moon and the wild. I adorned myself in talismans and uttered incantations. I burned incense and tiny scrolls with written wishes curled up within. Together, the items and images I dwelled amongst formed a membrane of magic, a constellation of iconography that delineated sacred space. Crossing its threshold separated the mystical from the mundane, the ritualized from the routine. My childhood bedroom was a land of the liminal: studio, sanctuary, shrine.

In hindsight, it is clear that I was intuitively building a sort of cauldron for myself—a distinct and protected container wherein deep transmutations could take place. But back then I saw my arts and crafts to be related to, yet still bifurcated *from*, my witchcraft. It wasn't until I got older that I realized my magical praxis and my creative expression were two sides of the same sparkling coin.

In Defense of Magic

I make my living now as a writer and a witch. (Believe me, I'm as surprised as you are on both counts.) The process of weaving these roles together was a gradual one, developed over years of study and lots of trial and error—or trial and triumph as I prefer to look at it. It also took me a long time to lay claim to either of those titles, at least out loud. But two of the truest things about me are that I have always loved magic and I have always loved making things. And those fascinations have only grown more vivid and more fervent as I've aged.

I'm often asked when I realized I was a witch, and while I wish I had some sexy occult origin story—being zapped between the eyes by a bolt of lightning! getting anointed in the woods by a mysterious crone!—the truth is, I simply can't remember a time when I wasn't whatever witchly being I am. My interest in magic was born out of a love of fairy tales and myths, '80s cartoons, '90s glitter grrrl rock, Surrealist art, Henson-Froud films, Vertigo comics, suburban new age shops, and books like the Time-Life *Mysteries of the Unknown* series, the twenty-nine-volume *Man, Myth and Magic* set, and, my all-time favorite, *The Encyclopedia of Things that Never Were*.

I recently rediscovered a haiku I wrote when I was ten. It goes like this:

> *Metaphysicians.*
> *They all study fantasy.*
> *I want to be one.*

It is accompanied by a self-portrait in crayon of my idealized grown-up self, wearing red lipstick and a purple tunic with gold buttons and standing next to a shelf filled with books that have words like CHARMS and METAMORPHYSIS [*sic*] on their spines. Three decades later, it seems my reverie wasn't too far off. I don't have the prodigious Jersey bangs I envisioned, and I would now make the case that metaphysics is more than the study of "fantasy," but rather a field of inquiry that focuses on the immaterial, the mystical, the arcane. Still, this poem is a precious relic, a sort of manifestation spell rendered in cursive and Crayola.

My obsession with magic has become both a spiritual practice and a scholarly pursuit. And any way you slice it, I can tell you that it has given me a truly magnificent life. It has also shown me, time and time again, that occult topics make some people uncomfortable. In this so-called modern age, public engagement with magic is frequently either sensationalized or trivialized—something to be ashamed of and eradicate, or at least kept under wraps.

There are those that fear magic, framing it as diabolical or sinful and associating it with things unnatural, ungodly, or impure. These tend to be folks who have their own deep-seated religious beliefs, and anything outside of a narrow band of dogma must be avoided or snuffed out, lest it lead them and their cohort on a path to hell. They will argue that there is a difference between miracles (good!) and magic (bad!), and make the case that miracles come from a benevolent God, whereas magic is made by sinful humans—or far worse evil entities. They do not like it when you ask them the difference between saying a healing prayer or casting a protection spell. They might follow the prosperity gospel but reject abundance magic. They may believe in saints, angels, and a man who walks on water but feel uneasy when asked to consider the existence of other superhuman beings. They may drink the blood and eat the body of Christ each Sunday but find cauldrons creepy.

On the opposite side of the spectrum are the cynics. They will proclaim that a belief in magic is diametrically opposed to the dominions of science and logic, and they will dismiss anyone who feels otherwise as a superstitious ignoramus. They have a devoutly materialist worldview, believing the only thing that matters is, well, matter, and so to them, an interest in the immaterial is the mark of an immature, unsophisticated, or uninformed mind. Philosopher Theodor Adorno's 1947 "Theses Against Occultism" is emblematic of this thinking. In his nine-part takedown of astrologers, spiritualists, and their ilk, he writes: "Occultism is the metaphysic of dunces." Folks in Adorno's camp believe that anything that seems magical must have a scientific explanation. They bristle at the woo-woo (even that phrase is infantilizing). They deem anyone attempting to engage with the supernatural as naive or delusional, and characterize them as being anti-medicine, anti-progress, and anti-"reality." These "rationalists" devote themselves unquestionably to measurements and mechanics, despite the fact that the intricate workings of love, consciousness, death, and other central human concerns are still shrouded in mystery.

These cynics position themselves as having better critical thinking skills than the believers, yet they rarely acknowledge the roots of their own rationalist thinking. In his 1918 lecture "Science as a Vocation," German sociologist Max Weber spoke about how the Age of Enlightenment led to the "disenchantment" of the world (he used the word *Entzauberung*, which essentially translates to "de-magic-ing"). In Weber's view, the dominance of science and secularization in the West removed the richness of life.

What is important to note is that this disenchantment occurred systematically over centuries, and that it closely tracks with the rise of capitalism. After all, more labor can be squeezed out of people if their magical beliefs are discouraged or even punished.

In her book *Caliban and the Witch*, Silvia Federici writes about how the European witch hunts were largely driven by groups of powerful men seeking to profit off the populace. In the seventeenth century, she argues, those who believed in spells, charms, divination, and the magical correspondences between, say, metals, planets, and herbs were less likely to work as relentlessly as those who didn't. Therefore, these beliefs had to be eliminated in order to extract the most labor—and therefore the most profit—from them. As Federici explains:

> Eradicating these practices was a necessary condition for the capitalist rationalization of work, since magic appeared as an illicit form of power and an instrument *to obtain what one wanted without work*, that is, a refusal of work in action. "Magic kills industry," lamented Francis Bacon, admitting that nothing repelled him so much as the assumption that one could obtain results with a few idle expedients, rather than with the sweat of one's brow.

IN DEFENSE OF MAGIC

Federici also explains how astrology in particular was problematic because a belief in auspicious and inauspicious days limits a worker's availability. If time is money, then disenchanting the calendar was a crucial step toward establishing as many workdays as possible. In a capitalist model, Magic Makers are difficult to schedule and even more difficult to own. To take things a step further, if the very earth is disenchanted, it becomes far easier to devalue it and see it as a resource ripe for plunder and profit rather than a holy place one can relate to with a sense of reverence, gratitude, and protection.

At any rate, these two groups—the religionists who fear magic and the hyper-rationalists who invalidate its very existence—are with us today. Though each of these positions may seem to be on opposite ends of the spectrum, what they share is a root of Western, patriarchal, colonizer mentality. God-fearing folks have been taught that any engagement with the spiritual world outside of organized religion is evil. Nonbelievers reject anything associated with the irrational or immaterial as being a threat to scientific—and often economic—progress. Yet despite both of these dominant stances, there are still countless groups and individuals around the world for whom a belief in spirits, magic, and other extraordinary forces is really, well, quite ordinary. Venerating ancestors, worshipping nature, and having relationships with nonhuman entities is still common practice in many Indigenous and diasporic cultures, as it has been for tens of thousands of years of human history overall. To qualify these systems as diabolical or primitive is part of the racist project of white supremacist colonialism, plain and simple.

We should also note that there are many examples of mystically minded scholars, from physicist Isaac Newton to mathematician Georg Cantor to botanist Robin Wall Kimmerer, who managed to integrate their spiritual beliefs with their scientific studies. One need not reject religion or science in order to embrace magic, and most of the Magic Makers I know are quite happy to have access to hospitals, computers, and electricity—even as many of them seek to make each of these modern developments more holistic and more equitably accessible. Furthermore, despite countless attempts from those who have tried to suppress its power or deny its existence altogether, magic can never be fully eradicated: if you have a lucky charm or wear a pair of lucky socks on game day, or if you have ever made a wish on a star, a coin toss into a fountain, or a cake full of birthday candles, you are casting a little spell, plain and simple. Magic belongs to everyone, and it isn't going anywhere anytime soon, so we might as well learn how to mindfully integrate it into modern life.

I believe that religion, science, and magic can coexist, as they historically always have. I know there are vast amounts of beauty, wisdom, and meaning to be found in religious texts and organized spiritual communities. And my fully vaccinated arms are helping me type these words on a laptop, so I'm certainly a fan of science as well. Generally speaking, I have no problem with folks who orient their lives around meaningful religious practice or rigorous scientific inquiry. But when extremists in either camp treat a belief in magic as some sort of a threat, whether to the soul or the intellect, I take issue.

I often describe myself as a pragmatic witch. I value analysis and critical thinking, and I have a strong aversion to bullshit. And while I love shiny objects, I despise shiny rhetoric if it's not supported by depth, nuance, and real results. If magic didn't work for me, I simply wouldn't bother with it.

My magical practice has helped me be a more centered, more compassionate, more creatively fulfilled human being. It has helped me become who I'm meant to be and do the work I'm meant to do in this lifetime.

IN DEFENSE OF MAGIC

And, as I've discovered over years of studying the topic, it has helped many makers—from authors to biochemists to CEOs—do the same, even if they felt resistant to it at first. In a 1988 *Mavis on 4* interview, Toni Morrison explains how embracing her family's ancestral magic aided her writing:

> My whole education, you know, was to make sure I didn't believe things like that, and I dismissed all sorts of things that were indigenous in my family: superstition and you know, the discredited information, the discredited way of knowing that discredited people always have. But when I began to write, that was the place where I had to go. That's where the information was. That's where the images were. That's where the language, the color came, in these tales, folktales, attitudes, the normal easy acceptance of signs. And then things began to happen that were really quite startling.

Now, before we go any further, it's important for me to state the following: I don't know *how* magic works, I just know that it *does*.

There are those who long for explanations—perhaps it's the power of suggestion that is causing us to associate our magical practices with the positive outcomes we have experienced; that when we act as though magic is real, we trick ourselves into thinking it's so. Maybe it's a sort of supernatural placebo effect that kicks in, or a self-fulfilling prophecy in which we act *as if*, thus becoming *what is*. It's entirely possible that going through the motions of magic gets our minds into a more open, receptive state, and that any productive outcomes are due to this more positive outlook.

I'm also aware of the pareidolia effect. This is the brain's tendency to make patterns out of random elements or to project meaning onto what some might consider meaningless. Seeing shapes in clouds, faces in tree trunks, or otherwise sifting seemingly recognizable imagery from ambiguous markings or textures are all considered to be examples of pareidolia at work. On a related note, apophenia refers to a propensity toward making connections between random things, and it is often used to describe conspiracy theories or obsessive-compulsive behaviors: "If I turn the key in the keyhole nine times, I will keep my apartment safe." I understand the rationalist urge to categorize someone's perception of magic as a mere misunderstanding of natural neurological processes, if not evidence of straight-up delusion. I get why people reject the idea of magic being "real."

I suppose my only rebuttal to these arguments is that as long as my involvement with magic is enhancing my life, increasing my creativity, and helping me be a more generative and generous person, then that's the reality I want to live in.

Perhaps the findings of quantum physics or future developments in psychology will come up with proven explanations for the magical experiences I've had, the wonders I've witnessed. Is it possible that casting a spell is just a means of agitating the quantum field somehow? Maybe it's a way of sending a message to another dimension, or to a future self. Who's to say? Albert Einstein was skeptical about quantum entanglement—or what he called "spooky action at a distance"—which is the idea that bonded particles can affect each other across vast distances, even if they're light-years apart. Yet in 2022, a Nobel Prize was awarded to three quantum physicists who proved this *is* possible. As science fiction writer Arthur C. Clarke famously stated: "Any sufficiently advanced technology is indistinguishable from magic."

All of this may be so. Personally, I think there's a difference between a music algorithm learning my taste well enough to determine which track to serve up next and a song playing over the grocery-store loudspeaker that synchronistically delivers me precisely the message I needed to hear at that very moment in my life. The first instance is technical, the second is magical.

I also can tell you that using the parameters of science to undercut the existence of magic is futile—and it's certainly no fun. Magic operates in the space of awe and artistry. It murmurs in the language of mythopoesis, and its symbolism will softly seduce you or sweep you clean off your feet if you let it. It is romantic and relational, and it responds best to imaginative methods, not pedestrian ones. When we make magic, we leap fervently into uncharted territory and trust that something nameless but numinous will be there to greet us midflight. And so it does, with wide, wild wings.

So What Is Magic Exactly?

My initial response to that question is to answer in the same way Supreme Court Justice Potter Stewart did when he was asked to define pornography: "I know it when I see it."

Better yet: I know it when I *sense* it.

Magic-making is a spiritual enterprise, but it is crucially also an *embodied* practice. It's a way of shifting one's entire mode of being in the direction of Creative Force and interacting with it in order to change oneself and one's circumstances. When magic is working properly, there is a feeling in the body of being *activated*. Power is raised. Ideas flow. Something outside of our egos is allowed entrance, and we respond to its visitation in kind. We converse with this force whenever we create, whether via ritual, spellwork, ideation, art. We offer this force the use of our gifts. And it gifts us with enchanted energy in turn, so we can keep making more magic for the world.

I sometimes refer to the entity behind this force as capital-*S* Spirit to connote its immensity and its immanence. Other names for this Spirit include Source, the divine, God, the Goddess, the gods, the One. Its power

SO WHAT IS MAGIC EXACTLY?

can be called the creative urge, life force, or what tarot expert Rachel Pollack has called "spirit force." Chinese mystics call this force qi or chi, to Hindu philosophers it is prana, and ancient Egyptians named it ka. I'm especially partial to the Celtic notion of awen, which refers to the flowing energy of inspiration said to have been brewed in the enchantress Ceridwen's cauldron. I also love the twelfth-century mystic Hildegard von Bingen's idea of viriditas, the green life force of creation. Whatever its name, this Creative Force is a vital power that's eternal and infinite, and it doesn't care what you call it (though I suspect it responds favorably to good intentions in that regard).

Magic is how we can interact with this Creative Force. However, *magic* is notoriously difficult to define—though many have tried. Even the spelling of the word has variation, with some choosing to add a *k* at the end—*magick*—to differentiate it from stage magic and other forms of illusory entertainment. That said, the use of the word *magic* to describe sleight-of-hand and other tricks didn't come into popularity until the nineteenth century. I prefer its standard spelling, primarily because I think it's somewhat pointless to split hairs between the "trickery" of performance and the pageantry of ceremonial acts, as the two are interrelated—particularly when we consider the shared histories of magical performative arts like shamanism, theater, and ritualized dance.

Etymologically, the word *magic* is most likely derived from the Proto-Indo-European root word *magh-*, meaning "to be able" or "to have power." This theoretically evolved into the Old Persian word *magush*, from which we get the Latin words *magus* (singular) or *magi* (plural), which originally referred to a specific priestly, magic-wielding class of Persians (e.g., the Three Wise Men or Magi of the New Testament). This later turned into words such as *magikos* (Greek), *magique* (French), and the late-fourteenth-century English *magikē*, which the *Online Etymology Dictionary* defines as the "art of influencing or predicting events and producing marvels using hidden natural forces."

To be sure, "producing marvels using hidden natural forces" is the part that gets my blood pumping, and I'm guessing that notion appeals to you as well. But let's take a look at some other definitions.

In his book *Transcendental Magic*, nineteenth-century French occultist Éliphas Lévi defined magic as "the traditional science of the secrets of Nature which has been transmitted to us from the Magi."

In 1929, British ceremonial magician and notorious provocateur Aleister Crowley wrote *Magick in Theory and Practice*, and in it he says, "Magick is the Science and Art of causing Change to occur in conformity with Will." Occult practitioner and author Dion Fortune revised this to state that magic is "the art of causing changes *in consciousness* at will" (emphasis mine), as relayed by her student W. E. Butler in his 1952 book *Magic: Its Ritual, Power and Purpose*. The implication here is that magic is about changing one's subjective experience and perhaps even about changing a shared consciousness between multiple people. If perception is reality, then modifying consciousness as one desires—whether on the individual or collective level—is a valid magical aim.

In his 1954 book, *Witchcraft Today*, Wicca pioneer and cheeky rascal Gerald Gardner simply puts it, "magic is the art of getting results." OK then, Gerald! It seems he was a pragmatic witch as well.

I was introduced to one of my favorite descriptions when I interviewed *Tarot for Change* author, Jessica Dore, on my podcast. She told me that "Magic is using the subtle to influence the dense." She picked this up from an anonymous Christian mystic (most likely Valentin Tomberg) in their book, *Meditations on the Tarot*, which was written in 1967 and published in 1980.

Here's my best attempt at a definition: magic is an intentional means of collaborating with Creative Force in order to transform a state of being.

People from all backgrounds and vocations have flirted with magic, but it's clear that artists and other creative folks are particularly susceptible to its charms. Whether composing music, painting a picture, or scrawling a poem, the maker seeks to create something new that will stir the soul, and cause a splendid disruption. They want to leave the listener, the viewer, the reader *changed*. And in the process of making, they undergo a transformation themselves. Emotions surge. Electricity sparks. There is a marked gear shift that happens in the process of making. And the maker's intention is to transfer that strange, consciousness-shifting magic to whomever bears witness to the new thing they have made.

It's easy to talk about creativity and magic as being metaphorically related, but there are those like me who take things a step further, and posit that creativity *is* a sort of magic. In his seminal 1957 art history survey, *L'Art magique,* André Breton sought to trace the evolution of magical artwork, from prehistoric cave paintings to the medium-spanning creations of the Surrealist movement he cofounded and led. In his introduction to the text, he writes that even if a work of art doesn't appear obviously magical or have a magical intent, it is always at least derived from magic:

> ... [T]he work of art obeys its own laws: whether or not it decides to adapt itself to magical ends, we are unable to forget that *it is from magic itself that it draws its origin*. Even if it aims to be purely "realist," there is no avoiding the fact that it owes the greater part of its resources to magic. In this sense, all art is magical at least in its genesis.

Beat iconoclast William S. Burroughs wrote about how art's original purpose was as a magical device. In his essay about friend and artistic collaborator Brion Gysin for the 1977 book *Contemporary Artists*, Burroughs states, "It is to be remembered that all art is magical in origin—music sculpture writing painting—and by magical I mean intended to produce very definite results. Paintings were originally formulae to make what is painted happen."

Others contend that art and magic are essentially analogous, if not synonymous, since they operate in a similar transformational fashion. Legendary comics writer Alan Moore has said, "Magic in its earliest form is often referred to as 'the art.' I believe this is completely literal. I believe that magic is art and that art, whether that be writing, music, sculpture, or any other form, is literally magic. Art is, like magic, the science of manipulating symbols, words, or images, to achieve changes in consciousness." And my friend, the fine artist and NYU professor Jesse Bransford, has written, "I think magic and art are essentially the same thing. The two activities lead to a place of immanence or transcendence that point and direct all human endeavors." These two creators are each highly prolific artists and occult scholars in their own right, and so we would be wise to heed their declarations.

The Artful Occult

A note on that word, *occult*. Though it now has associations with suspect goings-on in candlelit, subterranean vaults (sign me up!), it is a word that simply means "hidden" or "concealed." It refers to anything that is not immediately or easily perceived, and it indicates that actions must be taken and work must be done in order to reveal buried wisdom. Pulp novels and horror films have given the word a frisson of the forbidden, but contrary to its titillating reputation, there is nothing inherently evil about the occult. Those who engage in it are generally curious sorts looking to expand their knowledge about themselves and the universe. The goal of occult study is to unearth hidden truths and bring them out into the light.

Creative work is occult work. Artists are spelunkers, and they must have the courage and skill to explore the darkened caverns of consciousness and re-emerge with pocketfuls of dirt, bones, and the occasional glowing gem.

It's understandable then why so many "occult" societies have been made up of craftspeople and artists of all stripes. The Freemasons allege that they began as a fraternal order of stonemasons and cite the builders of ancient Egypt and the Temple of Solomon as part of their mystic lineage, if not their literal one. Their references to "the Craft," geometry, and "The Great Architect of the Universe" belie a belief in the divinity of construction. The nineteenth-century Spiritualist movement was based on the idea that one could communicate with the spirits of the deceased, and it birthed some of the earliest makers of what we now call nonfigurative or abstract art. Spiritualist artists Georgiana Houghton, Hilma af Klint, and Anna Cassel used their work as a means to visually translate the messages they were receiving from guides on the other side. The Hermetic Order of the Golden Dawn was a late nineteenth- and early twentieth-century group of bohemian seekers that counted poet William Butler Yeats, actress Florence Farr, supernatural author Arthur Machen, and Rider-Waite-Smith tarot illustrator Pamela Colman Smith amongst its ranks. The esoteric studies and creative output of many of the Golden Dawn's members are inextricably linked.

Golden Dawn member Aleister Crowley would go on to start his own occult society—the Ordo Templi Orientis (OTO). In addition to writing poetry and reams of magical liturgy for the OTO and others, Crowley also painted and, with artist Lady Frieda Harris, developed the Thoth tarot deck. Tellingly, perhaps, the notoriously distemperate Crowley replaced the Temperance card with the Art card in their deck. In *The Book of Thoth* (1944), Crowley writes that his Art card depicts a fertile and unifying phase of the alchemical process: "This state of the great Work therefore consisted in the mingling of the contradictory elements in a cauldron." The card depicts the communion of opposite forces, in other words. It shows a two-headed, multi-breasted being who mixes together fire and water. The two halves of this figure are made up of the alchemical king and queen who, combined together, form a magnificent androgyne version of the lunar goddess Diana the Huntress (or Artemis of Ephesus). For Crowley, the Art card depicts an important step in magical development. It's a process-oriented card, and one that "foreshadowed the final stage of the Great Work." Through Art, we can become closer to alchemical refinement, to divinity. As Crowley writes in *Magick in Theory and Practice*: "All Art is Magick . . . There is no more potent means than Art of calling forth true Gods to visible appearance."

The Theosophical Society, cofounded by Madame Helena Blavatsky, Henry Steel Olcott, and William Quan Judge in 1875, is still in existence, and its influence on the Modern Art movement and contemporary culture overall cannot be overstated. It popularized the notion that there is one universal truth behind all world religions, and it borrowed liberally from Eastern mystical ideas about spiritual evolution, reincarnation, and the possibility of attaining enlightenment. Oz series author L. Frank Baum was a Theosophist, and one can see clear Theosophical and magical themes throughout his work. One of my favorite examples of this is how in his first book, *The Wonderful Wizard of Oz* (1900), each of the adventurers sees a different version of the wizard. Dorothy encounters him as a giant disembodied head as she does in the subsequent MGM film, but the Scarecrow sees him as a regal green lady with wings, the Tin Woodman sees him as a woolly rhinoceros-headed beast with five eyes, five arms, and five legs, and the Lion sees him as a Ball of Fire. The "wizard" is eventually revealed when Toto knocks over the screen he is standing behind, and the truth comes tumbling out. To me, this feels like a Theosophist parable about the different veils that religion wears, when in fact they are all man-made attempts to point to a unifying Absolute. Still, there is true magic represented in this book, in the form of the Silver Shoes (made ruby in the film). Once Dorothy learns how to wield them properly, she is able to click herself back home.

The founding of the abstract art movement has roots in Theosophy as well. The 1905 illustrated book *Thought-Forms* by Theosophists Annie Besant and C. W. Leadbeater is another early example of nonfigurative, spiritual art, and it too influenced Hilma af Klint, as well as Wassily Kandinsky, Piet Mondrian, and other titans of Modernism. In Kandinsky's 1911 book *Concerning the Spiritual in Art*, he writes admiringly of "a tremendous spiritual movement which today includes a large number of people and has even assumed a material form in the THEOSOPHICAL SOCIETY. This society consists of groups who seek to approach the problem of the spirit by way of the INNER knowledge." He goes on to write, "Every man who steeps himself in the spiritual possibilities of his art is a valuable helper in the building of the spiritual pyramid which will some day reach to heaven." His own paintings attempt to interface with the invisible and perhaps even bring heaven down to earth.

Several nineteenth-century art movements, from the Pre-Raphaelites to the Symbolists, were steeped in spiritual thought and mythological tropes, particularly the work that sprang from French mystic Joséphin Péladan's Rosicrucian-inspired cultural salon series, the Salon de la Rose + Croix. My favorite art movement, Surrealism, is a clear early twentieth-century successor to this magical lineage. In 1917, French poet Guillaume Apollinaire coined the term "surrealism," describing it as "the point of departure for a whole series of Manifestations of the New Spirit that is making itself felt today and that will certainly appeal to our best minds." Spearheaded at first by writers such as André Breton, the movement would eventually be best known for the visual art it incubated and proliferated, including phantasmagorical paintings, collages, sculptures, and films by such Magic Makers as Max Ernst, Giorgio de Chirico, René Magritte, Salvador Dalí, Luis Buñuel, Leonora Carrington, Remedios Varo, Victor Brauner, Leonor Fini, and Méret Oppenheim. Influenced by the then-nascent fields of psychology and anthropology, the Surrealists believed that by plumbing the unconscious, one could access a veritable wonderland of dream, myth, ritual, and desire that all humans purportedly traverse. Ceremonial objects such as masks and statues from various Indigenous cultures were also magically inspiring to them (if problematically so, as they were often viewed through the lens of exoticization), as were tarot cards and other methods of divination.

The early work of mid-twentieth-century Abstract Expressionist artists such as Jackson Pollock and Mark Rothko could be considered specimens of the late Surrealist movement, focused as they are on depictions of shamanism and mythology (see Pollock's *Guardians of the Secret* [1943] and Rothko's *Rites of Lilith* [1945] for example). Eventually they and their contemporaries would veer away from figurative painting altogether, instead attempting to express a metaphysical experience using more primary—and perhaps more direct—elements of color, movement, and line.

To this day, the Abstract and AbEx movements remain widely misunderstood. There are many who still dismiss nonfigurative art with a "my kid could paint that" wave. And while they certainly don't have to like the work, I find that these detractors often miss the point that these movements are deeply spiritual ones. Abstract artists were attempting to represent the divinely unrepresentable, to transmit the feeling of transcendence through imagery, to visually inject the viewer with a sense of the sacred.

I remember taking my in-laws to the Museum of Modern Art and standing them in front of Barnett Newman's 1950–51 Abstract Expressionist painting *Vir Heroicus Sublimis*. At first they weren't sure what to make of it, as it's a giant field of red with a few vertical stripes of color slashed throughout it. An initial impression of it feels, well, kind of simple (though your kid would definitely need a ladder to paint its nearly eighteen-foot-long, eight-foot-high canvas, not to mention a steady hand). But I instructed them to stand so close to it that it filled their entire field of vision, as Newman intended. To let the painting engulf them, and to feel the energy that the painting emanates. Suddenly, they got it. They invited in the power of the work, and engaged with it using their spirits and bodies rather than their analytical minds. In other words, they received the artist's offering with a kind of metaphysical openness. As Newman stated in his 1943–1945 essay *The Plasmic Image*, "The present painter is concerned not with his own feelings or with the mystery of his own personality but with the penetration into the world-mystery. His imagination is therefore attempting to dig into metaphysical secrets. To that extent, his art is concerned with the sublime." My in-laws may not have walked away from Newman's red painting as new AbEx fans, but the experience certainly made an impression on them, and it changed their point of view about what art can do.

    Rothko also believed deeply in the spiritual effect of engaging with wide washes of color. His secular meditation sanctuary in Houston, the Rothko Chapel, is an octagonal space hung with fourteen large canvases that at first seem filled with nothing but strokes of black paint. These paintings surround the viewer on all sides, and there are benches positioned at various angles in the center of the chapel so that one might view the works from any angle. The first time I visited the chapel I was touched by how holy books from various faiths, from the Quran to the Bible to the Zoroastrian Khordeh Avesta, are provided for those who choose to make use of them. I was also struck by the ways in which the longer I sat in front of the paintings, the more I could discern fine details and depth that weren't clear in the reproductions I'd seen in books or online. Rather than being mere monochrome paintings, I noticed varying gradations in hue, from tenebrous violet to midnight onyx. There was also a variety of textures and different densities of pigment. And there was a surprising feeling of motion and making, even amidst the stillness; when viewed in person, Rothko's thousands of individual brushstrokes become apparent. There was also a sense of immensity, and deep, gaping awe. Sitting there made me contemplate things like the vastness of space and my place in it. I thought about time and longing and the terror of the void and the promise of new beginnings. Mostly, though, I felt that strange combination of broad calm and magical activation that comes whenever I am brought face-to-face with Mystery. Like I am noctilucent and dreaming while wide awake.

If there is one branch of Western occultism that has influenced me the most, it is undoubtedly the modern witchcraft movement. Though many proclaim it to be a revival of ancient Pagan practices (and evidence of that is somewhat spotty), we know for a fact that the modern practice of witchcraft got popularized in British and American circles in the mid-twentieth century thanks to Wicca progenitor, writer, and all-around witchy hype man Gerald Gardner. And while much has been written elsewhere by myself and many others about Wicca's cultural influence, for our purposes I'll stay focused on the creative aspects of this "new-old" religion, which are extensive.

Freemasonry was one of the many esoteric influences on Gardner when he was codifying the texts and rituals of the religion that would come to be called Wicca. And though Masons call their practice "the

Craft," when one hears that term in mainstream conversation today, it's safe to assume it's not referring to Masonic practice but to witchcraft in general (if not the Wicca-drenched 1996 teen witch film of the same name). Though Freemasonry has lodges around the world and has lasted for centuries, it still feels somewhat shrouded in secrecy, and it remains primarily an organization by and for men. The modern witchcraft movement is, by contrast, decentralized, feminine-leaning, and constantly evolving. And though Wicca has had a large hand in making the practice of witchcraft a bit less marginalized than before, there are many witches today who, like me, don't consider themselves Wiccan. This fluidity of the modern witchcraft movement makes it appealing for creative-minded folks who are attracted to its spirituality and magic rituals but who don't cleave to dogma or prescriptive religious tradition.

The development of Wicca itself is a study in creative innovation and adaptation. Many of the earliest rituals were written by Gardner, who borrowed extensively from many other writers and occult societies. His magical collaborator, the Wiccan High Priestess Doreen Valiente, went on to embellish and expand Gardner's ideas. Through her influence, more emphasis was put on the Goddess and the divine feminine overall. She also elevated his writing with her own poetic flair and contributed much of her original writing and research to the Wiccan canon, including her much-loved invocation, "The Charge of the Goddess."

Gerald Gardner's groundbreaking book, *Witchcraft Today*, came out in 1954. That Valiente released her own book called *Witchcraft for Tomorrow* twenty-four years later speaks volumes about her desire to keep witchcraft relevant and alive for future generations. Throughout the book she includes her own original poems and invocations and offers suggestions for how aspiring witches might go about fashioning their own magical tools and adornments. After all, there was nowhere near the proliferation of occult supply shops in her lifetime as there are now. This is why the collections of the Museum of Witchcraft and Magic in Boscastle, England, and The Buckland Museum of Witchcraft and Magic in Cleveland, Ohio, are full of handmade magical artifacts. When Wicca and its offshoots were burgeoning, the witches had no choice but to resort to crafting their own ritual wares. And despite the popularity of witchy websites and storefronts today, there are many practitioners who still prefer the handmade approach, believing that making one's own tools infuses each object with personal power.

One of the things I love best about Valiente's book is her insistence that witches don't fret about doing things perfectly; they remain open to improvising. "Use your own ingenuity . . . It is your effort and visualization that make a magic circle, not material things like twine or carpet," she writes. She is also a staunch advocate of self-transformation, insisting that anyone can choose to become a witch if they feel called to, and they may induct themselves into their own coven of one: "Many people, I know, will question the idea of self-initiation, as given in this book. To them I will address one simple question: who initiated the first witch?" Though there are certainly elders and leaders to be found in modern witchcraft, there is no requisite mediator between a witch and the divine. Each practitioner is empowered to be creative and commune with Spirit in their own style. The witch is free to make her own magic, just as the artist is free to make theirs.

Maker as Magician

Makers are magicians. They are intermediaries between realms who use their craft to transform Creative Force into a material offering for the world.

The Magician card of the tarot is, to my mind, one of the most profoundly illuminating depictions of the creative process there is. My favorite rendering of this particular tarot card is the one done by Pamela Colman Smith in 1909 for what's come to be known as the Rider-Waite-Smith tarot. In Smith's version, the Magician is an ambiguously gendered figure (likely modeled after either British stage star Ellen Terry or queer suffragist Edith "Edy" Craig). They stand behind a table laden with the tools of magic: a wand, a sword, a chalice, and a pentacle, each symbolizing the four elements of fire, air, water, and earth. These are also the symbols of the four suits of the tarot deck, thus representing the Magician's ability to work with the very components of life itself in equal measure. The Magician is anyone on the precipice of generativity: artist, inventor, craftsperson, producer of the new. The Magician is a coconspirator with mystery. An occult collaborator with the unknown, they midwife magic and partner with unseen powers. They stand at the ready, arms wide, heart bared. They are here to make something, an act that is paradoxically one of surrender and decisive doingness. They are present and patient and fully empowered.

The Magician is also considered the initiate of the tarot. Modern decks often start with the Fool as the first card, though it is numbered as card 0—and in the past has sometimes been numbered 22 as the final card of the Major Arcana, or else left unnumbered and free to float anywhere in the seventy-eight-card stack. The Magician—or its older equivalents—is usually card 1. In readings, this is a card that turns up at the beginning of the creative process, a figure standing tall in anticipation of the great transformations to come.

In Smith's illustration, the Magician's belt is an ouroboros—the alchemical snake eating its own tail—and floating above the Magician's head is the infinity sign (a lemniscate, or horizontal figure eight). Both of these images symbolize that creativity is an infinite process of giving and receiving, of admission and expression, of attraction and action. These cycles are ongoing, and though at any given moment the creative person's amounts of input or output may change, overall they swirl eternally in perfect equilibrium.

Most striking is the stance the Magician takes, with one arm raised upward to the heavens and the other arm lowered downward, with their hand pointing to the earth. They have become a bridge between the celestial and terrestrial realms. The upper hand holds a double-headed wand, a lightning rod for prima materia, the creative source material that surrounds them always but must have a container to fill so that it might become realized. The lower hand is empty; the Magician shall soon choose which of the tools before them is best suited to translate these divine transmissions and shape them into earthly forms.

Though Smith's twentieth-century depiction of the Magician has become rather ubiquitous—emblazoned on T-shirts, posters, tote bags, and the like—hers is only the most popular rendition. Her Magician card is a relatively modern example of a figure that appeared in much earlier tarot decks, whether used for their original purpose as playing cards or later as fortune-telling devices. Over centuries, this character's iterations include the Artixan or artisan; Il Bagatto, which is interpreted as a sleight-of-hand artist or street performer; and Le Bateleur, which colloquially became referred to in English as "The Juggler." While the illustrators' implications about each card's meaning certainly varied—from craftsperson to swindler to entertainer to conjuror—there is an occult connective tissue between them, indicating a state of play, the shaping of reality, and the subtle manipulation of materials for the purpose of affecting an intended audience. I would argue that these are all key aspects of the creative process in general.

Smith and her tarot collaborator (and commissioner) A. E. Waite were undoubtedly inspired by Oswald Wirth's 1889 rendition of Le Bateleur in his twenty-two-card deck, *Les 22 Arcanes du Tarot Kabbalistique*. A follower of French occultist Éliphas Lévi, Wirth incorporated Lévi's description of this card as being associated with the Hebrew letter Aleph (א), which Kabbalists associated with divine oneness. Wirth includes the Aleph beneath his illustration and emphasizes Le Bateleur's Aleph-shaped posture with one arm raised and one lowered.

And Éliphas Lévi himself makes use of this upward-downward pose, most famously—or infamously, depending on whom you ask—with his illustration of Baphomet or the Sabbatic Goat as seen in his double-volume nineteenth-century classic, *Dogme et Rituel de la Haute Magie* (*Dogma and Ritual of High Magic*). A popular image with heavy metal bands and other goth provocateurs, it is one of the most widely misunderstood symbols of Western mysticism. In actuality, this chimeric horned creature is no devil but, as Lévi describes it, a "sphinx of occult sciences . . . an innocent and even pious hieroglyph." His intention was to create an anthropomorphized depiction of the balance of opposites, no different in intent than, say, the yin-yang symbol of Chinese cosmology, the Hindu shatkona, or the Seal of Solomon hexagram of Jewish and Muslim mysticism. Lévi definitely brings the drama though, I'll give him that! His Baphomet drawing transcends species and gender, with its goat head, angelic wings, feminine breasts, and caducean phallus. The Latin word *Solve* is written on its raised arm and *Coagula* is written on its lowered arm, per Heinrich Khunrath's sixteenth-century engraving that's come to be known as *The Hermaphrodite*. (Four hundred or so years later, tarot scholar and *Doom Patrol* comics author Rachel Pollack would also decide to tattoo these words on the arms of her character, Coagula, the first transgender superhero.) The phrase *solve et coagula* refers to the alchemical cycle of dissolving something and then rebuilding it into something new.

This one-arm-up/one-arm-down stance is a motif that spans geographies and centuries.

According to Buddhist lore, after the baby Siddhartha was born, he took seven steps representing each of the seven directions, proclaimed "I alone am the World-Honored One," and then pointed up with one hand and down with the other, to indicate that he would unite heaven and earth.

The first time I witnessed the Sufi dervishes do their cosmic whirling dance in Istanbul, I noticed each of their arms would slowly extend as they spun, with one hand pointing up at the sky and the other pointing down to the earth. I later learned that the upward hand is meant to receive the blessings of Allah, while the downward hand is meant to share that grace with the world.

Hermes (Greek) or Mercury (Roman), the winged-footed classical god of communication and divine messages, is often shown midflight, with one hand holding his wand-like caduceus up to the sky and his other hand gesturing downward. Known as a psychopomp and a messenger of the gods, it is believed that he can cross boundaries and travel between the realms of the underworld, earth, and celestial Mount Olympus. No surprise then that many mystics associate the Magician card with Mercury.

In modern witchcraft, one of our most beloved practices is an act we call Drawing Down the Moon. During this ritual, the witch reaches out to the heavens and invites the Goddess herself to descend from her lunar throne and enter the witch's own body. Like any visitation, it's a dual operation of borrowing and becoming. We willingly offer ourselves to a force that is effulgent and enchanting, and we let it take over for a while. It's an act of apotheosis—of transforming into a divine entity for a time. In this unifying moment, the Goddess is both our guest and our host. I am Her, She is me. And though it's considered a temporary state, anyone who has experienced it will be forever changed.

Over the past few years, though, I've incorporated a new maneuver into my magical practice, which I call Striking Magician's Pose. Before I embark on a new creative undertaking, I cast my magic circle and then extend one hand up to the sky and one hand down to the earth. My eyes are closed, my spine is straight, and my feet are rooted firmly on the ground. I slow my breathing and I clearly invite Spirit to join me in my making. I ask for my work to be worthy, to be of service to something greater than me, and to reach the people it's meant to reach so that it might bring about the most possible good for the world. I ask for Spirit to collaborate with me and to help me bring its magic into matter. As I hold this pose, I imagine a sort of electrical current from above gilding my raised fingertips and then flowing down and through my arm like ichor. It then spreads around and within my whole body, eventually shooting through my lowered hand, into the material world. Then I envision it looping back from the earth into the downward hand and up my limbs and torso, until my raised hand offers it skyward. I become the Magician.

Creativity is an energy exchange. Do you remember learning how to make a potato battery in science class? The experiment used zinc, copper, wires, a potato, and an LED light. When connected just so, the potato closes the circuit between the opposite charges and the light becomes illuminated.

When creating something new, the maker also closes the circuit of an energetic exchange of opposing forces. Creative Force is a current, and the Magic Maker is the connector allowing it to flow, from *Out There* to *In Here*, and back again.

In other words: the Magician is the potato.

And as with any energetic exchange, there are opposing forces that the maker must bring into some kind of harmony, even if the results of this resolution are dissonant or seemingly erratic. (Our goal is not smoothness, it's *synthesis*.)

The Magician is the great reconciler of opposites, transcender of boundaries, bringer of balance between contrasting components. Some of the binary pairs that the Magician spans include:

MAGIC MAKER

CELESTIAL—TERRESTRIAL

MASCULINE—FEMININE

ORDER—CHAOS

LIGHT—DARK

SUBTLE—DENSE

ANALYTICAL—INTUITIVE

INTELLECTUAL—EMOTIONAL

LOVE—FEAR

MASTERY—MYSTERY

CREATION—DESTRUCTION

LIFE—DEATH

It is sometimes said that in the best creative alchemy, one plus one equals three. It's a beguilingly simple saying that points to the miraculous occurrence of two seemingly disparate elements combining to make something entirely new. The Magic Maker's job is to become a bridge between binaries, manifesting their integration and eventual mutation into an independent, unique result.

Numerous magical makers have spoken about this both/and orientation of engaging with the world. Often they write about employing different ways of seeing at the same time.

In his book *On Alchemy*, Brian Cotnoir writes, "One of the goals of alchemy is to unify the inner and outer aspects, that is, to see with both eyes." In other words, the alchemist must be cognizant of the esoteric and the exoteric, the micro and the macro. As the famous alchemical adage goes, "as above, so below"—or per Cotnoir's translation: "the highest is from the lowest and the lowest is from the highest."

On a similar note, in Leonora Carrington's imaginal memoir, *Down*

Below, she writes: "To possess a telescope without its other essential half—the microscope—seems to me a symbol of the darkest incomprehension. The task of the right eye is to peer into the telescope, while the left eye peers into the microscope." To fully comprehend reality, one must look at it with both removed objectivity and absolute intimacy.

Pagan ecofeminist writer Starhawk has differentiated between what she calls "flashlight vision" and "starlight vision." In her book *The Spiral Dance*, she writes that flashlight vision "sees the world as fixed; it focuses on one thing at a time, isolating it from its surroundings . . ." Whereas starlight vision is "the other mode of perception that is broad, holistic, and undifferentiated, see[ing] patterns and relationships rather than fixed objects . . . Starlight vision, the 'other way of knowing,' is the mode of perception of the unconscious, rather than the conscious mind." For Starhawk, flashlight vision is associated with the literal, the linear, and the rational. Starlight vision is intuitive, magical, and expansive. Switching between these two visions—or perhaps using them at the same time—allows us a multidimensional view of the world.

Self-proclaimed "writer who draws" and creativity author Austin Kleon has written extensively about creative dichotomies as well. His zine *Aristotle's "Doctrine of the Mean"* takes the philosopher's theories about how virtue is a midpoint between two extreme vices and applies this thinking to the idea of the importance of creative tension. The push/pull between polarities is where the interesting stuff happens. It forms its own force field where strange reactions and rapturous revelations occur. On his blog, Kleon has also cited Heraclitus's passage "The cosmos works by harmony of tensions, like the lyre and the bow." As a lifelong devotee of Artemis, Greek goddess of the hunt and the moon, the more resonant metaphor for me is one of archery. Only through the perfect tension of the bow and string can an arrow be shot with precision.

Friedrich Nietzsche's 1872 book *The Birth of Tragedy* popularized the Apollonion–Dionysian binary, named after the Greek gods Apollo and Dionysus. This philosophy states that there are both Apollonian artistic impulses of order, control, and logic, and oppositional Dionysian artistic impulses of frenzy, instinct, and passion. Nietzsche argued that Greek tragedies exhibited a successful fusion of these forces, though many have since made the case that these tensions are and always have been in, well, everything that humans have made.

In his 1802 novel *Heinrich von Ofterdingen,* Novalis writes that in every poem, "chaos must shimmer through the veil of order." This reminds me of when stitchers flip their embroideries over and one sees that behind the pristine picture is an unruly riot of threads and knots. In the Book of Genesis, God is said to bring forth order from tohu wa-bohu (והבו והת), which is sometimes translated to mean "formlessness and void." By extension, if we are all allegedly made in God's image, then creating is a truly divine act. Our job as makers is to take formlessness— the chaos—and shape it into something ordered and shimmering.

It's no wonder why modern and contemporary artists have felt a kinship with the Magician card and its theme of connecting the heavenly to the earthly, of transmuting immaterial elements into material creations. Surrealist painters from Victor Brauner (*The Surrealist*, 1947) to Leonora Carrington (*El Nigromante* [*The Conjurer*], ca. 1950) to Remedios Varo (*The Juggler* [*The Magician*], 1956) have each paid homage to this tarot icon, no doubt relating to the experience of being able to conjure realm-traversing, consciousness-shifting magic with their art. The Magician/Juggler made such an impression on Surrealist artist Kurt Seligmann that it is the only tarot card to which he devoted an entire chapter of his 1948 occult survey, *The Mirror of Magic*, writing, "He is the Aleph, the master-spirit of the universe which stretches before him like the juggler's table. All things of creation are tossed about by him as if they were the juggler's objects." In a 1946 article titled "Magic and the Arts," Seligmann writes,

> To the magician, All is contained in All—and All is *One*. God and the Universe are o n e. . . . Moreover: *what is above, is also below*, the visible and the invisible world reflect one another . . .
>
> The universe is harmony, and its multiplicity brought into One by a mysterious law. These principles, can they not be applied to every good work of art? Is it not the painter's task to express the marvelous manifoldness of nature through the variety of forms he depicts? And does he not, following the law which he sees in the universe, strive to bring all these forms into one organic whole?

Salvador Dalí certainly related to this magic-making archetype. In his own custom-designed tarot deck from 1984, he cast none other than himself as El Mago/The Magician. In the card, Dalí stands behind a table that is covered with elements from some of his most iconic paintings, including a melting clock from *The Persistence of Memory* (1931) and the wineglass and broken bread from *The Sacrament of the Last Supper* (1955). The Magician conjures forms and forms connections, and so it is the ideal avatar for artists and for anyone who feels called to follow their creative impulse.

Magic-Made

It's my belief that everyone is born with innate creative gifts, and that sharing those gifts with the world is our magical mission. Honing the skills we've been granted takes no small amount of labor and courage, but luckily we have help on our side. Spirit *wants* us to make use of these gifts, and it will do everything in its power to assist us in the process.

Our job as Magic Makers is to meet Spirit halfway.

We can do this by consciously inviting it to work with us and setting up the best possible circumstances that allow its presence to come through with clarity and ease. This means making it feel welcome and wanted, and opening oneself up to being a gracious receiver of its messages. It means fully committing to the craft of shaping the inspired information that Spirit sends us into a suitable, useful, even beautiful form. And it means staying with the magic, no matter what distractions, doubts, and other demons arrive to try to undermine the process.

We begin by readying ourselves to cocreate something with Spirit that wasn't there before.

MAGIC-MADE

We make believe, we make way, we make fun.

We make fools of ourselves. We make Magicians of ourselves.

We show up and stand tall, trusting that whatever we make will be of use, because in the making of it we keep Creative Force flowering and flowing. We enter the magic chamber with one arm skyward and one arm earthward, poised to pull ragged lightning and raw sparks down from the heavens and form them into fire.

We begin.

PART II

*Supernatural
Preparation*

As a witch I know that before I do any sort of magic working, there are ways in which I must prepare myself. There are special words I utter, specific tools I utilize, secret latches I unfasten. The methods I use vary depending on how much time I have or wherever I happen to be. What remains consistent is that I always make sure to signal to Spirit that I am ready for us to work together. When I do this, there is a palpable change that occurs and a different place that I seem to be operating from. I'm me, but I'm also Not Me. A version of my Self emerges, enchanted and enhanced. I slip into a new sphere, my senses heightened like some sort of crepuscular creature. It feels as if I have taken steps beyond myself toward an occult Other. I have opened a great gateway with my own private key. I have become a bridge between the usual and the super-usual, and magic crosses over and through me.

Over time I've learned that the mystical methods I use to prepare myself for my witchcraft can be implemented before I begin any sort of creative activity. And so, before I sit down to write, I now go through a quick series of exercises to help recalibrate myself and reaffirm my connection to divine, generative flow. I call this shifting into Magician Mode. When I'm working from this way of being, I find my ideation is more easeful and my production more fruitful.

Whether I'm casting a spell or writing an essay, what's required is a fair amount of unbroken focus, a sense of timelessness (even when—*especially* when—I'm on deadline), and an openness to what I'll call otherworldly input. Switching into Magician Mode before I start working helps me reach this heightened state of being. I get there by taking a few steps to help my body, my mind, and my space merge into a shared site of expansion and creative expression. Before a game, a basketball player changes into their uniform, does some exercises, and psychs themselves up to play as well as possible before they take the court. They may even ask for assistance from a godly being or guide. Creative folks can likewise benefit from preparatory rituals, and in my experience, magical ones are especially useful.

Something to note is that this preparation doesn't need to take long or be elaborate. Those of us who make things don't often have the luxury of designated workspaces or countless hours of time. I have become self-employed relatively recently, and even now I find myself having to write between meetings or in tandem with the many other projects that help me pay the bills, not to mention the obligations to family and community that fill my days. Before this, I worked at a corporate office for fourteen years, always in a cubicle with zero privacy. Still, I managed to get my creative work done by slipping it into whatever spaces I could find. And though there are certainly artists with giant studios, assistants, nannies, and enough funding to work for long stretches, they are by far the exception. Most of us are making things with limited resources, and when we finally do find the time to create, we can feel incredible pressure to make something worthy. All of this is to say: I understand why the idea of adding a whole extra step of preparation before making something can feel daunting.

But what I've found is that shifting into Magician Mode actually saves time in the long run because it helps me focus more quickly and quiets

SUPERNATURAL PREPARATION

the voices in my head that tell me I'm tired, I'm too busy, I'm not good enough, my work is a waste. Magical preparation actually helps me get out of my own way and into the path of Creative Force. And I can do it anywhere and with as much or as little fuss and fanfare as I wish.

The other wonderful thing about switching into this mode is that the effects of doing it have been cumulative. By incorporating this practice into my routine over years and myriad projects, I've built trust between myself and Spirit. I now know that if I take a few moments to intentionally shift orientation away from my small self, the grand Something will be there to greet me, even on days when I'm feeling unmotivated or unsure about my work. It's a trust fall into magic. And magic always, always catches me.

Now you may be shifting into Magician Mode to some extent already whether you realize it or not. Many of us have a favorite mug we like to drink out of when we're working or a preferred pen we like to use when we're jotting down big ideas. I've known musicians who always light a candle before they start composing a song and screenwriters who like their desk to be arranged just so before they begin hammering out a scene. Some of this behavior may be chalked up to habit, superstition, or even outright compulsion. To be clear, I don't believe one has to do the exact same thing every time or else their project is somehow jinxed. So if you arrive at the library one day and find someone else sitting in your cherished Special Writing Chair, have no fear! A codependency on lucky charms or rote routines is not what we're after. But there are healthy, intentional ways that a magical approach can be applied to the start of our creative processes, even before we write one word or paint a single stroke.

Please note that, as with the entirety of this book, the examples that follow are not meant to be prescriptive. You may choose to implement only some or even just one of these techniques. You may add to or subtract from them at any given time, swap between them, or swirl them together. You may distill them down or embellish them to high heaven. Your creative opening ceremony might take a moment, a half hour, or an entire week. The only requirement is that you try incorporating some ritualized way of drawing a boundary between the sacred and the mundane. Of separating THAT/THERE/THEN from THIS/HERE/NOW.

Here are some ways you can do a bit of supernatural preparation and switch into your own Magician Mode whenever you choose.

Cleansing/Clearing

It's sometimes said that a writer's house is never cleaner than when they have a looming assignment. They become convinced that they can't possibly work unless their desk is tidy, their laundry is folded, and their floor is polished to a lakelike sheen. And while it's true that a sudden swell of neat-freakery is often just a means of procrastination, I do think the urge to declutter before starting to create is an instinctive one. When we bring something new into the world, whether an idea or an ice sculpture, space must be made for it. However, this space need not be physical. There are time-tested techniques that can help us clarify our thoughts, land back in our bodies, and cast a line out to the divine.

At Shangri-La, the legendary Malibu music studio run by Grammy-laden producer Rick Rubin, all of the rooms are painted white and there is no art on the walls in order to encourage the visiting musicians to feel clear and able to more easily connect to their own artistic current. Rubin's employees not only clean the space and burn purifying incense between each session, they also repaint all of the interiors white so that the next guest can have as pristine a creative environment as possible. Home organization books like Marie Kondo's *The Life-Changing Magic of Tidying Up* and Margareta Magnusson's *The Gentle Art of Swedish Death Cleaning* have popularized the notion that clearing out clutter is good for one's emotional landscape. And certainly, when our environment is dirty or crammed with stuff we don't need, we can become distracted and energy stagnates. There isn't only psychological reasoning behind this. Animistic systems purport that all things have a spirit. In Japanese Shinto practice, it is believed that everything from trees to rice to doorways are imbued with their own specific deities called kami. Marie Kondo spent five years as a Shinto shrine maiden—or miko—and she credits this with helping her develop some of her signature tidying rituals such as greeting every house she enters with a prolonged bow and thanking every object before discarding it. So if you feel compelled to clean your carpets before chipping away at your novel, by all means go for it. Your house spirits might appreciate it.

But what I'm more interested in for our purposes is how we cleanse *ourselves* in order to make room for new magic. Call me lazy, but I confess I'm less concerned about organizing my papers into neat piles than I am about clearing out the spiritual cobwebs before I sit down to write, lead a ceremony, or do any other sort of arts-and-crafting. The idea here is to let go of the residue of the mundane. And while there are highly involved cleansing rites some choose to engage in, such as silent retreats (maybe someday), fasting (no thank you), or abstinence (*fuck* no), lucky for us, some of the finest magical cleansing agents are the simplest. I tend to think about these elementally, and incorporating even just one of them into your magico-creative prep can work wonders.

✳ Air ✳

The first cleansing method is the most readily available, because all it requires is you and your lovely lungs. Intentional, focused breathing is

CLEANSING/CLEARING

beguilingly uncomplicated, but it has an immediate effect. Stop what you're doing right now, close your eyes, and take three slow, deep breaths.

I'll wait.

Now check in and see how you feel. Calmer? Less rushed? More present? Many of us have been led in some sort of breathwork exercise over the years, thanks to the popularity of yoga and other such practices. But I now begin every personal ritual and every workshop I lead by taking three deep, delicious breaths. And when I'm podcasting, I sometimes lead my guest in breathing with me before we start to record, to get us both feeling focused and in sync with one another.

Of course, there are much more elaborate versions of breathwork, from square breathing to quell anxiety and Breath of Fire to increase energy. Entire breath-focused books and a legion of YouTube videos exist offering exercises one can follow as well as physiological evidence as to how deep breathing positively affects our biochemistry and cognitive function. The simple act of inhaling and exhaling with measured attention is tremendously good for our health, no question.

But I also love breathwork because it connects me to Spirit in the most primary way. Life is sacred, and taking a moment to deliberately fill my body with divine vitality reminds me that Spirit is immanent—it infuses everything and everyone, including me. When we focus on our breath, we also invite inspiration to enter us. *Respiration* and *inspiration* are spiritual sisters. The word *inspire* means "breathe or blow into," and per its original connotation, the one breathing into the recipient is an external, supernatural being. If inspiration is the breath of the gods, I welcome their presence with each inhalation.

As Grammy-winning musical enchantress Stevie Nicks told *Creem* magazine in 1982, "I feel there are good spirits everywhere when I am writing my songs, helping me. I just feel them and feel good. And it's not stupid or mystical or weird. I just get good feelings from—I don't know—the air."

So breathe, and let the air cleanse you. And let Spirit breathe into you too.

✳ Fire ✳

Candle lighting is an essential part of my practice, and it is an immediate way to shift the atmosphere of a space, mark the start of sacred work, and connect to Creative Force. That said, the element of fire bears other gifts in addition to the inner and outer illumination it brings. When used in a safe and controlled manner, it also helps cleanse negativity and rid us of unwanted presences. As Phyllis Curott writes in her book *Witch Crafting*, "fire is often used for banishings because of its unique energy that transforms by consuming."

We don't often think of fire as having cleansing properties other than to turn raw food into something safer to ingest. That said, there have always been people who incorporate burning into their purification rituals. The Pagan holiday Beltane is a celebration of fertility and the hot-blooded sensuality of spring, and etymologists have proposed that its name comes from a Celtic word meaning "bright fire." Modern witches celebrate this holiday by dancing around a maypole with colorful ribbons to symbolize sexual union, and by building a bonfire to honor the life-giving power of the sun. However, it is believed that the original Gaelic custom was for celebrants to build two fires and to walk their cattle between them to get purified and receive protective blessings from the gods. Other contemporary Pagan rituals include jumping over a fire or a candle to symbolize a transition from one phase of being to another, with the smoke as a purifying force here too. By burning away the old, and leaping over a flaming threshold between past and future, we can start anew.

The Indigenous American practice of smudging has likewise been popularized—and many would argue appropriated—by non-Native people. And though the term *smudge* and the white sage often used for this purpose are both best left to the tribes who originated the practice, burning other plants with magical intent is something that is available to everyone. Lighting incense or herb bundles—especially those that are ethically harvested or locally procured—is an extremely effective way of clearing negative energy and shifting the self into another state. Smoke is also believed to deliver messages to the gods, so you are not only cleansing your surroundings when you burn incense, you are also employing a sacred courier service—and one that's divinely scented to boot.

Taking a smoke bath is also something I do regularly before working. I simply hold some lit incense or dried herbs in one hand and pass this over myself, making sure that as much of my body as possible gets touched by smoke. I envision it forming a perfumed cocoon around me, swirling me into my next metamorphic stage. Afterward I always feel lighter and ready to take wing.

✴ Water ✴

Certainly the most literal way to cleanse is to wash grime away with water. But the beauty of this is that it's easy to add magic to the cleaning that is already part of our daily routine. I've known many brujas to add Florida water to their floor washes, and there are now entire lines of house cleaning products that include ingredients believed to be both energetically and physically cleansing. (HausWitch's Counter Magick products and supernatural home cleaners come to mind.)

Submerging oneself in water is a far more intimate act than housekeeping, and one many of us engage in each day for purposes of hygiene and general upkeep. But this mundane activity can be elevated with awareness and an added intentional ingredient or two. Soaps made with any number of magical herbs and oils can be easily found in shops or online, and same goes for bathing mixtures full of various potions and petals. Burnish yourself in their beauty, and as you use them, envision any stresses or distractions of the day sliding off of you and down the drain. Those of us who are fortunate enough to have a tub or shower in our homes essentially have twenty-four-hour access to a full-body cauldron.

My favorite way to cleanse before any creative work is to take a salt bath (unprocessed natural salt, not table salt). I adore the idea of immersing myself in crystals. As I soak, I picture them drawing out impurities while fortifying me with their mineral magic. Taking a dip outdoors is also transformative, whether it be in an ocean, river, lake, or waterfall. Each of these bodies of water has their own current and their own mythopoetic way of renewing and replenishing.

In Christianity, the watery ritual of baptism is meant to wash away sin and initiate someone into the faith, and there are four different methods that can be used. Total submersion and partial immersion are when all or part of the body is surrounded in water. Aspersion refers to sprinkling holy water on the body (and is an example of how language mutates over time, as the phrase *casting aspersions* now colloquially carries a negative connotation). Affusion, the most common means of baptism, is when holy water is poured on the body, usually the forehead. Customary blessings and ges-

CLEANSING/CLEARING

tures designate this as a specifically Christian rite, such as repeating the aqueous action three times to symbolize the holy trinity. However, the origin of the word *baptize* means simply "to dip" or "to steep," and there are many non-Christian examples of similar rites. To that end, one may choose submersion, immersion, aspersion, or affusion for their own cleansing ritual, and symbolically cast out any pollutant to one's creative process.

After my book *Waking the Witch* came out in 2019, I decided to take part in my very first mikvah, the Jewish bathing ritual of purification. I had poured so many years of creative energy into that project, and now that it had finally been released into the world, I felt called to mark the occasion and begin the next phase of life with a clean slate. Judaism is an important part of my ancestral heritage (I sometimes refer to myself as "Jewitch"), but I'm not particularly religious. I do love the tradition of going to the mikvah to purify oneself for certain milestones, holy moments, and rites of passage. The feminist in me does, however, take issue with the Orthodox Jewish belief that a menstruating person is so unclean that conjugal relations (and in some cases, any touching at all) between a wife and her husband are forbidden until she cleanses herself in the mikvah. Still, I was sure to be respectful and delayed my visit until a week after my period stopped, as I understood that I was a guest in someone else's sacred space, and so I should adhere to their house rules as much as possible.

As with entering other public pools or baths (Japanese onsen come to mind) there is also a requisite pre-cleansing one must undergo before immersing oneself in communally shared water. For the mikvah, this means washing in a private bathroom on the premises and removing any dirt, detritus, or human-made accoutrements from the entire body, including jewelry, makeup, nail polish, bandages, contact lenses, even dentures. After I fully prepared myself, I stepped into a quiet, softly lit room containing a small pool of naturally flowing water (using pumped or carried water is prohibited according to Jewish law). An attendant held my robe for me and guided my squinting, corrective-lens-less self into the liquid warmth. Interestingly, in Jewish custom there is also a triple immersion during the mikvah rites, usually done once before reciting a prayer and two consecutive times after that. In my case, I brought three different Hebrew prayers that spoke to me, making sure to dunk my entire head after each recitation from my soggy printout.

The walk back to my apartment was more of a floatation. Experiencing the mikvah filled me with a sense of peace I hadn't been able to access during the months of excitement and anxiety leading up to my book's publication. It also deepened the connection to my ancestors, as if the cord of blood and magic that ties us together was somehow reinforced. Drifting home with damp hair and a cleansed soul, I felt remade, and ready to receive whatever new projects and pathways awaited me.

✲ Earth ✲

It may seem counterintuitive at first to cleanse using earth. We're taught that dirt is, well, dirty—something to wash *off* and not *with*. But communing with earth can be extremely purifying, not to mention how it brings us closer to the very element where so much growth and transmutation occurs. The word *alchemy*, after all, is born from the dirt: it comes from *kēme*—the word Egyptians had for their country, which is derived from *khmi* or "black earth." The dark color of Egypt's soil denoted fertility—as opposed to the miles of beige desert sands that surrounded it.

The Aztecs were devotees of Tlazoltéotl, the goddess of dirt. She is a deity of dualities: of misdeed and holiness; adulterers and midwives; transgression and forgiveness. She is often depicted with dirt or excrement around her mouth, and one of her epithets is the Eater of Ordure. By ingesting the filth of sin, she purifies it and turns the vices of her believers into virtue and revitalization.

On my desk is a clear plastic container filled with blessed dirt from El Santuario de Chimayo, an over two-hundred-year-old Roman Catholic church about forty minutes outside of Santa Fe. Visitors make pilgrimages there, many on foot, some from hundreds of miles away. Beyond the beautiful grounds and sanctuary, one finds a modest back room where miracles are said to occur. Here is El Pocito, or "The Little Well," which despite its watery moniker is actually a hole in the floor said to be filled with holy dirt. It is believed that if you rub some on your body, you will be blessed, and your ailments will become healed. The passageway to this room is filled with abandoned crutches and braces, evidence of cleared maladies, purged pain.

One need not venture far to find sacred ground, however. All earth is holy, and so connecting with it as a cleansing practice is quite easy to do. The expression "touch grass" has become an offhand way to gently admonish someone for losing perspective. But I will say that going for a walk or simply standing outside and envisioning myself rooting downward is remarkably effective at making me feel anchored, and at helping me let go of stress and anxious thoughts. The Grounding Movement encourages people to spend time with their bare feet on earth, as it is thought that this allows one's body to absorb negatively charged electrons and neutralize harmful free radicals. Whether or not this is the case remains to be scientifically proven, but I can say from experience that doing it makes me feel better—held and more present.

The Japanese practice of shinrin-yoku, or forest bathing, has become quite popular of late. Essentially a mindfulness technique, it's a form of nature walk that is slow-paced, not strenuous, and focused on one's sensory experience. It's considered to be therapeutic on multiple levels, soothing for one's inner terrain, a balm for spirit and mind. Trees also emit volatile oils called phytoncides that have antimicrobial properties and may have positive effects on the immune system—and so biochemically there seems to be benefits to shinrin-yoku as well. I imagine this is also why gardening buffs find their pastime so peaceful. Plants are pacifying, and dirt is medicine.

I'm going to confess something shameful to you now, which is this: Despite all of the encouraging evidence that the outdoors is a vast temple of healing—despite the fact that I'm a *witch*, for fuck's sake!—sometimes I just really don't want to leave my house. This, my friend, is what magic gemstones are for. And before you ask, no, I don't know how crystals work, or if they're pseudoscience or keepers of ancient terrestrial wisdom. They may work like Dumbo's feather—something we clutch, thinking it's the reason we can do challenging things that, in actuality, we could have done on our own. What I do know is that they are beautiful, and that many Magic Makers, such as my favorite painter Remedios Varo, have surrounded themselves with crystals and other spiritually supportive stones when they do their work. Clear quartz is said to be particularly effective for cleansing as well as for bringing through messages from the other side with truthfulness and clarity. This is also the stone many tarot readers use between sessions to clear energy from their decks. Whatever cleansing rocks you select for your own creative preparation, just make sure you get them from ethically sourced suppliers—or even better, get over your own indoor-kid tendencies and go out and gather them yourself.

Circling/Centering

Before I sit down to write, lead a workshop, cast a spell, or do any sort of other magical work, I always call circle. While my cleansing and clearing methods beforehand may vary, calling circle is a nonnegotiable act for me. Psychedelics experts talk about the influence that "set and setting" have on someone's trip. The idea is that a calm mindset and a comfortable environment are key factors in encouraging a positive psychedelic experience. The same is true for any consciousness-altering activity. Casting a circle before I make my magic is the way in which I take care of both set and setting in one fell swoop. It helps quiet inner chatter and bring my focus into the present. And it builds an energetic cauldron around me, no matter my physical surroundings. By calling in benevolent, supportive energies, I'm drawing Creative Force toward me, as well as setting up a spiritual safety net to help keep the bad stuff out. I've cast elaborate circles at the top of my lungs in public ceremony on a moonlit Grecian beach, and I've muttered quick circle castings under my breath while riding the subway. I'm currently at our little house in the hills of upstate New York, and I cast a circle in my office before I began typing these words. It is the primary way I shift into Magician Mode, and it's something that anyone can do, anywhere.

The topic of magic circles may remind you of that scene in *The Craft* where the four teen witches "call the corners" in a windswept, fiery ring near the ocean. And while the god they invoke was invented for the film (pour one out for Manon), the language they use was based on real Wiccan rites. However, the crafting of sacred circles is a far older practice, and a universal one at that. Structures from Bighorn Medicine Wheel in Wyoming to Britain's Stonehenge are evidence of a long history of humans using circles as both ceremonial gathering spaces and technologies to track and connect with the cosmos.

A circle doesn't have to be constructed out of megaliths in order to be effective. Salt, chalk, candles, flower petals, a hoop scratched in the dirt, a group of people dancing in the round, a single body twirling under the night sky—all of these can form an enclosure for generating magic and sealing the maker safely within.

Best of all, you can make a magic circle using nothing but your words. The important thing is to invite in elements and/or entities to surround you from all directions. Many modern witches call in the Spirits of Air in the East, Fire in the South, Water in the West, Earth in the North, and Spirit in the Center. My teacher, the green witch Robin Rose Bennett, taught me to cast circle seven directions–style, and to include the Spirits of Below and the Spirits of Above just before calling in the Center.

Remember: the construct of the four or five elements is just that—a construct. The notion of the four classical elements of Fire, Air, Water, and Earth was put forth by the Greek philosopher Empedocles during the fifth century BCE. (He also believed that there were two other elements, Love and Strife, which would interact with and influence the other four. If you feel like inviting them to your magic circle as well, be my guest, though I imagine Strife is a bit of a wet blanket.) In the fourth century BCE, Aristotle went and added his own fifth element to Empedocles's system. He called this Aether, and unlike the other four terrestrial elements, it was celestial and moved in a circle. Other names for Aether are Quintessence or simply "the fifth element," and today it has evolved into symbolizing Spirit, Mystery, or Mind, depending on whom you ask. The five-pointed star, or pentagram, has a long history of representing these five elements being in harmony.

Other cultures have their own elemental constructs. Chinese metaphysics uses a five-element system: Fire, Earth, Metal, Water, and Wood. In Vedic tradition there are also five elements, but these are Earth, Water, Fire, Wind, and Void. Either of these versions may feel appropriate to call on when casting your circle, depending upon your own ancestry or spiritual orientation.

And then there is the Judeo-Christian practice of calling circle by invoking the names of angels rather than elements. A Jewish variation traditionally uttered as part of bedtime prayers goes like this: "To my right, Michael, and to my left, Gabriel, in front of me, Uriel, and behind me, Raphael, and over my head, the Shekhinah." Shekinah is a feminine Hebrew word essentially meaning "divine presence," and so again, we see the notion of a fifth entity symbolizing some ineffable, holy force.

When I teach circle casting to my students, I sometimes give them an exercise where I have them fill in their own blanks with any elements or protective guides they would like:

To my right _____
and to my left _____
in front of me _____
and behind me _____
and over my head _____

The results are unfailingly delightful and often quite moving—and they don't always include the names of deities or angels. I've heard people surround themselves with the spirits of deceased grandparents and pets, tarot archetypes, artistic heroes, and folkloric characters from their personal spiritual paths. When beloved children's book author and illustrator Maurice Sendak was asked about his faith by Terry Gross on NPR's *Fresh Air*, he responded thusly:

> **Sendak:** Faith is—you know who my gods are, who I believe in fervently?
>
> **Gross:** Who?
>
> **Sendak:** Herman Melville, Emily Dickinson—she's probably the top. Mozart, Shakespeare, Keats. These are wonderful gods who have—who've gotten me through the narrow straits of life.

And though I'm fairly sure Sendak wasn't in the habit of casting magic circles himself, I think the sentiment is relevant for our purposes here. Anything, anyone, or any One is appropriate to call into your circle, so long as each helps you feel protected, fortified, and magically activated.

When I cast my own circle, I face each direction I'm calling in, and after invoking each one, I say "Blessed be." But there are no exact words one must use here. The important thing is to address the directions as if you are welcoming an honored guest. As with any invocation, I recommend using words that are respectful and inviting as opposed to commanding and controlling. Because, well, that's the kind of host I like to be. And while I tend to meet the moment and change the words I use every time I call circle, here is a short version you may use or riff on further if you find it helpful:

CIRCLING/CENTERING

Welcome to the Spirit of Air in the East,
Direction of Breath and New Beginnings.

Blessed be.

Welcome to the Spirit of Fire in the South,
Direction of Will and Creative Sparks.

Blessed be.

Welcome to the Spirit of Water in the West,
Direction of Flowing and Deep Dreams.

Blessed be.

Welcome to the Spirit of Earth in the North,
Direction of Fertility in all Its Forms.

Blessed be.

Welcome to the Spirit of Below, Direction of
Ancestors and the Wisdom of Shadows.

Blessed be.

Welcome to the Spirit of Above, Direction of
Shining Guides and Bright Possibilities.

Blessed be.

Welcome to the Spirit of the Center, Direction of
Enchantment, Magic, and Holy, Holy, Holy Love.

Blessed be.

The circle is cast. We are between worlds.

That last bit, "We are between worlds," is a standard phrase that many modern witches use, and it is always my favorite part. When I utter those words, I feel a palpable change. I have made the declaration that whatever occurs henceforth within this circle is happening in another realm. I'm in a heightened state, primed for marvels and supernatural surprises. And though the space I'm in may not have become visibly altered, I'm able to access another layer of it. A veil has been pulled back, a divine door is ajar, a portal is open. I am here, and I am Somewhere Else. Beyond time and space and self.

It's important to note that there is no correct routine or cadence for circle casting. In other words, some may choose to cast circle every time they sit at their desk to write or enter the sound booth to record. Others may choose to cast circle at the beginning of a new endeavor and then consider that circle to be intact throughout the entire duration of the project's life cycle. In either case, you just want to be sure to always open the circle back up once you have reached your stopping point. (I've been taught that we close or seal the circle when we cast it, and that we open or release the circle when we're done.) We open circle at the end of our magical activities by thanking and dismissing the elements in the opposite order we called them in.* Think of your circle as a boundary marker for a distinctly liminal zone where mundane rules don't apply. It is an active space until you deactivate it. While the circle is sealed and operational, you are dwelling within a space of infinite—and in-process—potential. When you are inside your circle, you are Queen of the In-Between, King of Making, Mage of Infinite Imagining.

I first encountered the phrase "betwixt and between" as an anthropology student at NYU when I was assigned Victor Turner's *The Forest of Symbols,* his 1967 book about Ndembu initiation practices. In it, Turner

---

*I've included an example of how I open circle on page 320.

writes about the concept of liminality—a transitional period that initiates experienced during rites of passage wherein they were no longer children but not yet adults. (Cue Britney Spears.) Turner says that liminality is "a realm of pure possibility whence novel configurations of ideas and relations may arise." And though he is describing an inner state of being, there are physical environments that can also give a sense of betwixt-and-betweenness. These are places that feel outside the norm, spaces of potential where anything may happen. The ancient Celts spoke of "thin places"—special locations that feel otherworldly, as if the heavens were touching earth. Others have written about an immaterial realm that one may access only during transcendent states. Occult artist Austin Osman Spare wrote about how to use meditation to reach a place of non-duality, which he referred to as "the mystic state of Neither-Neither." No matter its name or its geography, it's that sort of slippery space that I am trying to reach when I create, and casting a magic circle helps me get there.

As you've no doubt gathered by now, creative mysticism is full of seeming contradiction and paradox. Dwelling in liminality and entering a state that is between worlds is crucial, but feeling centered as I do so is equally important. The Magician is a bridge between worlds, and a bridge must be steady, unobstructed, and well-balanced. When a hose is bent, water doesn't flow as easily. When a wheel is off its axis, the ride is far more rickety. The same is true when we engage in the magic of making. Centering ourselves helps everything run more smoothly.

M. C. Richards writes about this beautifully in her book *Centering in Pottery, Poetry, and the Person*. When working at the potter's wheel, one must center the clay and maintain that centeredness as best one possibly can as they bring it into shape. Richards believes that the same is true whether she is writing poems, teaching her students, or just going about living her life. She realizes that by keeping herself centered, her perspective expands, and so does her soul. She writes, "The world is always bigger than one's own focus. And as we bring ourselves into center wherever we are, the more of that world we can bring into service, the larger will be the capacity of our action and our understanding." Here we see that centering not only helps with her pottery and other work, but helps her become more centered as a human being overall.

I'm mindful of staying centered throughout my creative process, but incorporating some intentional techniques during my prep time has been extremely helpful as well. I confess I'm an inconsistent meditator in the formal sense, but whenever I do it, I feel far more centered as an artist, a witch, a partner, a friend. There are so many styles of meditation: sitting or standing, counting breath or watching thoughts, listening to narration or music or total silence, with eyes open or closed or gazing into flame. Calling circle is a meditative practice for me: the rhythm of the words, the rotating and swaying of my body, the slide into a starry state. A couple of decades ago I took a weekend workshop in Primordial Sound Meditation, which is a mantra-based practice like the better-known Transcendental Meditation (or TM), but which, at the time, cost a third of the price to learn. I was taught to sit somewhere comfortable, close my eyes, and repeat the mantra I was given over and over in my head twice a day for twenty minutes a session. And while this was undoubtedly helpful when I was diligent about it in my younger days, I can tell you that doing this just once a day, or for shorter bursts, or even on an erratic as-it-occurs-to-me schedule, also works wonders.

I have deep admiration for David Lynch, who is one of my favorite filmmakers and who was an avid TM advocate. He didn't diverge from his twice-daily meditation practice for over fifty years, and he swore that this was the source of his well-being and his most powerful creative ideas. In his book *Catching the Big Fish: Meditation, Consciousness, and Creativity*, he writes, "Ideas are like fish. If you want to catch little fish, you can stay in the shallow water. But if you want to catch the big fish, you've got to go deeper. Down deep, the fish are more powerful, and more pure. They're huge and abstract. And they're very beautiful." Meditation is what kept Lynch centered and receptive to inspiration.

He also writes about how TM helped him access the Unified Field, a term that physicists and metaphysicians alike use to refer to an ultimate, interconnected source of being. No matter the reasoning for it, I know from my own experience that centering helps me feel closer to that Creative Force.

M. C. Richards comes to this conclusion too. She explains that centering is not about keeping the self separate but rather helping us commune with the life force overall. She writes, "We bring our self into a centering function, which brings it into union with all other elements. This is love. This is destruction of ego, in that its partialities are sacrificed to wholeness. Then the miracle happens." This is why casting circle, calling in the elements, and greeting each direction isn't about carving up the universe into bite-size units. Nor is meditation a cutting-off from reality. These practices are about merging with something that is greater than any one individual or component.

If you aren't a meditator or a circle caster, that's perfectly fine. I center myself in other ways too. Listening to music is one of the primary tools that helps me shift into—and maintain—Magician Mode. There is a specific album that I find particularly centering, and that's Lykanthea's *Migration* EP. I listen to it at least once whenever I write, and as soon as I put it on, something inside me recognizes that this is a time for magic-making.

I love it so much, in fact, that her track "Hand and Eye" is the theme song of my podcast *The Witch Wave*. And while I don't believe in shortcuts to creativity per se, Lykanthea's music is definitely an enchantment accelerant for me. Perhaps there is a talismanic song or album that you can listen to as an auditory anchor. After all, the root of *enchant* is the Latin *cantare*, which means "to sing."

Finally, one of the simplest centering techniques I know of is Striking Magician's Pose. I stand in the middle of the room, raise one arm up toward the sky, and stretch one arm down toward the earth, and I feel my body linking together the realms of the celestial and the terrestrial. As I do so, I envision magic flowing to and from me, charging me up with creative energy from the divine Life Source itself.

Try it now. Plant your feet steady on the ground. Extend one hand to the sphere above and one hand to the sphere below. Say "I am the Magician. I am the Magician. I am the Magician!"

And presto change-o, so you are.

Invocation/Altar-cation

My friend Susan Aberth is a professor of art history at Bard College who also happens to be one of the most magical people I know. She once told me this about spirits: "They can't help you if you don't ask!" She encouraged me to request assistance from the unseen world whenever I need it, because in her experience, spirits need permission to be able to intervene. And while I don't pretend to understand the full mechanics of circumventing phantasmic red tape, it seems to me like sensible advice.

Since that conversation, I've been in the habit of asking for help from invisible entities throughout my day-to-day goings-on, and especially when doing any sort of creative work. I usually feel that this makes my life run more smoothly and my creative obstacles more easily dissolved. On my more skeptical days, I figure it can't hurt. As thousands of years of history have shown us, requesting otherworldly assistance is an extremely human thing to do.

It's often said that artists must court the Muse, a celestial being who bestows creative inspiration upon those who win her favor. In ancient Greece, it was believed that there were nine muses, each with a different area of specialty, including Calliope, the muse of epic poetry, and Thalia, the muse of comedy. If connecting with any of them gives you confidence, then I'm sure they would love to hear from you.

When I was younger, angels weren't really my thing; the only depictions I was exposed to seemed vanilla and a little vapid. My local Hallmark store had shelves of angelic figurines wearing porcelain gowns and schmoopey gazes, and I just didn't see the appeal. Eventually I would learn that the original meaning of the word *angel* is "messenger," and that they could come in any form: a beam of light, a million-eyed mass of whirling feathers, an R&B-crooning subway busker in disguise.

Poet Federico García Lorca famously had disdain for muses and angels, much preferring a darker creative spirit that he and his Spanish brethren called duende. In his 1933 lecture "The Theory and Play of Duende," he describes this entity as being associated with soulfulness, earthiness, and emotional depth. He writes that duende has "wings made of rusty knives" and that it "loves the edge, the wound, and draws close to places where forms fuse in a yearning beyond visible expression." There is a romantic whiff of death about duende, and both the teenage demi-goth and the crone-to-be inside of me find this to be positively irresistible. It makes me think of how the underworldly word *chthonic* is the true opposite of celestial (and also one of David Bowie's most overused words according to his 1998 *Vanity Fair* Proust Questionnaire). A work of art's duende-quotient is something I think about a lot, and when I don't respond well to a song or film that's otherwise been celebrated by the masses, it's usually because there's not enough duende in it for my taste. All of this to say, if you want to be like Lorca and "Reject the angel, and give the Muse a kick," you're not alone. Duende is there to wrap you in its dark, delicious shadow.

I'm going to let you in on a little secret: you're allowed to ask for help from anyone or any One. It can be God, the Messiah, or Mnemosyne. It can be the Great Mother, Mother Mary, or Mother Goose. It can be Buddha, Batman, or Bilbo Baggins. It can be your great-great-grandmothers or the Great

INVOCATION/ALTAR-CATION

Pumpkin, the triple Goddess or Ganesha. In other words, you can ask for help from any inspiring being that ignites you and fills your heart with creative fire.

When I invite in the presences I work with, I always do so out loud—even if it's just a whisper. The root word of *invoke* is *vocare*, "to call," and it's related to words like *vox*, *voice*, and *vocal*. The voice is an instrument of vibration and resonance. It requires breath. It runs on rhythm. It is a powerful tool for calling in any incorporeal collaborators, and the way we use it helps us shift into a different energetic frequency. I'm a great admirer of my friend and frequent co-teacher, the occult poet Janaka Stucky. When he recites his poems, he uses what he calls his magical voice. His sounds are rounder, more voluminous, and somehow mesmeric, as if polished, musical stones are tumbling out of his mouth. When he does this, he is operating from an altered state, and using a voice that he senses the gods respond to.

Invocation need not be performative, though. As long as we are speaking with clarity and humility, our creative guides will feel welcome. We do this by orienting ourselves toward magical forces in a respectful, interrelational manner. In the 1923 book *I and Thou* by philosopher Martin Buber, the author expounds upon the difference between addressing another being as "Thou" rather than "It." He says that in an "I-It" relationship, there is a separateness: the I is always objectifying the It and treating it as an other thing. In an "I-Thou" relationship, there is a shared subjectivity. When you refer to someone or something as "Thou," it feels more reverential, as if you are speaking to them as a greatly respected equal and treating them as an envoy of holiness. It reminds me of how the Sanskrit phrase *namaste* is sometimes translated to mean "I bow to the divine in you." When we treat an Other as an extension or expression of the divine, the relationship is elevated. This is true whether we are addressing close friends or strangers, animals or plant life, a manuscript we're writing or a menu we're devising, a fountain pen we're holding or a glitching printer we're negotiating with. Magic is how we communicate with the Thou in everything.

And so I approach Spirit, my muses, my guides, and my work as if each is a Thou rather than an It. I don't necessarily use the word *Thou* when I'm communicating with them, but the Thou is implied in my attitude toward them and in the way I handle myself when I'm inviting their influence.

As we already established, I always welcome the seven directions when I cast my magic circle, but there are other presences I invoke as well. I will sometimes call upon specific ancestors by name, as well as specific deities that relate to the work I'll be doing. For my magico-creative practice, there are three Greco-Roman deities that I've been invoking of late. These are entities who bolster and embolden me, and so perhaps one or more of them will arrive when you call upon them too.

The first I've discussed at length already, and that is Mercury (Roman) or Hermes (Greek). As a messenger god who flits between realms, I invoke him to help with clear communication, boundary-crossing, and world-traversing. He is helpful for anyone who is hoping to get their message across no matter their field. That said, he has deep associations with those working in the humanities, which is why the craters of the planet Mercury are named after people who have made significant contributions to the arts, e.g., Angelou, Beckett, Caravaggio. Talk about goals! In addition to a small statue of Mercury that is centered on one of my altars, I also keep a vial of quicksilver nearby. On Wednesdays I give him extra love, as that's the day of the week said to be sacred to him according to old astrological magic. On Mercury's Day, I burn special incense for him that's blended with herbs associated with his planetary energies. Sometimes I'll slip on my Mercury dime necklace. Though these coins actually depict an image of Lady Liberty wearing a winged cap, many have interpreted this as being a representation of Mercury, and magic practitioners of various backgrounds have used it as such. Ever the protean being, I imagine Mercury doesn't mind this one bit. Mercury the magician helps me stay fluid as I labor to shape supernatural transmissions into crafted earthly forms.

Artemis is my matron goddess, and she has been with me for so long I can't quite recall when I first made her acquaintance. She became a pronounced presence for me in my teen years, which is no surprise, as adolescent girls are said to be under her protection. At her temple in Brauron, the young female initiates who worshipped her would engage in the arkteia, a ritual dance in which they "became" she-bears. A Greek lunar deity associated with freedom and the wilderness, she supports the balance of unfettered thinking and arrow-sharp precision. She is also said to be a goddess of midwifery, and despite the fact that it's become a bit cliché to compare writing a book to, say, having a literal child, I'll take any creative help I can get! My collection of Artemis moons, arrows, bears, and deer are too numerous to count, and our house in the hills is dedicated to her. My whole life can be considered an Artemis devotional, and certainly my work as a writer and a witch is a significant part of that offering.

Then there is a goddess who is a much newer mystical companion of mine, though I've admired her from afar for quite some time. This would be Iris, the Greek goddess of rainbows. Like Hermes, she is a messenger deity, and she is often also depicted holding a caduceus, the double-serpent staff of Olympian heralds. Iris signifies beauty, hope, and divine messages (especially those that seem to suddenly appear out of thin air), and so I find her to be a perfect deity to collaborate with for any type of art-working. The iris of the eye and the flower kingdom are both named after her, as is the word *iridescent*. One of the things that appeals to me most about her is that there is very little surviving evidence of Iris worship.

While she appears on the west pediment of the Parthenon and is mentioned in a few myths, not much is known about how human beings interacted with her, so we are even more free to adore her as we wish. Any rainbow, prism, or prismatic stone can help bring her closer, as can highly chromatic artwork or spaces of any kind. I feel her presence when I consider Ellsworth Kelly's multicolored art chapel at the Blanton Museum in Austin or when I gaze upon the 1936 painting *Creative Forces* by Transcendentalist artist Emil Bisttram. I have a playlist of rainbow-themed songs I listen to when I'd like to commune with her—it's playing as I type this. And on January 1 of this year, a stroll in my beloved Green-Wood Cemetery led me to stumble upon a sign that read "Iris Path." I lit some incense for her as I curved along its cobblestones, and quietly requested her blessings on my writing and on my year overall.

When I invoke these deities, I often do so using whichever words come to me in the moment. I ask them to guide and bless my work, and I thank them for their presence. Sometimes I use preexisting invocations such as *The Orphic Hymns*. More often, I select favorite poems or songs that contain their names or evoke their mythical properties. Magic is timeless, and so it truly doesn't matter if you play music by Mahler or Mitski to honor your celestial guests. The important thing is that you call upon them adoringly and enthusiastically. After all, with its roots being *en* meaning "in" and *theos* meaning "god," the word *enthusiasm* literally means to be entered or possessed by a god. Collaborating with these entities can keep us feeling enthusiastic about what we are making. It can allow us to loosen our grip on the creative process a bit, for we can trust that someone else is with us. Together, we steward a new bit of beauteousness, and help it become earthbound.

In addition to working with invocations, I have these beings represented on various altars throughout my living and workspaces. I also

INVOCATION/ALTAR-CATION

have altars for specific projects—there is, indeed, a book altar I've been tending for this very project. Designating physical space where wondrous things can happen is a time-tested technique. We see examples of this when we visit the hallowed halls of museums and mosques or kneel before shrines or souvenir-filled shoeboxes.

In ancient Greece, a tract of land that was marked for a deity or a noble was called a temenos. This derived from the word *temno*, meaning "I cut." This was a place cut off from more mundane matters, set apart as special and reserved for finer doings. The term was popularized in English by psychoanalyst Carl Jung, who likened the temenos to the inner space where psychological transformation could occur. Just as casting a circle can create a temenos where magic can happen, an altar is a temenos for divine visitors. By setting up a sanctified physical area, we make Spirit in any form feel welcome, and we give it a clear place to land. An altar doesn't need to be grand or take up a lot of room. It can be a window ledge, a cabinet, a shelf. I've even known folks to make a discreet miniature altar inside an Altoids tin that they can slip safely in a drawer or pocket when not in use. Some altars are festooned with photographs, figurines, and feathers, or overflow with fresh bouquets. Others may contain a simple bowl of water or a single candle that's lit at specific times. But a crucial aspect of an altar is that it is treated as separate from the everyday spaces and objects that we're otherwise surrounded by. I don't put my cell phone on my altar or casually toss my house keys on it when I pass by. An altar is a sanctuary for the sacred, and by extension, for the most precious parts of the self. Altar-keeping has elevated both my witchcraft and my writing practices. Maintaining temenos wherever I dwell means that I'm keeping the spirit world close, and that I'm giving it my tender attention whenever possible.

Anointment/Adornment

A friend recently gave me a vial of Abramelin oil that he made, and I anoint myself with it whenever I need a magical boost. This blend is based on an ancient sanctification oil used by Jewish priests, as described in Exodus 30:22–25:

> Moreover the Lord spoke to Moses, saying: "Also take for yourself quality spices—five hundred *shekels* of liquid myrrh, half as much sweet-smelling cinnamon (two hundred and fifty *shekels*), two hundred and fifty *shekels* of sweet-smelling cane, five hundred *shekels* of cassia, according to the *shekel* of the sanctuary, and a hin of olive oil. And you shall make from these a holy anointing oil, an ointment compounded according to the art of the perfumer. It shall be a holy anointing oil."

The recipe has been adapted over centuries and repopularized by twentieth-century occultists S. L. MacGregor Mathers and Aleister Crowley. I imagine my friend took liberties with the ingredients and amounts, per availability. Magic is scrappy. It's made out of whatever materials we have to hand, using the best of our abilities. Perfection is never the point.

ANOINTMENT/ADORNMENT

When I anoint myself with any sacred oil, I start with the crown of my head and then my third eye (I sometimes draw a pentacle—the encircled star that symbolizes the unity of the sacred elements). If I'm feeling particularly formal, I'll then anoint the rest of the meridian points down my center: throat, heart, solar plexus, sacrum, root. In common parlance, these are often referred to as the seven chakras, though this popular paradigm is a clear example of cultural appropriation: nineteenth-century Theosophists "borrowed," reinterpreted, and modified this system from Hindu Tantrism and recodified it for a Western audience via books such as Arthur Avalon's *The Serpent Power* (1919) and C. W. Leadbeater's *The Chakras* (1927). In actual Tantrism, there are varying numbers of chakras and location points throughout the body. Color assignments and energetic associations for each chakra were also added by various Western New Age proponents throughout the twentieth century. (For more on this topic, see the excellent writings and lectures by Kurt Leland, particularly his book *Rainbow Body*.) I mention this not only to give credit where credit is due, but to also liberate you from the idea that there is any one correct way to anoint oneself. I sometimes rub the oil on the soles of my feet, down my arms, throughout my hair, and so on, depending on mood and instinct. The important part is to bless oneself with gentleness. To gild the body with sanctified liquid and use the touch of the gods.

Our magical tools are also worthy of anointment, whether that's a wand, paintbrush, piccolo, or pen.

Pioneering reggae producer Lee "Scratch" Perry did precisely this at his Kingston recording studio, the Black Ark. In Michael Veal's book *Dub: Soundscapes and Shattered Songs in Jamaican Reggae* he describes Perry's "personal brand of eccentric mysticism and alchemy" wherein the magic and the materials of his engineering process were quite literally mixed together:

He would often "bless" his recording equipment with mystical invocations, blow ganja smoke onto his tapes while recording, bury unprotected tapes in the soil outside of his studio, and surround himself with burning candles and incense, whose wax and dust remnants were allowed to infest his electronic recording equipment. He would also spray tapes with a variety of fluids, including urine, blood and whisky, ostensibly to enhance their spiritual properties.

These techniques not only seemed to boost the creative output of Perry and his collaborators, it also changed the texture of the sounds he was producing, giving them a distinct musical signature. Many musicians have raved that working with Perry was a highlight of their careers thanks to his innovative approach and its potent sonic results.

I'm not recommending going to the extremes that Perry did—his equipment certainly suffered for it (the Black Ark would eventually burn to the ground), and by some accounts his mental health did for a while as well. All was not lost, however. He saw a renewed interest in his music later in life, eventually working with everyone from the Beastie Boys to the Clash to Paul McCartney, and went on to win a Grammy. As he told the *Vancouver Sun* in 2016, "I am just a messenger of his holiness and majesty (Haile Selassie I) and the righteous message of godliness from Rastafari . . . [T]he music was created most essentially to heal and bring everyone together in one love. We are just vessels to bring sacrament to heal mind and spirit and that is what my life work is." I love the way Perry saw his spirituality, his recording gear, and his sounds as extensions of one another, and imbued them all with blessings.

I do most of my writing from home and can work all day in my pajamas if I choose to. I rarely do though. Something about getting dressed

ANOINTMENT/ADORNMENT

in the morning signals to my psyche that I am in productivity mode, ready to concentrate and create. I don't wear a specific uniform when I write or otherwise conjure, but I can see the appeal of having one. Scrubs, chef's whites, army fatigues, or a three-piece suit each offer varying degrees of protection, and they also differentiate the wearer from the general public. Just as significantly, a change of clothes also shifts something on the inside. When a gardener puts on their gloves and overalls, they are not only prepared to work in practical terms—they also project the identity of *gardener* to themselves. They feel ready to do the weeding, planting, and dirt-working because they dressed the part.

Ceremonial garments operate in a similar fashion, pun intended. A priest's vestments, a graduation gown, and a wedding dress may vary in style and symbolism, but the donning of each demarcates a distinct *beingness*. These outfits are special. They are worn during heightened spiritual states and bring about a sense of transition, transformation, and elevation.

On a pragmatic level, wearing the same work outfit means that you have one less decision to make, thereby decreasing cognitive load and preserving that mental energy for other creative tasks. Steve Jobs famously wore a black turtleneck, blue jeans, and white New Balance sneakers every day for this reason. Saatchi and Saatchi art director Matilda Kahl's black-and-white "work uniform" became so popular that her company hosted a "Dress Like Matilda Day." And President Barack Obama told *Vanity Fair*, "You'll see I wear only gray or blue suits . . . I'm trying to pare down decisions. I don't want to make decisions about what I'm eating or wearing. Because I have too many other decisions to make." By implementing a uniform you can stave off decision fatigue and apply that time and energy to more important matters.

I would argue that those garments also serve another purpose: they act as their own cloaking devices, and they provide protection from unwanted attention. They also project an intentional image outward. At some point, Obama, Jobs, Kahl, and other uniform devotees decided upon those garments. The colors, fabrics, and cuts of each uniform telegraph an idea about who the wearer is and how they would like to be perceived. In this regard, it's also a kind of psychic armoring that allows each of them to feel more centered in their power.

In a 2019 *Witch Wave* interview, goth rock star Chelsea Wolfe explained to me how adorning herself in witchy, haute-occult fashions for her live shows helps her shift into her own version of Magician Mode when she performs:

> I've always found it important to at least try to step into a confident place on stage, even though that's in direct contrast to the stage fright that I felt for a really long time, and I still have occasionally . . . I always wanted the live show and even some of the imagery and stuff to just feel very empowering for whoever was into it or was listening or watching. And for myself to be able to really actually lose myself into the music, I really had to prepare myself backstage . . . I started to really think of getting dressed and putting on makeup and stuff as like putting on this sort of armor for myself so that I could step out and be like a more confident version of myself.

I can attest firsthand that her method is highly effective, as Wolfe is an absolute powerhouse on stage.

Modern witches don't have one specific uniform per se, but during certain ceremonies we may don robes or cloaks, or dress in specific hues that have magical associations. The members of my coven each have their own

ANOINTMENT/ADORNMENT

(fabulous) style, and there is no dress code for when we meet. Still, it's true that for certain ceremonies or holy days there is a high representation of black clothing, swirling fabrics, and sparkling jewels. We know that we have gathered to accompany each other into the liminal realm, and our garments reflect that. As Martin Duffy writes in *The Devil's Raiments* (2012), "In 'wearing' symbols of the very powers we seek to mediate, we are able to read the many secrets therein encrypted, the colours, forms and uses of the adornments becoming a veritable cipher of the mysteries." When we do ritual together, my coven mates and I are directly interfacing with those mysteries, and so we dress like the night itself.

Some witches choose to go "sky-clad" and wear nothing at all. Many magical folks encourage nakedness during ritual, believing it helps them be a more potent conductor of divine energy. In his 1899 witchcraft treatise, *Aradia, Gospel of Witches*, Charles Godfrey Leland writes:

> And as the sign that ye are truly free,
> > Ye shall be naked in your rites, both men
> > And women also . . .

Wicca progenitor Gerald Gardner incorporated a great deal of Leland's ideas and language into the Wiccan rites he developed, and he was also an ardent "naturist," or nudist. Gardner believed that nudism was responsible for curing an illness of his, and he wrote that "there is something in the nature of an electromagnetic field surrounding all living bodies . . ."

For Gardner, nakedness was a means of making sure this field, or "nerve force" as he called it, could flow unimpeded.

Benjamin Franklin was also a proponent of spending time in the nude. He was known to disrobe completely near an open window for thirty to sixty minutes at a time, believing that fresh air on naked flesh would bring about physical health and invigorated spirits. These daily "air baths" as he called them were taken no matter the weather, and he would often write and engage in other creative contemplation during these sessions. Perhaps his theories of electricity were sparked during these air baths. Perhaps the nude body is its own lightning rod in the creative sense as well as the literal one.

What we wear—or don't wear—as Magic Makers can certainly have other social implications. Victor Hugo's wife, Adèle Foucher, wrote about how her husband procrastinated writing *Notre-Dame de Paris* (more commonly known as *The Hunchback of Notre-Dame*) for months on end. Finally, he decided to go on a self-imposed writer's retreat, only what he was retreating from was his usual wardrobe. As Foucher writes: "He bought himself a bottle of ink and a huge gray knitted shawl, which swathed him from head to foot, locked his formal clothes away so that he would not be tempted to go out and entered his novel as if it were a prison." By depriving himself of his usual clothing, Hugo voluntarily rendered himself a social pariah. And while his giant gray shawl was intended as an isolation costume of sorts, I can't help but draw a parallel to the robes, capes, and other shrouds so often worn in magic ceremony. I like to imagine Hugo as some kind of writing wraith, drifting between worlds as he guided Quasimodo across the veil with his quill.

An entire outfit or lack thereof is not required for magical adornment. The origin of the witchly/wizardly pointy hat is debatable, but there are certainly numerous examples of people sporting ritual headgear throughout history. Conical hats in particular have been worn cross-culturally. The mummified remains of women found in the eastern part of central Asia dating from the fourth to second centuries BCE are often referred to as

ANOINTMENT/ADORNMENT

"the witches of Subeshi" due to the tall, pointy black hats they were buried in. The Judenhut was a conical hat worn by Jews in medieval Europe—first as part of traditional dress but later made mandatory to identify them to the antisemites in power. (Some believe this is the precursor to the pointed hats associated with witches, though many other theories abound.)

There are those who believe that elongated hats can help capture energy. The headgear we now call a dunce cap was originally inspired by the ideas of fourteenth-century Scottish philosopher John Duns Scotus—also known as the Subtle Doctor due to his complex and nuanced thinking. Duns believed that the conical hats worn by alleged wizards were supposed to funnel wisdom down from the heavens and into their heads, and so his followers—or "Dunsmen"—wore similarly styled skull toppers. Duns's mystical theories eventually fell out of favor, and over the centuries the terms *dunce* and *dunce cap* came to signify idiocy and disgrace.

Still, the idea of a hat being a sort of power beacon has persisted. The new wave band Devo became as famous for their iconic red, tiered hats as they did for their music. Though the hat resembles LEGOs or an upside-down flowerpot, the official name for it is the Energy Dome. And while it was meant to be a playful costume, the band members were inspired by Aztec ziggurat mounds, which were believed to collect and circulate energy. Twentieth-century German psychoanalyst Wilhelm Reich put forth ideas about what he called orgone, or life force, and this played into Devo's hat design as well. As the band's co-founder and bass player Gerald "Jerry" Casale put it:

> [T]he Dome collects the Orgone energy that escapes from the crown of the human head and pushes it back into the Medulla Oblongata for increased mental energy. It's very important that you use the

foam insert (which is included with every Dome when purchased from ClubDevo.com), or better yet, get a plastic hardhat liner, adjust it to your head size and affix it with duct tape or Super Glue to the inside of the Dome. This allows the Dome to "float" just above the cranium and thus do its job. Unfortunately, sans foam insert or hardhat liner, the recirculation of energy WILL NOT occur.

Whether or not wearing an Energy Dome works is up for debate, but it has certainly been a mighty merchandizing opportunity for Devo and their Devo-tees.

Performance artist Marina Abramović has also explored ideas about adornment and power via her *Energy Clothes* series. In 2001, Abramović invited gallery participants to dress up in brightly colored prostheses meant to collect and strengthen the wearer's energy fields. Per the exhibition's description:

> *The Energy Clothes* were built to activate some energy points of the body (head, eyes, heart, solar plexus, spine) by means of circular magnets based on the shape of the cone, which, since the times of medieval witches, carries within itself the purpose of intensifying strength, perception, and the ability to change the world. Such prostheses, including a hat over a meter high, were made with silks in bright colors: purple, lilac, dark pink, pale pink, green, blue, red, yellow. The colors were also chosen by the artist as conductors of light and psychological energy.

Abramović revisited this series in subsequent years, and one can see photographs of her gardening in a giant green Energy Hat, reading in a fetching red version, and my personal favorite, bathing while crowned with an enormous, pointed blue one.

Her work brings to mind the hat collection of writer-illustrator Theodor Geisel, better known as Dr. Seuss. Though haberdashery played a crucial role in Seuss's bestseller *The Cat in the Hat*, as well as his earlier children's book *The 500 Hats of Bartholomew Cubbins*, these were fictions based somewhat in fact. Seuss collected hundreds of hats throughout his life and was known to wear one when he needed writing inspiration. According to *The New York Times*, one of Seuss's editors, Michael Frith, was also pulled into his madcap creative antics: "When they were stumped by a word choice, Mr. Frith said, Geisel would often bound to the closet and grab a hat for each of them—a sombrero, or perhaps a fez." Whether this was a magical act or a psychological trick is beside the point. A costume change is a change in perception.

I'm not wearing a pointy witch's hat, or even a thinking cap, as of this writing, though I'm now seriously tempted to go out and find an absurdly lavish one, so watch this (head)space. However, I am mindful about the jewelry I adorn myself with, and I vary it depending on my magical needs. This morning I woke up a bit groggy, full of mind-mist and fatigue. And so I put on one of my favorite necklaces depicting my arrow-wielding matron goddess, Artemis. Her balance of precision and wild abandon is what I'm tapping into today as I tap on the keyboard. She is helping me to focus but not second-guess (the latter of which will come with the editing process down the road). This is one of many talismans I wear when I'm in need of some bewitching backup.

Legendary fashion designer Christian Dior incorporated magic into his career and his clothing. He regularly consulted psychics and is said to have had his tarot cards read before every catwalk show. This is one of the reasons why his recent successor, Maria Grazia Chiuri, designed several tarot-themed collections during her tenure as Dior's creative director. Dior himself would have no doubt appreciated the gesture. He believed not only in the ability of clothing to change how one is perceived, but also in the power of talismanic fashion. As reported in *T Australia*, Dior "sewed sprigs of lily of the valley—his 'lucky flower' and a French symbol of good luck and happiness—into the hems of garments for his fashion shows in an effort to will his creations into success."

The word *talisman* comes from the Greek *telesma*, meaning "religious rite" or "payment." It has its roots in the notion of completion: the verb *teleō* (τελέω) translating to "I complete, perform a rite." A talisman is used ceremonially. Worn, held, hung, or hidden, it helps bring about a magical result. While the words *talisman* and *amulet* are now often used interchangeably, an amulet is traditionally associated with apotropaic—or protective—magic, whereas a talisman can also attract what one desires and manifest change. Talismans can come in virtually any form: stone, bone, scroll, bowl. Often they are worn on the body, as power pendants and magic rings. Crystals are used talismanically: carnelian for creativity, lapis lazuli for self-expression. Slip a spell around your neck, your wrist. Spangle your ears with magic. What messages do you hear?

Shape-Shifting/Name-Taking

Masks are a key aspect of Mexican wrestling, or lucha libre. A luchador must keep his mask on at all times in the ring, and if an opponent removes it during a match, it is considered the ultimate dishonor. One of my favorite wrestlers, Rey Mysterio, is a high-flying luchador who wrestles for the WWE. I often think about one of his matches, part of WWE's 2009 pay-per-view show *The Bash*. He is fighting Chris Jericho for the Intercontinental Championship title, and it's a solid twenty minutes of beefy grappling punctuated by the occasional signature Mysterio flip. Suddenly Jericho puts Mysterio in a submission hold and snatches Mysterio's mask off: horror of horrors! It seems the match has come to an end. But then the camera cuts to Mysterio, and—SURPRISE!—he had *another* mask on underneath the whole time! His face is still hidden! His honor is preserved!! With some kicks, a spin, and a dive-bomb off the ropes, Mysterio pins Jericho and wins the match, his second mask and his dignity intact.

Masks have held a prominent place in pop culture for decades, from villains like Darth Vader and Ghostface to heroes like Spiderman and

Zorro. In fiction, a mask is a disguise, a protective device that allows the wearer's true identity to remain hidden while also empowering them to behave with more daring and less fear. But masks are potent tools in real life too. Donning a mask is still a prevalent Halloween tradition, and there's a solid argument to be made that the act of wearing makeup is a form of daily masking. Masks bestow a feeling of disinhibition, and that means that they can be as revealing as they are concealing. When our pedestrian identity is somehow obscured, some other energy is unleashed to express itself through us. This is why musicians like Sia, Orville Peck, Leikeli47, Glass Beams, and the Knife have chosen to be masked or otherwise obscure their faces when they perform. In addition to preserving their day-to-day privacy to some extent, their preferred masks allow them to feel more free on stage.

These performers are part of a long lineage of masked Magic Makers. Virtually every known culture has a tradition of masked rituals if you go back far enough, and many are still with us today. Often these masks are in the shape of an animal head or depict a deity's visage. Many believe that a shaman or ritual dancer becomes one with their mask, and that during ceremony they become an embodiment of the represented being in an act of theurgy. This belief would eventually evolve into the foundations of what we now call theater. Formalized Greek drama originally began in the sixth century BCE, and its original function was to honor Dionysus, god of wine, fertility, and ecstasy. The actors at these festivals were always masked, and the comedy-tragedy icon of theater is derived from this tradition. One of the god's epithets, Dionysus Eleutherius, means Dionysus the Liberator, due to the shedding of inhibitions that he is said to bring about.

The ancient Japanese ceremonial dance kagura translates to "entertainment of the gods." It was a performance that started as a reenactment of a Shinto myth wherein the sun goddess, Amaterasu, was coaxed out of her cave with a bawdy dance from the gods led by Ame-no-Uzume, the goddess of mirth and the arts. (It's a remarkably similar story to the part of the Persephone myth wherein the old crone Baubo flashes her genitals at agricultural goddess Demeter to make her laugh, thus lifting Demeter's spirits enough so that she does not give up looking for her abducted daughter. Never underestimate the power of a little perversity!) In kagura, a female shamanic dancer becomes a god, first entering a trance state and then moving wildly once the transformation has occurred. This practice is derived from older dances wherein imperial shrine maidens would wear masks and reenact the dance of the gods by temporarily becoming them. These magical performances eventually evolved into masked Noh theater, which still exists today.

If the root of theatrical performance is apotheosis—temporarily becoming the deity you are impersonating (or: dress for the god you want to be)—then it's understandable why so many makers have developed full-blown alter egos to help them tap into Magician Mode. Crafting a persona is a sort of full-body masking in which one creates an entire character whose skin they may slip into whenever they wish to metamorphosize into something Other. Beyoncé famously developed the character Sasha Fierce to help her feel more emboldened as a performer. Though she spoke about her alter ego publicly as part of her 2008 *I Am . . . Sasha Fierce* double-disc album promo tour, she also stated that she'd been working privately with the character since her 2003 smash hit with Jay-Z, *Crazy in Love*. In a statement about *I Am . . . Sasha Fierce*, Beyoncé explained how the first half of the album contained more personal songs about who she is "underneath all the make-up, underneath the lights, and underneath all the exciting star drama." The second half of the album was from the Sasha Fierce perspective: "the fun, more sensual, more aggressive, more outspoken side and more glamorous side that comes out when I'm working and when I'm on the stage." She also explained how the Sasha Fierce persona helped her tap into her confidence when she was getting ready to perform. As she told Oprah Winfrey:

> Usually, when I hear the crowd, when I put on my stilettos . . . the moment right before, when you're nervous and that other thing kinda takes over for you, then Sasha Fierce appears, and my posture and the way I speak and everything is different . . . It's kinda like when I do a movie, becoming the character, once you put on the wig and once you put on the clothes, you walk different . . .

Crucially, the electro-tinged songs Beyoncé created from the Fierce perspective also allowed her to stretch beyond the R&B sounds she had previously been associated with. By temporarily shape-shifting into another being, she was able to break through preconceived notions and perhaps even self-imposed limitations about the kind of music she was "supposed to" make. Letting another entity inhabit her was a creatively liberating act.

The Beyoncé/Sasha Fierce dichotomy is one example among many of artists who have used alter egos to unlock their power and defy expectations. Eminem's Slim Shady, Bono's MacPhisto, Janelle Monáe's Cindi Mayweather, and the Beatles' Sgt. Pepper's Lonely Hearts Club Band have each helped the artists in question tune into different frequencies and access new facets of their creative expression. In 1999, American country musician Garth Brooks released an album of "greatest hits" by an Australian rock star persona Brooks invented named Chris Gaines.

SHAPE-SHIFTING/NAME-TAKING

The project was originally intended to lead up to a film about the peaks and valleys of a fictional rocker's career, and though that never came to fruition, Brooks remains committed to writing and performing as Gaines for future albums. Clearly something about creating under the guise of Gaines has proven to be continuously beneficial to Brooks. It's also worth noting that performers aren't the only ones to use this technique: Surrealist artist Max Ernst had a bird alter ego named Loplop who appears in several of his paintings and collages, and who represents his magical, subconscious self.

Incorporating alter egos into one's work can help keep the maker engaged by staving off the boredom of repetition and introducing a fresh perspective. The employment of personas can signal to both the creator and the audience that something new and different has arrived. Sometimes these invented entities prove so potent that their maker chooses to work with them throughout their lifetime, as with Norma Jean Baker's platinum phenom Marilyn Monroe, Paul Reubens's manic man-child Pee-wee Herman, and Cassandra Peterson's bewitchingly bodacious Elvira. In other instances, the cohabitation is occasional or short-lived, conjured to serve a specific body of work.

David Bowie is considered by many to be the ultimate musical chameleon. Over his five-decade career he developed multiple alter egos including Ziggy Stardust, Aladdin Sane, and the Thin White Duke, each with their own distinct style and sound. (And even "David Bowie" can be considered the artistic alter ego to his first given identity of David Robert Jones.) Mime, kabuki, clowning, and other forms of performance art were hugely influential on him, and his application of these shape-shifting arts to popular music was one of his many great innovations. By playing with the plasticity of the rock star archetype, he was able to explore themes of fame, alienation, loneliness, and transcendence. As he told the *Daily Express* in 1976, "I'm Pierrot. I'm Everyman. What I'm doing is theatre, and only theatre . . . I'm using myself as a canvas and trying to paint the truth of our time on it." As with Beyoncé and Sasha Fierce, Bowie's characters also served an amuletic, internal purpose by helping him overcome performance anxiety when he was starting out. Though it's difficult to believe due to his out-of-this-world charisma and scintillating wit, he's stated in interviews with journalist Paul Du Noyer: "I'm not a particularly gregarious person" and "I had an unbearable shyness; it was much easier for me to keep on with the Ziggy thing, off the stage as well as on the stage. . . . Who was David Bowie and who was Ziggy Stardust? But I think it was motivated by shyness."

Bowie was also one of many creators who has played with gender in his work, adorning himself in the makeup and high-heeled boots that other glam rockers were experimenting with in the 1960s and '70s. He went on to wear full drag in the video for his tongue-in-cheek, toxic-masculinity-skewering 1979 single, "Boys Keep Swinging." In it, Bowie is dressed as three different female backup singers: a brunette-beehive-sporting '60s housewife, a red-headed fashion model, and a blond senior in a skirt-suit. At the end of the video, the brunette and the redhead pull off their wigs and smear their lipstick, and the blond blows a steely-eyed kiss to camera. Bowie reminds us that gender is just another costume that each of us wears—and so it can be cast off, swapped out, deconstructed, or remade however and whenever one wishes.

For some, shape-shifting across the gender spectrum can help them access new levels of creation and become more fully realized makers. And though the gender essentialist notion of a feminine/masculine binary is being rightly called into question in the modern era, it can be a wildly enriching experience for those who intentionally call in energies that are different than those they usually present to the outside world. Tapping into the magic of gender expression is one means of expanding one's creative outlook and output.

In 1986, Prince recorded an entire album under the name Camille, his feminine alter ego. He wrote songs from a woman's perspective and shifted his vocal pitch to a higher register in the studio. He originally intended to release the record anonymously, so that his Camille tracks would be received—and presumably assessed—independent of his involvement. Though this plan was eventually scrapped, many of these songs, such as "If I Was Your Girlfriend," were later folded into his 1987 *Sign o' the Times* album.

Dada art daddy Marcel Duchamp began his infamous gender-bending exploration (and lampoonery) in 1919 by painting a mustache on a Mona Lisa postcard, which he called *L.H.O.O.Q.* or *La Jaconde*. (The letters spoken aloud in French sound like *Elle a chaud au cul* or "There is fire down below.") Shortly thereafter he developed a female alter ego named Rrose Sélavy, whose name was a play on the French adage "Eros, c'est la vie" or "Eros, that's life." Duchamp's Rrose modeled in fashionable hats and flamboyant outerwear for several Man Ray photographs beginning in the early 1920s, and she was also credited as the creator of her own works, including the 1926 animated film "Anemic Cinema."

Lady Gaga also found crossing gender lines to be a source of inspiration when she came up with the character of Jo Calderone, a chain-smoking Italian American guy from New Jersey with black sideburns and smoldering machismo. For Gaga, becoming Calderone was a way to push back against society's limited ideals of attractiveness. As she told *V Magazine* in 2011: "In a culture that attempts to quantify beauty with a visual paradigm and almost mathematical standard, how can we fuck with the malleable minds of onlookers and shift the world's perspective on what's beautiful? I asked myself this question. And the answer? Drag."

Like many, I've fallen deeply under RuPaul's spangled-and-spackled spell. As an avid spectator of *RuPaul's Drag Race*, I've become entranced by the ways in which drag artists bring their alter egos to life. Many transform themselves into a fully materialized fantasy of traditional femininity, from gamine to glamazon. On my podcast, two-time *Drag Race* winner, Jinkx Monsoon, explained to me her formula for devising her drag character: "I always say that the best way to start when creating a drag persona is to kind of create a recipe of three to five personal divas that contribute to your drag persona. And mine changes over time, but I think the five that stay constant are Carol Burnett, Bette Davis, Lucille Ball, Madeline Kahn, and Bette Midler." She later clarified, "I've always said that even though I have all these other influences, essentially I'm just channeling my mother." Since then, Jinkx's drag has evolved as she has. By adding more witchy elements to her performances, she pays homage to anyone who has been marginalized or othered while also honoring her own real-life witchcraft practice. Other drag queens blur the lines of the gender binary in their act, or opt to embody opulent, chimeric creatures that are beyond human.

When Ru reminds us "We're all born naked, and the rest is drag," he's not only talking about how gender performance is an illusion but also about the malleability of image in general. Certainly, this can be taken to mean that everything is artifice. But in his book *GuRu*, RuPaul explains how dressing in drag can give people license to be their grandest selves:

SHAPE-SHIFTING/NAME-TAKING

> I know how to make magic. I have the ability to help people cross over to their greatness and realize their potential . . . Drag for me has always been my superhero costume. I feel powerful in drag. I think other people see that and believe they can do the same thing.

When I watch Ru, Jinkx, or my other favorite queens perform, I certainly feel inspired to express myself more vibrantly too, and to expand beyond my self-imposed limitations. In Vedic tradition, there is the concept of māyā, which is often translated to mean "illusion." But another interpretation of this term is closer to "magic" or "creative manifestation." As Sanskrit scholar Christopher D. Wallis writes, māyā is "the creative power of consciousness to emanate a universe, *not* illusion." Perhaps māyā is a paradox: like any sort of mask, it simultaneously reveals as it conceals. The magic of alter egos is that they can help the maker access the universes that dwell within each of us and awaken us to power that was there all along.

If coming up with an elaborately costumed character to get you into Magician Mode feels too ambitious for you, fret not. For many makers, simply using another name can be magic enough.

For Afrofuturist jazz pioneer Herman Poole Blount, his Egyptian-god-meets-extraterrestrial costumes were important, but his chosen name, Le Sony'r Ra, later shortened to Sun Ra, signified a permanent self-transformation. When asked about his birth name, he responded: "That's an imaginary person, never existed . . . Any name that I use other than Ra is a pseudonym." There are myriad examples of performers whose stage names dwarf their given names, whether through their own insistence or just due to reinforcement by the public over time. But a chosen name can also be a key to accessing new levels of creative energy, whether it is used by the Magic Maker full time or just in certain contexts.

There are many reasons why someone might create under a different name. It may be about protecting one's anonymity, as with street artist and activist Banksy. More often it's about managing public perception. Amantine-Lucile-Aurore Dupin chose George Sand as her nom de plume, knowing that male authors at the time were taken more seriously. Stephen King's pen name, Richard Bachman, was developed for practical purposes, as he wanted to write more than one book a year and was told by his publisher that putting out too many books under the King name would oversaturate the market. Bestselling romance novelist Nora Roberts writes crime thrillers under the name J. D. Robb—a pseudonym that went on to become a bestselling author in its own right.

Releasing work under a different name is not only clarifying for the audience, it can also be freeing for the maker in that it gives internal permission for them to explore uncharted imaginative terrain. According to her grandson on the official Agatha Christie website, Christie wrote books under the name Mary Westmacott because "it gave my grandmother the chance to better explore the human psychology she was so intrigued by, freed from the expectations of her mystery fans." And sometimes using different names is just fun. Bob Dylan (né Robert Zimmerman) has released work under such names as Lucky Wilbury, Sergei Petrov, and Jack Frost. Bewitching Surrealist Remedios Varo developed the character Felina Caprino-Mandrágora, a sort of fanciful version of herself who wrote fantastical recipes and spells. Gothic-comic illustrator and writer Edward Gorey created under many different pseudonyms, each an anagram of his given name. Some of these include Ogden Weary, Miss D. Awdrey-Gore, Garrod Weedy, and my personal favorite, Madame Groeda Weyrd, who is cited as the "interpreter" of Gorey's Fantod

SHAPE-SHIFTING/NAME-TAKING

Pack oracle deck and the author of its accompanying guidebook. Madame Weyrd, we're told,

> has devoted her life to divination, and is the author of, among a shelf of other works, "Floating Tambourines," a collection of esoteric verse, and "The Future Speaks Through Entrails." Her career as one of the most celebrated of trance mediums came to a close when she lost two and a third fingers as a result of a contretemps during an ectoplasmic manifestation.

Naming is powerful magic. In Talmudic Jewish tradition, the Creator's true name, sometimes referred to as the Tetragrammaton, is so powerful that one must not utter it out loud. Myriad alternate names and epithets for the Creator are found throughout the Torah, and many observant Jews use the term *HaShem*, which simply means "The Name." In fact, according to Jewish folklore, Adam's first wife, Lilith, was cast out of Eden not only because she refused to lie beneath Adam and insisted on being his equal, but also because she spoke the Ineffable Name.

Calling someone by their "true" name in order to exert some kind of power over them is a common trope in stories, from the fairy tale "Rumpelstiltskin" to Ursula K. Le Guin's Earthsea Cycle series. An Egyptian myth tells of how the goddess Isis wanted to rule jointly with the god Ra, but she couldn't unless she discovered his true, secret name. So she sent a snake to bite Ra, knowing that only she could cure him. As Ra writhed in pain from the poison, Isis told him that she would save his life in exchange for his true name. At first he resisted, boasting about his mighty powers and giving her other names instead. Isis didn't fall for the ruse, and at last he caved and transmitted the name to her. Isis then used her magic to heal him and become queen of the gods.

Naming someone or something is considered a holy act in many traditions. In the book of Genesis, Adam is given the gift of bestowing names upon all of the animals, signifying that human beings are active participants in the making of the world. Baby-naming ceremonies exist cross-culturally, as do rituals wherein someone receives a new name as part of an initiation. During confirmation in Catholic tradition, it is customary for the confirmed to take on the name of a saint. Native American ceremonies vary depending on the tribe, and new names can be given at significant moments of a member's life. These names are often derived from nature and reveal something about the recipient's personality or purpose. In the 1979 book, and subsequent 1984 film, *The NeverEnding Story*, protagonist Bastian Balthazar Bux must give the Childlike Empress a new name in order to save the fantastical realm she reigns over. (That her new name is Moon Child belies author Michael Ende's familiarity with occult philosophy, including Aleister Crowley's writings, just as the double-snaked Auryn symbol is a variation on the alchemical ouroboros.)

Like many, I have been given multiple names. Though I go by Pam in most situations, my full name, Pamela, is said to mean "all-honey"—hence my deep connection to bees and their magic. Those who love and know me well sometimes call me Pammy, and there are other nicknames from beloveds too numerous or intimate to list here. I've also experienced a spiritual name change: My parents' rabbi gave me the name Pesha Yashara during my Hebrew baby-naming ceremony. When we transferred to a different synagogue, the new rabbi was horrified, saying that the word *pesha* in Hebrew meant something bad, and so he changed the first half of my name to *Peninah*, meaning "pearl." (I later found out that *pesha* means something like "transgressor," which turned out to be rather apt!) Each of these names elicits a certain energy, for they signify a relationship between me and the person using the name in question.

Then there are secret names I will never share publicly, as well as pseudonyms I've worked under or plan to work under in the future. These are names I have chosen for myself, and so I treat them with extra care. Some versions of these names I only use in select groups or during solo ceremonies when I am conjuring something specific. Others may emerge for an audience if and when the time is right. When I use these other names—my magical names—my orientation to myself and what I'm making changes. I look at the world through newly bejeweled eyes, and possibilities blossom.

Taking on a magical name, whether self-selected or from someone else, occurs in many initiatory traditions. In modern Pagan practice, some use numerology to generate a name, believing that letters and numbers have specific energetic associations. Others choose a name based on personally resonant symbolism or allusions to goddesses, gods, or nature spirits with which they feel a connection. A new name may be acquired at any time, and may be bestowed through ceremony, secret utterance, or by simply writing it down somewhere safe. We each have the power to name ourselves whatever we wish, whenever we choose. And we may switch the names we use when we feel called to as well. A name is a device of activation and identity. It is perhaps the first spell that is cast upon us when we enter this world, and its meaning is reinforced with every incantation. Therefore, a name may also be cast off when it no longer fits. You should love your names and call yourself whatever brings your own creation into being.

The same is true of any magical mask we wear or any shape we shift into as we're making our magic. We may morph at any time, and we are meant to.

Beyoncé recently stated that her Fierce days are behind her. As she told *Allure* in 2010: "Sasha Fierce is done. I killed her . . . I don't need Sasha Fierce anymore, because I've grown, and now I'm able to merge the two." If her three-album project that began with *Renaissance* has proven anything, it's that she can ricochet from Church Girl to Alien Superstar to Cowboy Carter and still be Bey. She brings to mind Walt Whitman's elated declaration, "I am large. I contain multitudes." Through a profound amount of skill and artistry, Beyoncé has turned her multifaceted self into one gargantuan, goddess-like gem.

Then there are those like Rey Mysterio who will never be unmasked in the ring, whose creative persona is made up of masks on masks. Watching his match was not only exhilarating for me but surprisingly moving. By witnessing his skillful bit of stagecraft, I was bewitched by his commitment to his persona, his pride, and his sense of selves. And who is to say that Rey Mysterio is any less real than Óscar Gutiérrez Rubio, who wears his visage? "The self might just be an agglomeration of masks," the author Sandra Newman has written. When you step into your own magic ring, why not keep choosing whichever mask makes you feel the most vital and valorous?

Shifting into Magician Mode looks different for each of us, but the goal is the same: to plug into a sacred socket and supercharge the creative process. We select what to wear, and we open ourselves to whatever entities may wear us. Through numinous names and other occult costumes, we reveal our most naked imaginative impulses. We veil ourselves as we tear the veil between worlds asunder. We welcome alteration. We become.

So go ahead: Don your mask and face the divine.

PART III
The Craft

I'm far from the first person to draw a parallel between craftspeople and magicians. The Old English word *craft* meant "power," "might," and "strength," and later evolved to signify "skill," "dexterity," and "talent." To craft something, whether with wood, words, or witchery, is to have the fortitude to turn the intangible tangible, to render the invisible visible, to take an idea from imaginal space and bring it into being. I love how this word seems to encompass the physical and the ethereal. To craft something is to wield creative power—to direct unseen energies with precision and purpose. "Frankly, the essence of everyday creativity is also the true essence of witchcraft," writes poet Dorothea Lasky in her essay "In Pursuit of a Lifelong Creativity." When we craft a poem, a quilt, a rocket ship, a spell, we nimbly transmute force into form. We give our visions volume. We make magic shapes.

Sometimes an idea will strike us at random, an electric epiphany that arrives when we're driving, washing the dishes, or doing some other mundane task. These moments are great gifts and are not to be ignored. They also teach us that some time away from our creative work is not a distraction but a necessary diversion, because in these more grounded states of being we are able to receive certain types of ethereal information. Our guard is down, and so our creative circuitry is unobscured by ego, self-doubt, and other "protective" barriers that often get in our way.

There is no predicting when these inspiring sparks will come, and no telling where exactly they come from. As songwriter and poet Leonard Cohen said in his acceptance speech for Spain's Prince of Asturias Letters Award: "Poetry comes from a place that no one commands, and no one conquers. So I feel somewhat like a charlatan to accept an award for an activity which I do not command. In other words, if I knew where the good songs came from I'd go there more often." The poet Jack Spicer wrote and lectured extensively about good poetry being "something from the Outside coming in."

I'm of the belief that ideas are all around us and that our job is to attract them, like spectral moths to our incandescent imaginations. Many other makers have described this feeling of being surrounded by ideas, of learning how to bring them from an exterior realm into their work. When speaking of songwriting, Nick Cave has said, "You are not the 'Great Creator' of your songs, you are simply their servant, and the songs will come to you when you have adequately prepared yourself to receive them. They are not inside you, unable to get out; rather, they are outside of you, unable to get in." I was introduced to that quote by Austin Kleon, who describes a similar orientation toward his own work as an author: "I never feel like I have a book *in* me. I always feel like there's a book *around* me." I can absolutely relate to this. Writing sometimes feels like catching fireflies. A single idea might give off a pretty twinkle, but if you gather enough of them with patience and persistence, you'll have a lantern you can use to navigate somewhere new.

Others have talked about how their work seems to have its own consciousness, gathering its components like a cloud gathers water droplets. If an idea is a seed or a fragment, a piece of art is a condensation of Creative Force.

When I'm working on something, it seems to have its own inner gravity, pulling more of itself to itself. The deeper I get into a project, the more connections to it I seem able to make. I'll also suddenly encounter relevant bits of research even when I'm not hunting for them: someone will unknowingly send me an article that's germane to a section of a book I'm writing, or they'll mention something in passing that perfectly coincides with a theme I've been teasing out. Creativity is a magnet. It draws what it needs toward the maker, and the maker amplifies this attraction by staying receptive, engaged, and aware.

Such an incident occurred yesterday: my husband surprised me with a book about one of my favorite filmmakers, the Japanese animation master Hayao Miyazaki. As I flipped through it, a Miyazaki quote in big bold letters caught my eye. He said, "The relationship is not one of me creating the film, but rather of the film forcing me to create it." I had to laugh at how perfectly relevant this felt to this very chapter I was writing, both in content and as an illustration of how this manuscript and I are creating together. Just as Miyazaki's films seem to take on a life of their own as he's working on them, this very book is pulling in what it needs. It's up to me to stay open enough to recognize when it's happening, and to do what I can to encourage it along.

Creative Force *wants* to coagulate. It wants to become something tangible and alive in the material world. As Magic Makers, our job is to receive those imaginal particles and help them find more of each other. We then use the best of our ability to weave those strands together and give them shape. And we infuse this form with our own magical signature before releasing it into the world to see what else it may attract—or be attracted to.

Remember the Magician standing with one arm raised to receive and the other arm pointed down to express? As Magic Makers, we receive spiritual energy using our powers of invitation and attention. We then use our

Spirit-given skills to discharge this energy with action and intention. The process of doing this in tandem—of blending the esoteric with the exoteric—is the Craft of creativity.

Across humankind there have always been different kinds of magic practitioners. There are those who stargaze to gain insights, and those who speak to the beloved dead. There are those who use cards for fortune-telling, and those who use plants for fortification. For our purposes, it doesn't matter if you're a witch, a ceremonial magician, a shaman, or a seer. You may have little to no experience with any "official" magical modalities, and that's absolutely fine too. These techniques are available for anyone to experiment with, both when gathering ideas and throughout the process of making something out of them—and often these two things are happening at the same time.

In the following pages, we'll delve into ways that magic can help us craft our work—both how to receive inspiration and ideas from Spirit and how to charge our work with our own magical intention. Due to the inherent linearity of the book format, we'll first talk about inputs and then talk about outputs, but this is by no means meant to imply a set order to the process of crafting! Sometimes inspiration doesn't strike until we are getting our hands dirty and physically working with materials. Sometimes a message from the muses comes through seemingly out of nowhere, and all we can do is sit back and listen before we figure out how to make sense of their musings. Usually for me, it's some combination of the two: a constant *bateleur* juggling act of giving and receiving. I've found that the esoteric and the exoteric often work best in collaborative tension with each other—and with a hopeful Magic Maker suspended somewhere between them, crafting steadily with supple hands.

INSPIRED INPUT

Though it's often depicted as being above us, the ethereal realm is everywhere. I think of the immaterial and material words as being layered over and throughout each other, an interdimensional palimpsest that requires certain skills to be able to translate. A Magic Maker knows secret ways to widen their own aperture. They have sensitive antennae that twitch in the presence of mystery. They see with triple vision and hear with more than just their ears.

In his 1979 book *The Timeless Way of Building*, architect and urban design theorist Christopher Alexander writes, "Your mind is a medium within which the creative spark that jumps between the pattern and the world can happen. You yourself are only the medium for this creative spark, not its originator." While he may have been using the word *medium* in the literal sense, the maker as spiritual medium is an apt metaphor. Mediums are mediators between disembodied presences and living beings. They are open and attuned, and they have honed their gift for conveying messages from the Great Beyond to the here and now.

This level of heightened receptivity is innate for some, but many of us can learn to sharpen our senses of perception or use time-tested tools that can bring forth more spirited communiqués. The preparatory methods we covered in the last section will help shift you into Magician Mode, and ready you to receive inspiration. The gods are with us always, exhaling ideas and fanning creative fire. But by implementing some of the following magical practices, you'll be better able to receive their input and get more direct downloads of information from on high.

Opening the Channel

The words *medium* and *channel* are often used interchangeably, but there is a distinction. A medium is anyone who acts as translator between the spiritual and material realms. They communicate with ghosts or other spirit entities, and they have the ability to relay messages to and from them. A channel allows the spirits to overtake their body—and sometimes their entire consciousness for a time. Generally speaking, spirits work *with* a medium and *through* a channel. Furthermore, some mediums are also channels, and vice versa. It simply depends on the modality that they are using at a given moment.

The first medium I remember seeing was Whoopi Goldberg's character Oda Mae Brown in the 1990 movie *Ghost*. When we first meet her, she's a charlatan, scamming people with fake readings and gold lamé–draped theatrics. Eventually she realizes that not only can she actually hear and speak to ghosts (mediumship), but that they can enter her body and speak through her (channeling). This is excellent news for the ghost of Patrick Swayze's character, Sam, who proceeds to use her to communicate with his grieving girlfriend, Molly, played by Demi Moore. In a pivotal scene, Goldberg allows Swayze's ghost to possess her so that he and Moore can physically touch each other across the veil. And while I was intrigued by the implied quasi-Sapphic slow dance between Goldberg/Swayze and Moore, I was mostly struck by the notion of the body as a vessel that another spirit can temporarily take over.

When someone is channeling or acting as a channel, they are opening themselves up to letting another energy flow through them. During a session, a professional channel might exhibit the mannerisms of the visiting entity, or their voice may take on a different register. Many years ago, I went to see the channel Paul Selig. When he first greeted me, he came across as a calm, soft-spoken man, even a bit professorial. Once our session began, his energy shifted. He sat with his eyes closed, and he spoke quickly and intensely in literal double-speak: first he would utter a bit of the message he received from his guides, and then he would repeat that same bit loudly to me before moving on to the next line and speaking that twice. It seemed like he was taking metaphysical minutes, first verifying that he heard their words correctly, then saying them again to me with more volume and more conviction. And so it went for nearly an hour, a cascade of twinned dispatches from the other side.

Such practices have been happening for centuries. The Oracle of Delphi in ancient Greece was said to enter a trance during which she would deliver prophetic messages from the god Apollo to those who sought his counsel. Some scholars say her utterances would be cryptic or frenzied, thus meriting further interpretation from her guests. And others suggest that her trance was perhaps induced by hallucinogenic fumes that came from the temple's proximity to a vaporous chasm (which might explain the cryptic, frenzied part).

The practice of allowing other entities to take the reins of the self occurs in many cultures. In Haitian Vodou, the spirits—or lwa—are said to "mount" or "ride" a practitioner during ceremony. When someone is being ridden by a lwa, they are overtaken by it, becoming the spirit's vehicle and mouthpiece. During these moments, the possessed person (known as the chwal or "horse") behaves differently than usual. The lwa may make them tremble, dance, or otherwise move with great intensity, speak in a voice different from their own, and take on the deity's characteristics. In this altered state, the chwal will share messages of guidance, blessing, or admonishment from the lwa to the other devotees present. It's a temporary trance that may last hours or even days, and it not only transforms the possessed but everyone bearing witness as well.

There is also an argument to be made that the glossolalia practice of modern Pentecostal Christians is a kind of channeling: when the spirit of Christ overtakes them, they begin speaking in tongues. The key point is that in all of these entrancing cases, the speech patterns, sounds, or images that the channel or medium emits are distinct from those they would normally use. The spirits are believed to be expressing themselves via the live bodies of human beings.

To be clear, each of these examples has their own religious and cultural contexts, as well as methods of containment to keep the situations under control. There is a distinct start and finish to these experiences, and the people involved generally participate with full consent. It's also important to be aware of one's emotional and mental stability when considering such techniques. Schizophrenia and other mental health dysregulations are serious conditions that must be treated with care, so if you have any of those types of diagnoses, experimenting with channeling may not be appropriate.

Disclaimers aside, many makers have referred to their creative processes as a type of channeling or have felt as if they were working from a trance state. They may use those terms figuratively to imply that ideas just flowed to them without much intervention on their part. As poet and author Robert Graves once told an interviewer, "No poem is worth anything unless it starts from a poetic trance, out of which you can be wakened by interruption as from a dream. In fact, it is the same thing." Others might literally believe that while they are creating, a separate spirit is at the wheel. Many creative people have spoken of being a kind of radio picking up signals from some cosmic broadcast, or else being a metaphysical stenographer taking dictation from above. Actors often talk about the experience of being a vessel who lets a character take over. Emmy-winning costar of *The Bear* Ebon Moss-Bachrach describes his belief in the spiritual aspects of acting on Sam Fragoso's *Talk Easy* podcast:

> To me it's very exciting to think about the spirit of something and having the spirit sort of come into you or you pick it up and you sort of carry it for a little while, and you're its protector. And you're its advocate. It feels heroic in a way to me. And it's also nice because you can kind of put your own stuff aside and say, Okay, for right now, I'm carrying this character. I'm carrying this idea, this person, this spirit of something.

No matter how it works or where the messages come from, the results from these channeled sessions are often wildly surprising and can lead to breakthroughs or take one's work in exciting new directions.

Spiritual Advisors

Cultural history is rife with ghostly consultancy sessions. And though celestial messages might come from one unified Spirit or from specific deities, sometimes the messengers are understood to be the spirits of the deceased. These encounters are frequently framed in a practice of ancestor veneration. Many cultures have traditions of keeping shrines for their dearly departed, visiting their graves, and leaving offerings to please and honor them. There is also a seemingly universal impulse to set aside specific holidays for ancestral remembrance, such as the Jewish Yizkor service during Yom Kippur and other holidays, the Mexican Día de Muertos, the Japanese Obon Festival, and the Hindu Pitru Paksha period to name but a few.

In contemporary Pagan practice, we have a holiday called Samhain (pronounced SOW-en), which falls on Halloween (or All Hallows' Eve, which is the night before All Hallows' Day and All Souls' Day—both Christian holidays of the dead). It is a modernized version of a much older Gaelic festival. Considered to be our Witches' New Year, Samhain is a time when we believe the veil between worlds is thinnest and spirit communication is at its clearest. Typical Samhain rituals include creating or reactivating an ancestor altar and having a Silent Supper, wherein a place setting with food is left for the spirits of our beloved dead. Many modern witches also engage in divination on this night, believing our ancestral guides are able to help deliver more powerful readings than usual.

However, one may commune with incorporeal collaborators at any time of year. My own experience of ancestor veneration is an ever-evolving one, and it includes the honoring of both my deceased blood relatives and my chosen spiritual family of friends, mentors, and creative heroes. On one of my altars is a tube of my grandma Sonya's electric pink (and incongruously named) Lilac Champagne Revlon Moon Drops lipstick. A prolifically talented and stylish visual artist—and a late-in-life metaphysical seeker—Sonya and her unconventional path continue to inspire me as I travel along mine. Hers is one of several names I invoke when I cast my magic circle and call upon my benevolent familial guides for support. I sense that this book in particular is being guided at least in part by her, as she and I connected deeply over our shared love of art when she was alive.

Likewise, it may seem appropriate to hold such a creative séance at nighttime accompanied by flickering candles or bathed with moonlight, but truly any time of day will do. Poet CAConrad has developed a morning practice of collaborating with their ancestors and other deceased loved ones to create what they call "(Soma)tic Poetry Rituals." In their book *Listen to the Golden Boomerang Return*, they state: "I do most of my writing at dawn when the voices of my dead friends, lovers, and family whisper in my ear to help me make poems. I have determined that they are always there for me, but that I am most relaxed and open in the morning and can distinguish their voices with more accuracy."

SPIRITUAL ADVISORS

Many Magic Makers have honed their own ghost-socializing techniques and developed realm-spanning relationships that turn into rich sources of inspiration. The Spiritualist movement of the nineteenth century was driven largely by women who believed that the dead could be contacted through such practices as séances and other channeled communications. (It also gave women one of the few legal means at the time to be able to speak in public for money, since it "wasn't really them" speaking, but rather the spirits who allegedly spoke through them.) We now know that the earliest Abstract artists were in fact Spiritualist women such as Georgiana Houghton, Hilma af Klint, and Anna Cassel. Much of their colorful, nonfigurative work was generated in channeling sessions and was delivered to and through them by various spirit guides.

Contact with the other side was also a goal of those with a more technological bent. Nineteenth-century "spirit photographers" such as William H. Mumler purported to use newly invented cameras to capture images of the dead so that those who mourned them might find comfort (his photo of Mary Todd Lincoln being embraced by a ghostly Abe is not to be missed). Even Thomas Edison jumped on the phantasmal bandwagon. In 1920 he told *American Magazine*: "I have been at work for some time, building an apparatus to see if it is possible for personalities which have left this earth to communicate with us." Though Edison's "Spirit Phone," as it came to be called, proved unsuccessful, inventors and tinkerers alike continue to build ghost-gabbing gadgets to this day via spirit boxes and other machines that allegedly capture electronic voice phenomena (EVP) and other "evidence" of afterlife conversation.

The Ouija board is a now-ubiquitous tool for afterlife engagement thanks, in large part, to Parker Brothers, who bought the rights to Ouija in 1966. These "talking boards" have been mass-produced in various iterations by them and, subsequently, Hasbro, which now owns the Ouija brand. My personal favorite is a 2008 bright pink version with its very own carrying case and the words "Asks the Questions Girls Want to Know" emblazoned on the box. Though today we associate Ouija with slumber parties and horror movies, the Ouija board as we've come to know it has been with us since 1890, when medium Helen Peters Nosworthy was asked to name a talking board that the Kennard Novelty Company was manufacturing. (She apparently asked the board what its name was, and it spelled out *OUIJA*, and then explained that it meant "good luck," though there's no direct linguistic translation for this term.) Though these companies sometimes get credit for "inventing" Ouija, they were merely capitalizing on the homemade talking boards that proliferated during the Spiritualist movement—and which arguably had much earlier roots. Some even trace the use of a spirit-controlled writing implement to the fuji method of China's Song dynasty in the first century AD, which involved a medium or group of mediums receiving messages via a stylus moving through a tray of sand or ash.

Origin stories aside, Ouija-style talking boards have captured the imaginations of many makers. Morrissey may not have been a believer when he released the song "Ouija Board, Ouija Board" in 1989, telling the press: "The only contact I ever made with the dead was when I spoke to a journalist from *The Sun*." But poet Sylvia Plath was definitely open to Ouija's possibilities. She and husband Ted Hughes would sometimes use a homemade talking board with an upside-down brandy glass to get spirited inspiration. Their most frequent ghostly guide was called Pan, and Plath scholar Kathleen Connors writes that Plath would consult Pan "for advice on poetry subjects, and sometimes to get numbers for horse races."

SPIRITUAL ADVISORS

In his 1982 *Grand Street* essay, "Sylvia Plath and Her Journals," Hughes also writes that Plath would communicate with spirits who she believed were delivering messages to her from her father, Otto, who died when she was eight. It seems Plath was ambivalent about the spiritual veracity of these Ouija sessions—and also felt this to be somewhat beside the point. In a 1958 journal entry, she wrote, "Even if our own hot subconscious pushes it (It says, when asked, that it is 'like us'), we had more fun than a movie." Her attempts to make contact with the other side were certainly creatively conducive, as she wrote several Ouija-themed poems as well as dark odes to Otto such as "Colossus" (1957) and "Daddy" (1965).

The most renowned Ouija-derived poetry is arguably that of James Merrill. Beginning in 1955, he and his partner, David Jackson, conducted hundreds of spirit writing sessions over the course of nearly forty years in their Stonington, Connecticut, house using their own homemade talking board. They made contact with deceased artistic heroes including poets W. H. Auden, Wallace Stevens, and W. B. Yeats, as well as their friend, the experimental filmmaker and Haitian Vodou researcher Maya Deren. However, the spirit of a Greek Jew named Ephraim proved to be their most consistent discarnate companion. Merrill's alphabetically organized, twenty-six-part poem, "The Book of Ephraim," is, at turns, an ecstatic and elegiac investigation into the workings of the cosmos, and it includes many of Ephraim's direct Ouija missives, quoted in capital letters throughout. The poem was included in Merrill's collection *Divine Comedies*, which was awarded the Pulitzer Prize in 1977. However, it would prove to be just one part of a much larger project, as the Ouija-generated long-form poems "Mirabell's Books of Number," "Scripts for the Pageant," and "Coda: The Higher Keys" followed suit. They, along with "The Book of Ephraim," were eventually compiled and released as one multipart epic poem called *The Changing Light at Sandover*, now considered Merrill's magnum opus.

Ouija also helped spark the spiritual writings of poet Lucille Clifton. In 1976, a silly Ouija session with two of her daughters turned serious when the planchette spelled out her mother's name, THELMA. According to Clifton scholar Marina Magloire, this session led Clifton "to automatic writing to, eventually, a spiritual state in which she could directly access the spirits without the need for writing." Clifton considered her poetry to be an extension of her mystical gifts. In the African American folk magic tradition of Hoodoo, "two-headed doctor" refers to a conjuror who can see into the spirit realm, and sometimes even see the future. The term resonated so much with Clifton that she titled her 1980 poetry collection *Two-headed Woman*. Much of Clifton's writing explores her identity as a Black spirit-worker who hails from a long, magical matrilineal line. In her poem "i was born with twelve fingers," she states that her extra digits were removed when she was an infant, just as her mother's and daughter's were, because "somebody was afraid we would learn to cast spells." Ancestor veneration is also central to Clifton's work and worldview. Her poem "daughters" is an homage to the spirit of her great-grandmother, and in it, Clifton recounts the lineage of supernaturally gifted women she comes from, including her "wild witch gran" and her "magic mama." One senses that her family members are both muses and mystic-artistic guides.

Automatic for the People

In stream-of-consciousness writing (also known as automatic writing) or other forms of creative free association, one makes work in an unedited and usually quick and fluid fashion. It's a means of creating without overthinking or analyzing, but rather letting the ideas flow, even if they seem silly, irrelevant, or otherwise odd. By employing techniques of automatic creation, our critical minds are temporarily set aside, and we make room for new insights and ideas that transcend our personal limitations. When we allow words or images to come in rapid succession, it often feels as if they're arriving from some other mysterious pocket of consciousness—whether from the deep recesses of the psyche or from an external, ethereal realm. There is a well-documented tradition of artists and others engaging in this technique from this latter and decidedly more occult perspective. Perhaps automatic writing, drawing, and so on are how a maker might bypass the borders of their own mind and invite in another spirit to collaborate.

The Irish poet William Butler Yeats was fascinated by esoteric thought, particularly the work of visionary artist and poet William Blake and proto-Spiritualist mystic Emanuel Swedenborg. Yeats himself was a member of the Theosophical Society, and later, the Hermetic Order of the Golden Dawn. In 1892, he stated: "Now as to magic. It is surely absurd to hold me 'weak' or otherwise because I choose to persist in a study which I decided deliberately four or five years ago to make, next to my poetry, the most important pursuit of my life . . . The mystical life is the center of all that I do and all that I think and all that I write."

His magical involvement escalated once he married Georgie "George" Hyde-Lees, a woman twenty-seven years his junior. He soon learned that she was a medium, and her method of receiving messages from the spirits was through automatic writing. By all accounts, Yeats's initially lukewarm feelings toward George heated up considerably upon this discovery, and they began engaging in these spiritual dictation sessions three or so times a week. Over three years, George and her guides generated nearly four thousand pages, which Yeats would use as the basis for his 1925 book (and subsequent 1937 revised version), *A Vision*, which is a cryptic philosophical treatise involving lunar phases, human evolution, and the poetic imagination. George asked that her name and her mediumship not be mentioned by Yeats in public, and so her lack of credit as co-creator was presumably not actually the sexist omission it may seem.

The Surrealists later experimented with their own version of uninterrupted creative sessions they dubbed "automatism." In 1920, the eventual co-founder of the Surrealist movement, André Breton, and the writer Philippe Soupault published their co-authored novel *Les Champs magnétiques* (*The Magnetic Fields*), which they generated using automatic writing. It is considered to be the first example of Surrealist literature. In Breton's 1924 *Surrealist Manifesto*, he went on to define Surrealism as:

AUTOMATIC FOR THE PEOPLE

> Psychic automatism in its pure state, by which one proposes to express—verbally, by means of the written word, or in any other manner—the actual functioning of thought. Dictated by the thought, in the absence of any control exercised by reason, exempt from any aesthetic or moral concern.

Breton and his brethren were responding to the burgeoning field of psychology as pioneered by Sigmund Freud, and they believed automatism allowed them to receive and express ideas in as unfiltered a manner as possible. Though Surrealism began as a means of mining the unconscious, it would eventually expand to encompass occult modalities, imagery, and techniques, as evidenced by the work of Max Ernst, Kurt Seligmann, Leonora Carrington, Remedios Varo, Victor Brauner, Ithell Colquhoun, and others. Breton himself grew more interested in the connections between magic and art, as evidenced by his 1957 book, *L'Art magique*. It was intended to be a deep dive into the history of magical art, though Breton grappled with the parameters of the subject. He writes,

> [T]he increasingly widespread use of the epithet 'magic,' applied nowadays to a whole category of contemporary as well as historical artworks, even if all too often it sanctions critical abdication, nonetheless attests to the need to understand such works from a quite different perspective from that of their manifest content: the propensity to bring more or less secret factors into their genesis.

Whether pure creativity is derived from the depths of the psyche or the superstratum of the spirit realm can be debated. Automatism remains an effective means of accessing new ideas, regardless of their origin.

I suspect that a primary factor in the power of automatic generation has to do with keeping things moving. If you speak, write, draw, freestyle, or play an instrument at the speed of intuition, you don't have time to overthink. This was affirmed for me during a writing class I took with the brilliant cartoonist Lynda Barry. She instructed us to keep our hands moving if we weren't sure what to write next. By writing the alphabet or doodling a stream of curlicues whenever we started to draw a blank, it would keep energy active and flowing. It worked: by staying kinetic during my moments of stuckness, new thoughts eventually arrived and streamed out of my hand and on to the page, as if by magic.

An important thing to note is that due to its unfiltered approach, a lot of what comes out of automatic sessions may seem like gibberish or a madcap unspooling of incongruous images. In many cases this technique is not going to generate a finished project. Just let go, and let the current of Creative Force flow through you without judgment or quality assessment. You can always sift through it later to find the gold.

Gettin' 'Mancy

Though it is possible to receive messages from Spirit directly into one's mind, many people throughout the ages have relied on other tools to help them converse with invisible energies and translate ethereal information. You are most likely familiar with tasseomancy, or the practice of reading tea leaves. The word conjures images of a wizened crone squinting into a teacup and telling fortunes from the soggy forms within. There doesn't seem to be anything that makes tea leaves specifically psychically charged, however, as people have used any manner of substances or items to inform or foretell. Throwing runes, stones, or bones; reading cards, palms, or facial features; analyzing the shapes of clouds or animal entrails are but a few of the myriad ways in which people have interrogated the unknown.

The word *mantic* means "prophetic," and in ancient Greece, a mantis, or seer, was a highly respected role. (The Greeks also allegedly named the praying mantis thusly because they believed it to be an auspicious insect.) The related suffix *-mancy* indicates some form of divination, and there are as many 'mancies as there are materials to make use of. In Dale Pendell's book *The Language of Birds: Some Notes on Chance and Divination*, he includes an alphabetized list of known divinatory methods including alectryomancy or "divination by roosters pecking grain," margaritomancy or "divination by heating and roasting pearls," and oinomancy or "divination by gazing into a glass of wine."

I'm particularly partial to oomancy, which refers to any technique of using eggs for prophecy. The most common method is to crack an egg into some heated water, and then analyze the shapes that egg whites make as they swirl, float, and solidify. Young seventeenth-century New England Puritans were said to sometimes secretly make a "Venus Glass," which was an egg cracked in water to foretell one's future love. Seeing a horse shape in the water might indicate that the girl would be traveling far away to get married, whereas a coffin might signify that her husband would die young. In fact, making a Venus Glass is likely one of the "little sorceries" that Cotton Mather accused the Salem girls Betty Parris and Abigail Williams of engaging in during the infamous Witch Trials. The Latin American purifying practice known as la limpia con huevo can also be considered a form of oomancy. During this ceremony, the curandera, or healer, waves an egg over a person's body to absorb negative energy. The egg is then cracked into some water and the colors and shapes therein are analyzed to determine the exact ailment the person might be suffering from.

Other shape-shifting materials can be used for 'mancy. Recently I was thrilled to learn of a practice in Jewish folk magic that makes use of ceromancy, or divination by wax in water. In Deatra Cohen and Adam Siegel's book *Ashkenazi Herbalism,* they write of an Eastern European opshprekherin, a medicine woman who specialized in prophecy and healing. If someone was believed to be suffering from the evil eye, an opshprekherin would hold a bowl of water over the afflicted person's head and then melt wax into it while uttering an incantation. The solidified wax would then be taken from the water, and its shapes would be interpreted. This was thought to help lift the curse, or at least provide insight as to how it could be lifted through subsequent actions.

Such supernatural shape-making has been used in all sorts of creative practices, particularly in the visual arts. The Surrealists popularized a technique called decalcomania, wherein they would smear paint between two pieces of material (almost like making a jelly sandwich) and then peel the pieces apart. The resulting texture would then be the basis for their artwork, dictating the shapes and images to follow. Max Ernst's *Alice in 1941* is a good example of this, as he clearly made the figure of Alice emerge from a wonderland of random, viscous paint. Other techniques that could be considered Surrealist art divination include fumage, which uses candle smoke to make patterns on paper, and soufflage, which involves blowing onto wet paint. Coulage is the Surrealist term for incorporating the cooled shapes of molten wax or metal into a work, and it is analogous to the ceromancy of my opshprekherin ancestors as far as I'm concerned.

The takeaway here is that any form that appears in a divinatory session can be used as a jumping-off point for more making. Lynda Barry is a big proponent of what she calls "water-skiing behind an image" while you are writing—of letting imagery lead you where it wants to go, and then writing down what you see. To expand upon this idea a bit further, I think the same is true for any image we encounter that has a particular vibration, resonance, or fascination for us. Divinely derived ideas often appear as imagery, and divinatory techniques can help us see them more clearly.

Cartomancy

One of the best-known forms of divination is cartomancy, which uses a deck of cards to divine spiritual messages. One version of this is tarot reading, which has roots stretching back to early fifteenth-century Italy where it began as a recreational card game. In 1781, the French occultist Antoine Court de Gébelin published what is considered to be the first explicitly occult interpretation of the tarot, and mystical writers including Etteilla, Éliphas Lévi, and Oswald Wirth are also credited with evolving such thinking in the centuries to follow. Likewise, there have been multiple versions of the tarot deck itself, with many of them riffing on or expanding upon those that came before. The Tarot of Marseilles from France became the most popular standardized deck in Europe in the eighteenth century, though its designs can be traced back to the late sixteenth century.

Today, the world's best-selling deck is known as the Rider-Waite-Smith deck (it's also known as the Smith-Waite deck or the Rider-Waite deck). It was co-created by esoteric writer A. E. Waite and artist Pamela Colman Smith (both members of the Hermetic Order of the Golden

Dawn) and published by William Rider & Son of London in 1909. This was the first mass-produced deck in which all seventy-eight cards had full illustrations, each consisting of symbolically rich vignettes (not just the Major Arcana and Court cards as in prior decks). This has arguably allowed for much deeper archetypal readings, and its imagery—from the lunar blue High Priestess to the triple-pierced heart of the Three of Swords card—has become iconic. In 1966 this deck went into public domain, and so not only has it remained widely available since then, but it has launched a proliferation of other "inspired-by" decks as well.

Though I've read tarot for myself since I was a preteen, my first ever professional reading was done for me by tarot scholar and writer Rachel Pollack when I was twenty-eight years old. As moved as I was by my reading from one of my mystic heroines, I was also impressed by the fact that the deck she used in the session was one she designed entirely herself, now known as the Shining Tribe Tarot. Meeting her and reading her books affirmed for me that tarot was a tool that could be used for more than day-to-day guidance; it could help unlock a door to a realm of infinite creative power. "Tarot readings help us to develop confidence in our own perceptions," Pollack has written. It makes sense then why so many makers have included tarot imagery in their work or have otherwise used tarot to assist them in solving their own creative problems.

Allusions to tarot have shown up in all kinds of artwork, including the paintings of Francesco Clemente, the T. S. Eliot poem *The Waste Land*, the Bob Dylan songs "Changing of the Guards" and "No Time to Think," and the SPELLLING album *The Turning Wheel*, to name but a few. Artist Niki de Saint Phalle was so inspired by the tarot that she created an entire sculpture garden filled with characters from the tarot's Major Arcana. De Saint Phalle and her collaborators began building *Il*

Giardino dei Tarocchi, or *The Tarot Garden,* in Tuscany beginning in the 1970s, and they continued working on it after it opened to the public in 1998. She even lived inside the Empress sculpture for seven years while working on the garden, using it as her studio and primary dwelling space. The Empress is the card of creative nurturing and feminine fecundity—a perfect and intentional symbol for a wildly prolific, vibrant Magic Maker such as de Saint Phalle.

Many visual artists go on to create their own versions of the tarot. Leonora Carrington, Ithell Colquhoun, and Salvador Dalí each developed partial or entire decks that vary in style from jewel-toned figuration to abstraction to collage. In the 1940s, a group of Surrealists created the fifty-two-card Jeu de Marseilles, which included images of many of their heroes such as Freud, Paracelsus, and the Marquis de Sade. Lately it seems a week can't go by without my hearing about a new deck from an artist I admire, and I welcome the bounty. I was particularly delighted to get the opportunity to write the guidebook for *Sabat Magazine*'s silver-inked Le Tarot de L'étoile Cachée, which was designed by Elisa Seitzinger. This allowed me to contemplate tarot symbolism from the inside out, as I came to understand the fluidity of the deck as each card was being reworked and finished. It's astounding to see how infinitely the tarot can be reinterpreted and remade.

There are also decks that don't hew to the tarot format at all but are still used for divinatory purposes. An oracle deck is a set of cards that can have virtually any theme, be designed in any style, and be offered in any amount. When I was a kid, my first oracle deck was Kathy Tyler and Joy Drake's Angel Cards. The cards were laminated strips, slightly bigger than what's found inside a fortune cookie. Each had a word on it like *Authenticity* or *Risk* printed in calligraphy, accompanied by a little angel illustration. When I pulled one of these cards, it made me feel as if I was getting some sort of direction—or directive—for the day.

One particularly groundbreaking—and decidedly more adult—oracle deck was created by the Surrealist collage artist Penny Slinger in 1977. Graphically bold and drawing on a plethora of mythic systems, the Secret Dakini Oracle deck combines Slinger's extensive studies of yoga, Tantra, and hermeticism with her lifelong devotion to feminist expression. She describes the deck as "a cycle of sixty-four archetypes conceived as moving around a central point—the Self." Though some of the cards such as Death/Transfiguration have distinct tarot analogs, others such as Cosmic Carrot are playful twists on spiritual themes.

Some of my favorite contemporary oracle decks include Kim Krans's Wild Unknown Archetypes deck; the Minimalist Oracle by Rachel Lieberman; the Uusi Supra Oracle; Rebekah Erev's Moon Angels deck; and Eht/Aht: A Netivot Wisdom Oracle by Kohenet Ketzirah 'haMa'agelet' Lesser. I also got to help develop and edit the MotherWitch Oracle, which was created by Bat for Lashes musician Natasha Khan. In the MotherWitch guidebook, there is not only an interpretation for each card but recommended books, films, music, and works of art to help the querant explore the cards' messages more deeply. And while I adore tarot and utilize it regularly, what I love about oracle decks is that they are often a bit more direct in their meanings—a card might be called something like Communal Bliss, as opposed to the 10 of Cups in tarot, which one must do a bit of extra work to understand. An oracle deck is also a complete world unto itself and offers the truly personal expression of its creator, since it is free of a preestablished structure. And artists love making them because they don't have to stick to a seventy-eight-card standard or be limited by tarot-centric iconography.

Regardless of whether you gravitate toward tarot decks, oracle decks, or some combination thereof, cartomancy is extremely useful in helping the querent navigate all sorts of creative matters. There are screenwriters such *Mad Men's* Matthew Weiner and *Chilling Adventures of Sabrina's* Joshua Conkel who have used tarot to help determine character choices and plot points in their TV shows. In fact, Weiner has said that Don Draper's pivotal tarot reading in the series was drawn from an exact reading he once got, including the Judgment, Sun, and World cards. (Weiner also uses the Sun card as the logo for his Weiner Bros. production company.) Fabulist author Italo Calvino called the tarot "a machine for constructing stories," and used it to help write his 1973 story collection, *The Castle of Crossed Destinies*. Rachel Pollack's *The Tarot of Perfection* (2008) is also a book of fiction based on her many divination sessions, and when I interviewed her on my podcast in 2020, she told me that she fell in love with tarot because "it reminded me of comic books in the best way"—and she was a devotee and writer of both. Pollack has also written that tarot is "an engine of pattern-making. Even one card may suggest events, characters, possibilities." By pulling a card, or several, you can uncover motifs, energies, and correspondences that lead you down a revelatory new path of meaning-making in your projects.

Cartomancy can also be a helpful coach in more general matters, such as how to break through writer's block or how to approach a project from a different angle. I know of several tarot readers such as Sarah Potter, Michelle Tea, and Jessa Crispin who specialize in working with artists of all stripes, and they are particularly sensitive regarding the issues that stir and plague those with creative souls. There are also themed oracle decks with a specific focus on providing creative guidance. Experimental musician Brian Eno and multimedia artist Peter Schmidt developed the

Oblique Strategies deck for precisely this purpose. Subtitled "Over one hundred worthwhile dilemmas," it's an elegantly designed black box filled with over one hundred white cards with simple prompts printed on them. The aesthetic is clean and minimalist, with no images to speak of. The cards say things on them like "Retrace your steps," "What would your closest friend do?" and "Infinitesimal gradations." Each is like a Zen koan, or a quick missive from a mysterious muse. First published in 1975, it's now in its sixth edition, has been translated into multiple languages, and has been a go-to deck for creatives of every field.

When doing any sort of divination, particularly cartomancy, it is always recommended you first clear and reacclimate your tools by shuffling them. While doing so, form a question in your mind. You may also choose to speak it out loud or write it down before you begin. The query can be as broad as "What do I need to know right now to help me with my creativity?" or as specific as "What new approach can I bring to the album I'm writing?" Sometimes it's useful to ask about specific friction points, such as "How can I overcome my perfectionism?" or "What should my novel's main character do next?"

You can then pull one card to receive your answer, or you may also choose to do an entire spread that can address multiple questions or different aspects of the same inquiry. But whatever you do, stay open to the messages that come through, and be prepared to sit with them over time. This isn't a pop quiz you're springing on Spirit! Sometimes the response might be immediately obvious to you, and sometimes its meaning will reveal itself as the days unfold. And as with any divinatory session, it's helpful to take notes so that you can remember and revisit this arcane information down the road.

Bibliomancy

Any 'mancy can serve as a powerful tool for inspiration or creative decision-making. These techniques arouse our creativity because they seem to tap into the magic of chance. Does divination operate on randomness or some kind of cosmically ordered synchronicity? No matter—it is *effective*, and countless creators have utilized these tools and methods to problem solve, iterate, and make surprising new work.

One of the most accessible 'mancies is bibliomancy, or divination through books. There is a long-standing tradition of flipping through a copy of the Bible and seeing what passage one's finger lands on, believing this to be a personal message from God. But truly, any book will do. This practice can be used for soliciting divine direction on a current project or simply to spark new ideas. When Janaka Stucky and I teach our Occult Writing workshop together, we always include a bibliomancy exercise. It's a wonderful way to generate writing prompts, and often our students find themselves coming up with exciting new turns of phrase or images beyond their usual scope.

BIBLIOMANCY

Another form of bibliomancy is about finding the "right" book in the first place. I'm sure many of us have had the experience of wandering into a bookstore or library and feeling pulled to a particular tome. There is a feeling of kismet to these literary encounters, and often people will remark that they seemed to find the perfect book at the perfect time. I sometimes do self-directed bibliomancy and pass my hand over the shelves to see which spine draws me to it. From there, I flip to a random page to see what lines my eyes land on. The book doesn't always come home with me, but the message certainly does.

Some believe these moments are guided by a sort of book deity. In Kabbalistic lore, Harahel or Herochiel is said to be a library angel, responsible for connecting readers with precisely the materials they need. In his essay "A Writer's Guide to the Library Oracle and Its Angel," librarian Justin Patrick Moore writes:

> Working at libraries for over a decade I have had the pleasure of tracking the many ways Herochiel acts as an interlocutor between the ideas contained in one's head and the feelings in one's heart, and what is continually being scanned back into the computer system of the library as I process recent returns . . . Herochiel delivers in outward reality, via the titles of books, movies, albums, and other materials vital messages corresponding to the burning questions of mind and soul. It is like bibliomancy on a vast scale . . .

There are also human beings who have this gift: clerks, librarians, and friends who intuitively know exactly the tome to recommend—book angels in the flesh. One such person I've encountered is a bookseller named Mari Granderson Lewis who worked at the Minneapolis airport's Simply

Books. Her recommendations are so surprising and precise that they feel oracular, and I always make sure to stop in whenever I'm passing through. (It seems I'm not the only one who has had this experience with Granderson Lewis, as she was given an MSP Nice Award in 2015.)

In my experience, the research process is often highly bibliomantic (or internetmantic, as the case may be). I'll have an idea of a topic I'd like to write about, but then my research takes me down different avenues that either enrich my original thinking or change it entirely. So many of my projects—including this very book—have been guided by bibliomancy that it would take a whole other book to write about it all, but I'll share one anecdote.

A few months ago, I noticed that a home-goods shop in my neighborhood had added a wall of books. I found myself drawn to an anthology called *Black Mountain Poems*. I've long admired the history of Black Mountain College, a mid-century liberal arts school in Black Mountain, North Carolina, that many artists and esotericists such as Ruth Asawa, Buckminster Fuller, and John Cage attended or taught at. I decided to flip to a random page in the book, and I landed on the poem "Often I Am Permitted to Return to a Meadow" by Robert Duncan. This happens to be one of my very favorite poems—in fact, I have a copy of it that I keep on my desk. Encountering it in the wild, seemingly randomly, made me *know* that I had to take this book home with me, which I did.

A week or so later, I was writing an episode of my podcast, and I decided to share this encounter as part of it. The topic of the show became about bibliomancy, and by way of illustration, I decided to flip to another random page of *Black Mountain Poems*. I landed on the poem "Concerts of Space" by M. C. Richards. And that very poem is *about bibliomancy*!

BIBLIOMANCY

But wait! There's more! A few days later, I ordered some books I've been wanting to read as part of researching *this* book. One of them is *Centering in Pottery, Poetry, and the Person*, which had been on my wish list for years. I decided to finally read it now, as I liked the idea of possibly including a potter's perspective in this book. So my copy of *Centering* arrives, and BAM! I notice that it is authored by none other than M. C. Richards, the very writer whose poem my bibliomancy had introduced me to in the *Black Mountain Poems* anthology! And, as evidenced by my reference to *Centering* in Part II earlier, you'll see that this trail ended up to being a fruitful one. Furthermore, Richards's book has become a personal touchstone for me, as it is truly one of the most beautifully written meditations on the creative process that I have ever encountered.

M. C. Richards passed away in 1999, long before I ever crossed paths with her work. Perhaps her spirit led me on this trail of books, somehow intervening in my bibliomantic quest. Perhaps you will feel called to pick up *Centering* yourself because of it (and I highly recommend you do), or you will be inspired to learn more about her pottery and her poems. A book is one of the finest time machines we have—an accessible and elegant way to commune with other minds across dimensions. Bibliomancy can provide a strange and subtle map to navigate this boundless highway.

Other Wordy Oracles

One of the oldest known divination texts is the I Ching from ancient China, which some date as far back as 1,000 BCE, though it is based on much older writings. Often translated in English to *Book of Changes*, it has gone through several permutations. (As Eliot Weinberger writes in "What Is the I Ching?," his wonderful *New York Review of Books* essay, "There is no book that has gone through as many changes as the *Book of Change*.") The I Ching system that has come to be most well-known is sometimes referred to as the "King Wen sequence" after its alleged founder. This is a set order of sixty-four hexagrams, or six-line symbols, each made up of solid lines, broken lines, or some combination thereof. Each hexagram corresponds to a different Taoist principle or meaning, and one usually finds out which hexagram "answers" their query by tossing sticks or coins. (When I randomly opened my copy of Stephen Karcher's *Total I Ching: Myths for Change* just now, I landed on hexagram 21 or Biting Through, interpreted by Karcher as "eating or biting through an obstacle with words or questions," which is how writing this section feels today. So using coin-less bibliomancy with the I Ching text clearly works too!)

Though there are many versions of the I Ching available today, Cary F. Baynes's 1950 English translation of Richard Wilhelm's 1924 German translation (often called the Wilhelm/Baynes version) is what helped this system catch on like wildfire in the West. Poets from Octavio Paz to Allen Ginsberg made use of it in their writing and in their lives, and Gary Snyder lists the *Book of Changes* as one of the works of "traditional magic" a writer should be familiar with in his 1967 poem "What You Should Know to Be a Poet." When writing his 1962 speculative fiction novel *The Man in the High Castle*, Philip K. Dick consulted the I Ching regularly, as did his characters. In a 1974 *Vertex* magazine interview, he explains that he's attracted to this method because it "gives advice beyond the particular, advice that transcends the immediate situation. The answers have a universal quality. . . . If you use the I Ching long enough and continually enough, it will begin to change and shape you as a person."

Avant-garde composer John Cage is considered a pioneer of "indeterminacy," a method of music-making that relies, at least in part, on elements of chance. Though he's become rather notorious for his 1952 "silent" composition *4'33"*, which involves a musician sitting without playing their instrument for four minutes and 33 seconds, his body of work is vast and varied. Much of it was created via an elaborate I Ching system that he developed for the purpose of writing music using what he called chance operations. In this method, he would use coin tosses to create charts of sixty-four squares, each corresponding to such musical variables as tempo, pitch, duration, and rhythm—acoustically based hexagrams, if you will. Then he would toss coins to select the squares at random and compose his pieces based on the results. His 1950 *Music of Changes* piano compositions are the most well-known of Cage's I Ching–devised pieces, though he would continue to use these charts and coin tosses to create much of his work. Eventually he came to use a hexagram-based randomizing computer program designed for him by Ed Kobrin, which allowed him to speed up his process significantly.

Though there are those who believe the I Ching to be imbued with its own divine consciousness, Cage was initially attracted to it because it helped eliminate any of his own aesthetic biases. Already a student of D. T. Suzuki and Zen Buddhism when he was introduced to the I Ching, Cage was determined to figure out ways of detaching his own ego and its tastes from his work. Still, Cage seems to think of the I Ching as being spiritually expansive, and not merely a force for powering some soulless sonic factory. He believed that relinquishing control and ego-based intention allowed him to make new discoveries and to stay loose. As he told Laurie Anderson in a 1992 interview in *Tricycle* magazine: "I use chance operations instead of operating according to my likes and dislikes. I use my work to change myself and I accept what the chance operations say." Doing so means he created music that asks the composer, the player, and the listener to let go of any preconceived notions and to greet the music with openness. For him, the purpose of art is "not self-expression but self-alteration," as he stated in the documentary *I Have Nothing to Say and I Am Saying It*. When we embrace the unexpected, we become more accepting and perhaps more evolved.

The term *aleatory* is sometimes used to describe such chance-based creative operations. Its Latin root, *alea*, is related to tossing dice, and it implies an association with accidental or unpredictable outcomes. The early twentieth-century Dada art movement was responsible for popularizing aleatory methods of writing, particularly through the cut-up technique. Tristan Tzara's 1920 *On Feeble Love and Bitter Love: Dada Manifesto* recounts his preferred cut-up strategy in Section VIII entitled "To Make a Dadaist Poem." He tells us to cut out each individual word of a newspaper article and then shake them together in a paper bag. At this point, you take out word after word from the bag, copying each down exactly in the order it appears. Ta-da! There you have it, a Dadaist poem (and the precursor to the Magnetic Poetry Kit gracing refrigerators around the globe since its debut in 1993).

One of the most celebrated aleatory writers is William S. Burroughs, who used the cut-up method to compose his Nova Trilogy (also known as the Cut-up Trilogy), which is composed of the books *The Soft Machine* (1961), *The Ticket That Exploded* (1962), and *Nova Express* (1964). Burroughs was introduced to this technique by the visual artist Brion Gysin, who stumbled upon it himself in the 1950s. Gysin used newspapers as a protective layer when he was cutting out other elements for his artwork with a Stanley blade. The resulting scraps of words captured his attention, and he began rearranging them to create new texts. Burroughs and Gysin would go on to develop this technique in various mediums such as film and recorded sound, as well as a 1960 book called *Minutes to Go*, which included cut-ups by the two of them, Sinclair Beiles, and Gregory Corso. Eventually Burroughs and Gysin would collaborate on their 1977 book, *The Third Mind*, which highlighted many of their cut-up theories and projects.

Though the Dadaists were known to court chaos and absurdity in their work, Gysin and Burroughs had a more occult take on these chance operations. They first met in Paris's (then unnamed) Beat Hotel, where they engaged in a whole host of metaphysical experimentation, including "mirror-gazing, scrying, trance and telepathy, all fuelled by a wide variety of mind-altering drugs," per Matthew Levi Stevens's book *The Magical Universe of William S. Burroughs*. And in his Gysin biography, *Nothing Is True Everything Is Permitted*, John Geiger quotes Timothy Leary's description of Gysin: "Brion dispenses blessings, visions, communications, poetic sermons, and wicked gossip—the world of the occult is his planet. Gysin is one of the great hedonic mystic teachers." Seen through the lens of magic, their cut-ups can be viewed as an extension of various practices of interfacing with the unknown to make art, and of inviting collaboration with otherworldly energies (not to mention each other). Burroughs would go on to discuss what he felt were the oracular aspects of cut-ups, noting how the final pieces would sometimes be eerily predictive. In his 1976 lecture "Origin and Theory of the Tape Cut-Ups," Burroughs states, "When you experiment with Cut-Ups over a period of time you find that some of the Cut-Ups in re-arranged texts seemed to refer to future events . . . when you cut into the Present the Future leaks out."

Whether or not cut-ups are used for divinatory purposes, the method certainly proved creatively contagious. Bob Dylan used cut-ups to develop lyrics for songs such as "Visions of Johanna," and Iggy Pop referred to the cut-up method as "a Ouija board for art people" (though as we've seen, an actual Ouija board would suffice!). As with John Cage's eventual move from analog I Ching tosses to digital ones, David Bowie was so taken with the Gysin-Burroughs cut-up system that he would eventually develop the Verbasizer computer program with programmer Ty Roberts, which could randomly mix inputted columns of words and generate wonderfully strange lyrical mutations. Bowie also remarked how cut-ups seemed to "predict things about the future or tell me a lot about the past. It's really quite an astonishing thing. I suppose it's a very Western tarot."

OTHER WORDY ORACLES

Later musicians including Genesis Breyer P-Orridge, Kurt Cobain, and Thom Yorke would employ the cut-up technique in their own songs, not to mention countless others who have used it for everything from generating kernels of ideas to entire compositions and everything in between. Today, engaging in the creative divination of cut-ups is as easy as going to a word-randomizing website—or even using an online version of the Bowie-Roberts Verbasizer at verbasizer.com. Or you can just use the good old-fashioned hands-on method: take a page of text, wield your scissors like a wand, and see what weird word magic they conjure.

Handy Advice

One rule of thumb, if you'll pardon the pun, is to let your nondominant hand lead when engaging in your divination sessions. This is the hand you can use to pull cards from a deck, toss runes or I Ching coins, or point to a passage in a randomly opened book. The nondominant hand is said to be your hand of intuition and receiving cosmic messages. I'm right-handed, which means that I use my left hand to select tarot cards or any other sort of divinatory gestures. If you are a lefty, you would simply do the reverse.

It's worth mentioning that there are those who associate left-handedness with anything occult, unnatural, or even diabolical. Though an estimated 10 percent of the population is left-handed, it's only fairly recent that left-handedness was even allowed in public because there was so much stigma around this trait. My grandma Trudy used to tell me stories about how she was born a lefty but was made to write with her right hand at school—and teachers would give her a swift rap on the knuckles if they caught her doing otherwise. She was forced to become a righty, and it was traumatizing for her to have to repress her genetic inclination. Many children of her generation and earlier experienced this—either being struck on the left hand or having it tied behind their back—in order to train them to use the "proper" right hand.

The reason for this is that throughout history, left-handedness was considered evil, as so many exceptional things are. In fact, the word *sinister* comes from Latin, and it originally meant "left" or "on the left side." The word *dexter* is Latin for "right," which is where we get the word *dexterity*, again implying that right-handedness is desirable. This is also why in a lot of Christian artwork, Jesus is shown on the right side of God and figures like Eve, who are considered evil, are shown on the left.

In the occult, we have an expression called the Left-Hand Path. Some associate this phrase with negative magic like hexes and curses, and the Right-Hand Path with healing and positive magic. That is, however, too reductive, as there are varying and far more nuanced breakdowns between these orientations. Many believe that practicing the Left-Hand Path implies that you embrace individualism, you're more comfortable utilizing subversive or transgressive techniques like sex magic, or you otherwise reject social convention in any number of ways. Clearly this rubric comes from old-fashioned superstitions and misguided understandings of a natural genetic permutation.

With all due respect to my left-handed readers, I do not believe there is anything more inherently magical about lefties—though if having a history of sinister associations delights or ignites you, by all means embrace it! For the purposes of divinatory work, however, the nondominant hand is considered the intuitive one, no matter which side that is for you. And if you're ambidextrous, just use whichever hand feels the most awkward or unnatural in any given divination situation. That's the hand considered to be your more supernaturally receptive one.

The Art of Augury

Though divinatory objects are plentiful and fun to use, one doesn't need cards, coins, or talking boards to communicate with Spirit. Inspiring signs swirl around us constantly, and all it takes to perceive them is a practice of paying attention. Augury is the interpretation of signs, and it is one of the most important skills a Magic Maker can develop.

Stop what you're doing. Be present to what's around you right now in this moment. What suddenly catches your eye? What song is playing from a passing car? What fragment of a stranger's conversation floats across your transom? Maybe there is a sign that keeps appearing to you over and over again: a fox shows up in your backyard, then in a novel you're reading, then on a mug you come across in a secondhand shop. It's probably time to do some research into foxes, I'd say, or perhaps to start drawing pictures of them or writing about them to see where they lead.

Augury can also be used when gathering materials for any sort of creative work. The legendary assemblage artist Betye Saar chooses found objects for her projects using her intuitive gift, which she refers to as "mother wit." She drifts through yard sales and thrift stores—not to mention the staggering collection of bric-a-brac she's amassed in her studio—and lets her mother wit lead her to the pieces as it may. She explained her sacred selection process to *T* magazine: "I've always felt that old objects hold a power . . . They've survived, and they have a sense of the previous owner. They have a spirit." Saar's art practice is led by a sort of second sight—or perhaps second *feel*. She follows the lead of the seemingly random objects she encounters and pays attention to signs and sensations she receives. She then constellates the various objects that she's collected, creating works that feel like altars, fetishes in the magical sense, and windows into other worlds. Her approach to synthesizing these spirit-objects is led by her intuition as well. She allows the work to take the form it is meant to and lets the process take as long as it needs to, not calling a piece finished until the elements click *just so*.

Experimental filmmaker and occultist Kenneth Anger also used a form of augury when selecting the soundtrack for his 1963 homoerotic short, *Scorpio Rising*. He was looking to complete a scene in which three motorcyclists adorn themselves in leather and chains in a ritualistic fashion but was unclear as to what song should underscore it. Anger intentionally opened himself up to sonic synchronicity and made his request to the powers that be. As P. Adams Sitney writes in his book *Visionary Film*, "Anger turned on his radio and exercised his will. Out came Bobby Vinton's 'She wore blue velvet,' which when joined to the episode created precisely the sexual ambiguity Anger wanted in this scene." The spirits of cinema had delivered his "Blue Velvet" answer.

And filmmaker John Wilson discussed the power of being open to synchronicity when making his pieces out of found footage. In an interview on Marc Maron's *WTF* podcast, Wilson explains the augury he used when creating his hit HBO show, *How To with John Wilson*:

> I'm usually an emotional wreck during the writing, especially, and the beginning of the shooting. Because I really don't know how any of it's going to shake down, and I'm just like constantly kind of whipping myself. It's like . . . "I don't know what this is," but then this kind of strange thing happens and I don't know how to explain it. I'm not this kind of person but there's just like this weird synchronicity or I don't know if it's manifestation or something but like just thinking about something constantly and looking everywhere for it . . . the universe will deliver it to you in really weird ways.

Opening your third eye, going spirit hunting, doing transcendental trail tracking—call it what you will. But signs are put in our path, and it's up to us to pay attention to them. Creative Force speaks to us in symbols and sensations. Sometimes it gently waves and whispers. Sometimes it smacks us with a scream. But it is always here, and it is always ready to be acknowledged by us and enlivened through us.

In ancient Rome, interpreters of signs from the gods were called augurs, and they had important roles in religious and social life. They were consulted for guidance in politics, war, business, and personal matters, and were well practiced in determining the divine meaning of natural occurrences, which they saw as omens. Though augury is often associated with the analysis of birds in particular—their behavior, flight, songs, and appearance—an augur would also pay attention to shifting weather patterns and other such phenomena. When an augur was working, it was said that they were "taking the auspices," and the word *auspicious* is related to this practice.

Today it's not unusual for someone to speak of a coincidence or meaningful appearance and say that it "felt like a sign." Many of us have deep associations with certain animals, insects, or plants, believing them to signify something magical when we suddenly encounter them. My mom believes that seagulls represent the spirit of her mother who passed away in 2001, and every time she sees one, she says, "Hi, Ma," and feels a sense of comfort. I know many people who think that finding a feather or coming across an animal bone is a sign of magic, or a message that they are on the right path.

But augury isn't only about nature. We can take the auspices in any environment or circumstance. One of the most magical occurrences that has ever happened to me unfolded over a twenty-four-hour period. In 2017, I decided to step away from my day job for what I thought would be a six-month unpaid sabbatical. It was a huge leap of faith, but I had reached a point where the call to devote my time and energy to my writing and other projects was so loud that I knew I would regret it forever if I didn't try it. I was burnt out on corporate life and feeling a burning desire to give my full attention to my passions. I realize I was very fortunate to have a little bit of savings squirreled away, as well as the relative stability of my husband's nonprofit day job. But I was forgoing a six-figure salary, so I had to figure out some way to hold up my end of our expenses or else do a lot of belt-tightening, and I had no clear idea what was next for me. What I did know was that the emotional and physical breakdowns I was beginning to experience would only worsen if I didn't take a time-out. And I also knew that I had sparks of inspiration that I longed to breathe into full creative conflagrations.

On my last day of work in the office, I was excited to be stepping away but also nervous as hell. Was I making the right decision? Was it foolhardy of me to press pause on what was then a rapidly escalating "successful" career? How would I afford this? What was I even doing? As I packed up my things from my desk, the head of my department called me into his office. He told me he wished me all the best on my break and that he was looking forward to seeing me when I returned in six months. And then he handed me a bottle of wine as a lovely send-off. When I looked at the label, I felt prickles of magic all over my body: it was from Stag's Leap winery, and the wine was called Artemis. My boss had no idea that Artemis has been my matron goddess for most of my life, and there's a chance he didn't even know what the word *Artemis* meant! But I took it as the goddess's way of signaling to me that I was on the right path, and that trusting my own vision and pull toward independence was absolutely what I was supposed to be doing.

If that wasn't enough, the next morning—my first morning of liberation—the clock radio woke me up to Jonathan Richman's song "Because Her Beauty Is Raw and Wild," which was randomly playing in the background of a story on NPR. Jonathan Richman is one of my all-time favorite musicians (talk about a Magic Maker), and the lyrics to this particular song describe the starry, wild beauty of a lady in a way that feels like an Artemisian ode. Further confirmation of my choice.

During those six months, I began working on my first full-length book, *Waking the Witch*, and I started my podcast, *The Witch Wave*. I felt fertile with inspiration, and creative energy poured out of me. But I knew the clock was ticking, and as the months flew by, I couldn't bear the thought of putting a stop to all of this productive magic. During the final month of my break, just when it was looking like I would have to return to my corporate gig as planned, my book sold and my podcast began attracting more advertisers. I wasn't making anything close to the income I'd had at my corporate job, but it was enough to skate by for a while longer. More importantly, I felt encouraged to focus on my creative purpose full time and to leave my job permanently. I sensed that the path would keep revealing itself to me if I trusted it to do so. And though there have been many ups and downs since then—financially and otherwise—the ability to do what I love for a living has been priceless. It's been eight years since I veered away from my corporate career, and it's one of the best decisions I've ever made.

I realize that not everyone has the ability to quit their day jobs. But I do believe that incorporating augury into one's life can be beneficial for most people. I'm often encouraging folks to follow the trail of cosmic breadcrumbs because I believe that these signs are sent to us to help guide our way into wonder. By becoming metaphysical detectives, we're better positioned to uncover clues about who we are and what we're meant to put our energy toward.

This is certainly true of any magical practice of making. Whether looking for inspiration, new areas of creative investigation, or just general direction in regard to one's life path, artful augury is a technique that anyone can develop. It requires a balance of intellect and intuition, of being highly perceptive while also willing to surrender to the supersensory. And this can happen whether we are wide awake or whether we are in a dream state.

Nocturnal Transmissions

The dream world is one of the most fecund spaces for receiving creative signs. Many makers have been inspired by a dream or reverie. In a recent episode of the *McCartney: A Life in Lyrics* podcast, Paul McCartney speaks about the mysterious way in which he discovered the tune of one of his most beloved Beatles songs: "the fact that I dreamed the song 'Yesterday' leads me to believe that it's not just quite as cut and dry as we think it is." In an episode of my podcast, *The Witch Wave,* BAFTA-winning actor Suranne Jones told me that the idea for her TV show *MaryLand* also came to her while asleep, just when she was stepping into more of a producer role in her life:

> When I was getting serious about developing stuff, I had a dream about two sisters that found a house. And when they went into the house, there was a funeral. And they were talking about this woman that they didn't know, but yet they saw these pictures on the wall of their mother. And then they suddenly discovered that their mother had a different life—another life they didn't know about. And the way she was being talked about was not their experience of her.

And that was it. That was my dream. And I wrote it down, and I didn't do anything with it for about three years. And I kept coming back to it . . . And then it needed to be developed . . . And that was our very first drama production.

Following her dream paid off, as *MaryLand* aired in 2023 on ITV in the UK and on PBS's *Masterpiece* series in the US.

These divine dream deliveries aren't exclusive to the arts. In 1862, the German chemist August Kekulé came up with the structure for the benzene molecule in a dream state. As the story goes, he was drifting off to sleep in front of a fire when suddenly he had a vision of an ouroboros, the alchemical symbol of the snake eating its own tail. When he fully awoke, he realized that benzene's six carbon atoms and six hydrogen atoms were arranged in a ring. Other allegedly dreamt-up scientific discoveries include the sewing machine, the structures of DNA and the atom, the periodic table, and Google.

Of course, oneiric engagement has an enormously long history, influencing everyone from the biblical Joseph to Sigmund Freud. Many ancient cultures had practices of dream incubation, or incubatio, wherein the dreamer would go to sleep with a specific issue or query in mind. The gods would then deliver the answer to them via overnight visions. In some instances, a person would travel to a sacred site for the purpose of receiving prophetic or healing dreams, sometimes referred to as temple sleep. In ancient Greece, this method was often utilized at the Sanctuary of Asclepius, who is the god of healing. This deity is also associated with snakes, which is why the Rod of Asclepius is still a symbol for medicine today. It is said that Asclepius's patients would go to sleep in the inner chambers of his temple, and that snakes would be let loose to crawl over their bodies and lick them, then thought to be a curative procedure. Upon waking, the patients would recount their dreams to the temple physicians, who would interpret them for further instructions regarding their treatment.

One needn't take a pilgrimage to a dream-steeped sanctuary nor bed some serpents to receive nocturnal secrets. Simply asking a question or holding a creative concern in your mind's eye as you drift off to sleep has proven effective for many slumber-curious creatives. Just be sure to keep a notebook and pen nearby so you can jot down any visions that come your way as soon as you wake up. This magic can be highly elusive, as those of us who struggle to remember seemingly vivid dreams can attest. I once dreamt the recipe for a flying potion, and I will forever lament the fact that I had no paper nearby to capture it on when I regained consciousness. Sorry, human race! I'll do better next time. (Come to think of it, losing the recipe for flight would make a wonderful story. . . .)

The beauty of dreaming, divination, and other forms of receiving inspired input is that we can do them no matter our mood or our surroundings. Anyone can read the messages that spirits scrawl for us in their symbolic lexicon. All we need to do is set an intention of reception and acceptance of whatever signs appear. In *Ideal Suggestions: Essays in Divinatory Poetics*, Selah Saterstrom writes: "Being an effective reader is contingent upon the quality of presence with which one positions oneself in the constant stream of information and texts. The stream is wherever you are, all of the time, in every grand place, and in every suffering pit." When we are present with Creative Force, we become fluent in lunar language, and we can confer with Spirit whenever we wish.

We believe, and we receive.

So go on.

Get open, let go, and let the magic flow into you.

ENCHANTED OUTPUT

It's time to turn our attention to the other half of the Craft process, and to focus on the work of the Magician's downward-facing hand. This is the hand that transforms all of that divinely inspired information into material reality. It is the hand of activating, of expressing, of giving. It doesn't matter what you're making. The final form is beside the point; whatever you are creating can be modified or otherwise refined later, and it will undoubtedly morph as it is brought to life by you and Spirit. For now, the focus is on the doing, and there are many time-tested practices that can be used to lace your project with magic while you are in the throes of writing, sketching, coding, painting, performing, or otherwise mixing together creative ingredients and starting to give them shape. Any of the following techniques can help infuse whatever you are making with energy and turn your ideas into more cohesive and intentional work.

As a witch, my frame of reference for an externalized expression of energy is spellcasting. Ecofeminist witch and writer Starhawk has written that "a spell is a symbolic act done in an altered state of consciousness, in order to cause a desired change." Spells are vehicles of intention and transformation. This is why I believe that the building blocks of any spell are similar to—if not the same as—those of an artwork or other creative offering. When crafting a spell, I'm mindful of the intention I'm putting into it as well as the words and symbols I use to bring it to the most enchanting and effective level I'm capable of.

Sometimes I have a specific goal in mind. There are spells I've cast to bless a home, remove an obstacle, find a mentor, or protect myself from harm. Other times I'm casting a spell with a broader purpose: to help me connect to the divine, to express gratitude, or to ask for general guidance. My art practice operates with similar fluidity. There are songs I've composed to generate swaggering strength or lullabied soothing; poems I've penned as pain containers, occult odes, and beauty balms; books I've written to excavate and celebrate the depths of feminine power. There are also things I make simply for the sake of making, without any specific intention other than to follow wherever the sweet leash of wonder leads me. Regardless of my initial ideas or assumptions, each creation is an opportunity to engage with the unseen and the unknown, and to share myself with that mystery. My fascinations and tastes are personal to me, as yours are to you. But no matter one's style, the root of making remains the same. Creating is always born of desire.

It's a complex word, *desire*, and one that can bring about feelings of discomfort. People often link it to sexuality and lust (and their too-often-related feelings of shame, guilt, and denial). In fact, *desire*'s Latin root is *de sidere*, or "from the stars." There is some debate as to what this actually means. Some interpret it as meaning "away from the stars"—that to follow one's desire denotes a dark swerve from one's loftier astrological fate. Others say it means "of the stars"—that desire's very origin is a starry one. For me it's a moot point since, according to astronomer Carl Sagan, "We are made of star-stuff." Desire, then, is celestial, sidereal, *and* it is embodied and held in every single one of our twinkling cells. It comes from the heavens and is felt in the self. By following our own stars of desire, we learn to trust our longings and curiosities, our wildest hopes and our truest wishes. When we make the work we're called to make, we are communicating a deep desire for some sort of change to occur in ourselves and in those with whom we share our creation. We want to affect the world somehow. We want there to be beautiful consequences. When we paint a picture, weave a tale, or shred a guitar, we are casting a spell. We are using our earthly bodies to realize our starriest desires, and we are creating a potentially transformative experience for those who chance upon our magic.

The downward-facing hand of the Magic Maker represents the expression of one's particular will, wants, and whims. But this does not come solely from a place of ego or id, as divine desire is not about ownership or impulse. Rather it is an engine that connects us to our higher purpose and that guides us to be a living expression of Creative Force that can positively affect those here on earth.

Bewitching Intentions

As any witch or magician will tell you, when casting a spell it is helpful to be clear about one's intent. What do you desire? What problem are you trying to solve? What outcome are you hoping to manifest? There are many kinds of spells that serve many different purposes, but broadly speaking they tend to either attract, repel, or do some combination thereof. In the attraction category are love spells, of course, as well as any magical operation that seeks to draw something to someone, whether that be a new home, an exciting opportunity, or an intriguing collaborator. Repelling spells are sometimes known as apotropaic magic, from the ancient Greek *apotrópaios*, meaning "to turn away." This category includes warding, banishing, or binding spells, all of which aim to protect a person or a place from unwanted attention or harm. Sprinkling a salt circle, hanging a hamsa, burning purifying incense, or wearing an evil eye charm are all examples of spellcraft that averts negative forces and fortifies one's magical protective barrier. What do you want your creation to draw toward it? What do you want it to drive away? Making is an act of manifestation, so it's helpful to envision the energies and intentions you want to weave into your crafting.

A note about magic that goes on the attack: As a witch, my own code of ethics means I don't cast hexes. I would rather cast a spell that fortifies me and/or whomever is in harm's way, or else do a working that keeps a perpetrator from enacting harm on others (e.g., banishing, binding). However, from a creative standpoint, there are certainly artists who have employed their magic on the offense to potent effect, whether that's via blistering rap battles or scalpel-sharp satire. And while these methods may not harm the intended recipient physically, they can certainly weaken or hurt them nonetheless. Alan Moore has even gone as far as to say that damning art can be even *more* damaging to someone than a traditional hex. As he told *Arthur* magazine in 2003:

> A bard, simply by using words, could do much worse things to you than a magician could. Yeah, a magician might put a curse upon you if you offended them. And what's that gonna do? It makes some of your hens lay funny, sends the milk sour, you have a baby with a club foot: these things are survivable. But if a bard were to put a satire on you, and if it was a good enough satire, then he could destroy you in your own eyes, if it was accurate enough satire, if it was BARBED enough, it could destroy you in the eyes of your friends, your family, your contemporaries. In fact if it was a good enough satire, it might well be remembered hundreds of years after you were dead. People might still be laughing at you, and your relatives, hundreds of years after you were dead. You might have become a shame to your entire bloodline.

BEWITCHING INTENTIONS

Our creative offerings can operate in the same way that spells do. We may make things with the intention to nourish, to heal, to entertain, to frighten, to arouse, to awaken, to condemn, to liberate. Our work may be filled with beauty or brutality, scintillating intellect or typhonic swells of emotion. A spell moves energy. As Magic Makers, we have the limitless ability to infuse our creations with whatever intentions we can imagine, and to put our divine desires in motion. It is worthwhile to check in with oneself periodically as one creates. To ask: What is my intention as a maker? What are the intentional energies and elements I feel called to bring to this particular work—or to my creativity overall? The answers may stay consistent throughout a project, or they may shift over time. But by considering our intentions as we make things, we ensure that as creators we remain aligned with spiritual purpose. (Consider the word *consider,* from Latin meaning "with the stars".)

Jazz saxophone pioneer John Coltrane was no stranger to the power of intentional creation. He stated that music was the spiritual expression of who he was, and as he got older and battled his way through addiction, he felt that his purpose as a musician became clearer. The music for his 1964 breakthrough jazz album, *A Love Supreme,* was received by Coltrane from the spiritual realm. As his wife, Alice (herself an ingenious and deeply spiritual musician), told *Ascent* magazine in 2006:

> It was so interesting, when he created *A Love Supreme.* He had meditated that week. I almost didn't see him downstairs. And it was so quiet! There was no sound, no practice! He was up there meditating, and when he came down he said, "I have a whole new music!" He said, "There is a new recording that I will do, I have it

all, everything." And it was so beautiful! He was like Moses coming down from the mountain. And when he recorded it, he knew everything, everything. He said this was the first time that he had all the music in his head at once to record. That was so beautiful.

When Coltrane recorded and released the album, he chose to include an extensive explanation of his spiritual intentions in the liner notes, as excerpted below:

> During the year 1957, I experienced, by the grace of God, a spiritual awakening which was to lead me to a richer, fuller, more productive life. At that time, in gratitude, I humbly asked to be given the means and privilege to make others happy through music. I feel this has been granted through His grace. ALL PRAISE TO GOD . . .
>
> . . . This album is a humble offering to Him. An attempt to say "THANK YOU GOD" through our work, even as we do in our hearts and with our tongues. May He help and strengthen all men in every good endeavor.

Coltrane also included a lyrical piece of writing that can be read as a prayer, a poem, and a cosmic manifesto for manifestation. It praises God, asks for humanity's fears and weaknesses to be resolved, and expresses Coltrane's belief that thought, vibration, and creativity are all connected to the divine. This writing, taken together with his music, makes crystal clear that *A Love Supreme* was intentionally created as a spiritual offering and a sonic spell to bring about love, happiness, and healing for the world. In 1966, just a few months before he passed away, he shared this vision with KPFK reporter Frank Kofsky, saying: "I want to be a force for real good. In other words, I know that there are bad forces. I know that there are forces out here that bring suffering to others and misery to the world, but I want to be the opposite force. I want to be the force, which is truly for good." Though he certainly had his struggles and left the material world far too young at the age of forty, his artistic intentions continue to reverberate through the magic of his music all these decades later.

That kind of intentional clarity doesn't need to be present at every moment of your process. Remember that when engaging in the creative act, it is absolutely fine (and often preferable!) if you start without any goal other than to just show up and see what happens. But even *that* is an intention to stay curious and committed to the process of discovery. Likewise, the actions you take to shift into Magician Mode are ways to attract ideas, inspiration, focus, and Spirited guidance, and to repel distraction, disruption, and other undermining forces. Still, as you are making something, the intentions you are putting into the work will most likely become clearer and clearer. Or you may start off thinking that your work is about one thing only to have its truer intentions revealed as you create. All of this is perfectly natural. But it becomes *super*natural when we stay mindful of the ways in which our Spirit-given gifts can impact others. It's not that we should necessarily tailor our work for a specific audience or to illicit a specific reaction per se—though many attempt to do just this, with varying success. As we'll discuss later, trying to control how your work is received and assessed is usually a futile exercise. But what you *can* control is the intention and energy you give to whatever you make as you are making it. And you can trust that if you create with magical intent, your work will resonate with the right recipient at the right time (even if you are not around to witness it).

In *How to Read a Poem . . . and Start a Poetry Circle*, Molly Peacock writes "a hold on life is what I got from my favorite poems, and I toted them around like amulets against the world, using them to ward off every evil . . . After a while it occurred to me that I could make these amulets myself." Everyone reacts differently to creative work, but it's fair to say that each of us has our own arsenal of precious creative spells cast by others that we carry with us throughout our lives. I've worn songs like armor, wept tears of recognition in movie theaters, and bravely gone on grand adventures just to bask in the beauty of my favorite works of art. When I listen to Björk's "Pluto" today, I feel as brazenly boundless as I did when I first heard that track as a yearning "please let me get the fuck out of this town" sixteen-year-old. Its energy is explosive and evolutionary. I have no doubt that when we encounter ideas that personally excite us, images that inspire us, or inventions that exhilarate us, we are in enchantment's thrall. Something in us connects to the current that the maker was tapping into when they were creating. And so, when *we* wear the mantle of Magic Maker, we owe it to ourselves, to each other, and to the Others to craft with intention. Your ballad can be a love spell, your matzah ball soup can be a healing spell. Your bildungsroman can be a protection spell for aching adolescents. And you'll be contributing to the sacred conversation of creation that humans have been having for centuries. It's humbling and heartening to know that what we make can affect others, and that the magic of creation changes us too.

Entrancing Energy

Spells are charged with energy, and the more energy generated while casting, the more effective a spell will be. We are the living embodiment of magic. And so it stands to reason that when we work with the rhythms of our bodies and of Spirit, we can increase the energetic charge of whatever we create. In doing so, not only do we add power and potency to what we make, we also make something that others will receive an energetic charge *from*, whether immediately or eventually. Creative magic transcends time and space, and so it carries its charge forward no matter when it is received. I find this to be one of its most beautiful properties. The fact that I can be rejuvenated by the energy of a string quartet composed by Haydn over 250 years ago, or made misty-eyed by a fragment of poetry penned by Sappho over 2,500 years ago, is as sure an argument as any that time travel is possible. And as I write these words, I am charging them with an energy that I hope will be felt by whomever it reaches, whenever that may be. (*You, now.*)

There are a number of ways to increase magical energy, and spirit-centric folks know this better than most. There's a reason that witches are often depicted dancing in a ring around a fire, Indigenous American tribes are known for drum circles and powwow dances, and the ancient Greek choreia circle dance evolved into the Bulgarian oro, the Jewish hora, and other iterations that continue today. Each of these is an example of people coming together with a shared purpose and using rhythmic practices to affirm their group's cohesion—as well as to grow their emotional and spiritual potential. These types of gatherings aren't always overtly mystical. Attending a live concert, sports match, or play can be an ecstatic experience even for the most secular among us. When a group of people gets together with ritualized intent, they tap into a heightened state of being that French sociologist Émile Durkheim coined "collective effervescence." This describes the phenomenon that happens when many individuals are engaged with the same thing: they feel connected to a larger, unifying force that many consider sacred. This force field can be harnessed and directed for metaphysical purposes, such as organizing a group prayer or doing a shared magical action (e.g., when members of a coven raise a cone of power together to increase a spell's effect). No matter the intent, one of the best ways to sync up everyone's attention is to get them to tap into the same rhythmic current. Sing-alongs, call-and-response exchanges, group recitations, unified movement, and chanting are all effective means of raising energy through the power of rhythm. This is why many collective magical rituals are punctuated by dancing, percussion, and song.

Examples of rhythmic magic are numerous and ubiquitous. I'm reminded of the Hasidic Jewish practice of rocking during prayer (known as shuckling), Pagan maypole dancing, Tantric chanting, and shamanic drum rituals. Some of the most affecting examples for me have been those I've experienced through the framework of art: Rooster drumming frantically for the giants at the end of Jez Butterworth's play *Jerusalem*. Heather Christian's *Terce: A Practical Breviary*, which is her divine feminine reimagining of a Catholic Mass as performed by thirty-plus singers and musicians playing instruments ranging from guitars to chimes to a vacuum cleaner to, my personal favorite, a broom handle fused to a shoe. The nocturnal, flame-lit meeting of women in Céline Sciamma's *Portrait of a Lady on Fire*; as they clap their hands they repeatedly sing the bewitching line "fugere non possum," which means "they come fly" according to the filmmaker. Whether I witnessed these in person or on-screen, I felt energetically activated and quite literally moved by each of these pulsing ceremonial rites.

This is one of the main principles of sex magic, a practice of spellcasting that some engage in with a partner, partners, or by oneself. Though it has a rather provocative reputation in places like the United States thanks in large part to our society's puritanical attitudes to sex in general, sex magic is simply a means of aligning visualization techniques with somatic actions. The person or people involved hold an image or pictured outcome in their mind, and they charge it up with their accelerating breath and movement. As they do so, the energy builds and Creative Force increases until they climax—whether orgasmically or otherwise—and the manifestation is released into the world, where it will ultimately materialize. Engaging in sex for the sake of experiencing and exchanging pleasure is already a great enough reason to have it as far as I'm concerned. But harnessing its powers of attraction and generativity can certainly be worthwhile, whether for procreation or for the creation of other marvels like works of art, new ideas, or exciting opportunities.

This sort of rhythmic energy-raising need not be done in the presence of anyone else. I am often a solitary maker, typing away at a laptop in the privacy of my office or scribbling words in a notebook for no one's eyes but my own. Likewise, I am often a solitary witch. Though I lead public rituals and attend my own coven's gatherings periodically, most of the time I'm lighting my candles and murmuring my incantations with no one around but a cat or two. Still, I've noticed over the years that even when I'm casting circle by myself, I tend to sway as I call in each direction. And when I write, I listen to specifically selected music that helps me stay in a state of energetic flow. These rhythms keep me company, but more importantly, they keep me undulating—sometimes outwardly, always internally. Call it an occult ocean if you will—this pulsating wavespace that I find myself submerged in when I'm in a state of making. Sometimes the rhythm is slow and mesmeric, sometimes it's rapidly propulsive. But I have come to learn that when I tap into these rhythms, they get transferred into whatever I'm creating.

Musica Magica

Dario Argento's 1977 art house horror film *Suspiria* played with the notion that a dance school could in fact be run by a secret coven of witches. It's a marvelous conceit, first, for its irresistible suggestion that a space of assumed genteel propriety could be a site of sinister doings. It also plays with ideas about how dance taps into primal—perhaps even chthonic—forces, and it imagines what would happen if this power was used for deadly purposes. When Thom Yorke was composing the soundtrack to Luca Guadagnino's 2018 *Suspiria* remake, he also found himself getting entranced by rhythms. As he described to *The Hollywood Reporter*, "There's a way of repeating in music that can hypnotize. I kept thinking to myself that it's a form of making spells. So when I was working in my studio I was making spells. I know it sounds really stupid, but that's how I was thinking about it." It doesn't sound stupid to me. Though Yorke is clearly self-conscious about fessing up to his magical experimentation, he stumbled upon a method of sonic conjuration that countless others have practiced throughout history.

Judee Sill described the music she wrote throughout the 1970s as "occult-holy-western-Baroque-gospel." She was light-years ahead of her time, and sadly gone far too soon due to a drug overdose. But during her brief years of brilliance, she began exploring the notion that a song could be a healing spell of a sort. Before performing her song "The Donor" on the BBC, she said:

> I thought I would take a different approach when I wrote this song . . . I thought one day when I was real depressed that—you know how when you're real depressed and you see everything comes to nothing? Well, I thought maybe I better take a different approach and write a song, instead of directed at people, that would somehow musically induce God into giving us all a break, cause I was getting a little fed up by this point . . . I'd like to sing this song for you and hope that you'll get a break.

For Sill, writing "The Donor" was her petition for divine intervention, and performing it was intended as an offering of spiritual support for her listeners. Here's hoping her audience members received the break that so tragically eluded her.

While Sill sonically invoked God, as Coltrane did with *The Love Supreme*, the early twentieth-century English composer Gustav Holst chose to write music that would express other supernatural energies. His interest in mysticism led him to study Hindu sacred texts and Vedic cosmology, and he would learn Sanskrit in order to write his *Choral Hymns from the Rig Veda* between 1908 and 1912. In 1913, a fateful vacation to Spain planted the seeds for what would become his most well-known work. It was there that conversations with the writer and Theosophist Clifford Bax turned to astrology, and though Holst was already interested in the topic prior to the trip, he felt encouraged to engage with it on a much deeper level. From then on, he studied astrology in earnest and would read the astrological charts of his friends throughout his life, calling it his "pet vice." Most significantly, from 1914 to 1917, he was inspired to write *The Planets*, a seven-part orchestral suite in which each movement expresses the astrological energies of seven planets. Many posit that his ideas about each planet's attributes were drawn from the writings of Alan Leo, an English astrologer who popularized the idea that astrology was not only a system for predicting events but also a means of analyzing one's own personality. (Leo's pamphlet "What Is a Horoscope and How Is It Cast?" and his book *The Art of Synthesis* are often cited as Holst's main sources.) However, Holst didn't speak publicly about these influences. As his daughter, Imogen, writes in her 1938 book, *Gustav Holst: A Biography*: "There were very few people with whom he could discuss astrology, and he seldom mentioned it for fear of embarrassing his listeners."

Though Holst reordered the planets in his composition per his own aesthetic preferences, he preserved many of Leo's ideas about each, even using Leo's language, "Mercury, the Winged Messenger" and "Neptune, the Mystic," to name two of the movements. Holst's own titles, including "Mars, the Bringer of War" and "Jupiter, the Bringer of Jollity," reflect the aspects, emotions, and energies of each planet that he intended his music to conjure in the listener. Despite initial mixed reactions, *The Planets* skyrocketed Holst's career shortly after it debuted, and it is still considered a masterpiece of classical music today. Even the very first public performance of some of *The Planets'* movements in 1918 had a palpable effect on those who heard it. Per Imogen Holst:

Even those listeners who had studied the score for months were taken aback by the unexpected clamour of Mars. During Jupiter the charwomen working in the corridors put down their scrubbing-brushes and began to dance. In Saturn the isolated listeners in the dark, half-empty hall felt themselves growing older at every bar. But it was the end of Neptune that was unforgettable, with its hidden chorus of women's voices growing fainter and fainter in the distance, until the imagination knew no difference between sound and silence.

She goes on to elaborate that when the final two alternating chords of "Neptune, the Mystic" were played, "for that one moment they opened the doors on an unknown world." Years later, after writing *The Planets*, Holst would clearly articulate his belief that art could give both the maker and the receiver a mystical experience. In his essay "The Mystic, The Philistine and the Artist," which he wrote for *The Quest* in 1920, Holst states, "All mystic experiences seem to be forms of union . . . But it is in Music that this feeling of unity shows itself most obviously and easily."

Björk's essay "Sonic Magic" (*Purple* magazine #44) delves into the various mystical components of her songwriting, production, and performance processes. For her, music is intrinsically magical: "I believe melodies have an inner magic written into them. Their snakelike shapes have inner tantric meanings." One of the most intriguing musical ideas is that an entire song may have transformative power, but also that the very notes themselves may hold magic. In his 1984 song "Hallelujah," Leonard Cohen sings about a Lord-pleasing "secret chord" that David was said to have played. And though Cohen is exercising poetic license here (in the actual Bible story, David plays music on the lyre for King Saul in order to soothe an evil spirit that the Lord sent to torment him), there are certainly those who believe that combining certain notes can have a divine effect. Russian composer and occultist Alexander Scriabin famously made use of a spellbinding chord in his 1910 piece "Prometheus: A Poem of Fire," which later scholars referred to as the "mystic chord," the "Promethean chord," or "the chord of the pleroma," though there is no evidence that Scriabin used any of these terms himself. It's a chord that clearly captivated him, and he continued to use variations of it in other mystical works. His unfinished *Mysterium* symphony in particular was intended to be performed as a week-long multimedia synesthesia extravaganza in the foothills of the Himalayas. The event as he envisioned it would be a grand artistic ritual meant to bring about the end of the world and usher in a more enlightened era. As music historian Simon Morrison writes, "This all-consuming spectacle would have used the chord and its brethren as an incantation, a kind of Symbolist 'Open Sesame' unveiling a realm of 'eternal freedom' where spirits commingle."

The current popularization of sound baths and the incorporation of "healing frequencies" in various alternative and New Age practices are worth mentioning here, as are the vast number of mystically minded new age and ambient artists, including Enya, Laraaji, Joanna Brouk, and Pauline Oliveros. Whether music changes brain waves, shifts our physical vibrations on a cellular level, or brings through the energy of benevolent spirits has long been a matter of discussion, and will continue to be. The specifics of how exactly these musical techniques are believed to work is beyond the scope of this book. But music has certainly been used as a means of healing—or used in conjunction with other healing modalities—for centuries. As composer Gao Yuan has pointed out, "Our ancestors believed that music had the power to harmonize a person's soul in ways that medicine could not. In ancient China, one of music's earliest purposes was for healing. The Chinese word, or character, for medicine actually comes from the character for music." Music therapy is now recognized as an evidence-based branch of psychology and medicine, and there are studies that show that relaxing music can help lower blood pressure and bring down one's heart rate. Its application to spiritual healing is harder to quantify, of course, but most of us have specific music we turn to in times of anguish to help ourselves feel soothed, purged, tethered, or uplifted.

By the same token, making music can also be a spiritually healing experience, and many songwriters and performers have reported as such. While Carrie Brownstein of the band Sleater-Kinney was working on their album *Little Rope* in 2022, she learned that her mother and stepfather had been killed in a car accident. Though much of the album's music was written already, playing the songs in the recording studio turned into a spiritual act for Brownstein, and the tone of the music shifted. As she told *The New Yorker*: "Finishing the record was basically my way of praying every day . . . I am not a religious person, but I had to ask. I had to wonder, I had to talk and commune with something that was beyond what I could see in front of me." She explained that playing this music also helped her transmute her pain into a kind of pleasure, saying that it "can add up to something that doesn't feel like grief at all. It could add up to something that feels really joyful. We could play it until it's not about grief."

The framework of ritual also heightens music's healing efficacy—or perhaps music enhances the potency of ritual. Many are now familiar with entheogenic plant medicines such as ayahuasca, psilocybin, and peyote, which Indigenous peoples have been working with to cure the physical and spiritual ailments of their communities for centuries. What is often lost when these medicines are used by non-Natives, however, is their highly ritualized contexts. Song is usually part of these ceremonies, and the healer's incantatory gifts are an important part of their practice. Throughout South America, *icaros,* or medicine songs, are sung or whistled by shamans during ayahuasca ceremonies, sometimes accompanied by flutes or rattles. These songs are either passed down by elders or "delivered" to a shaman directly from the gods during the shaman's ceremonial preparations.

One such singing healer, María Sabina, preferred the term "Wise Woman" to describe herself. Born at the end of the nineteenth century, she lived in the Oaxacan mountain village of Huautla de Jiménez, and spoke the regional language, Mazatec. When she was eleven, she witnessed a Wise Man cure her ailing uncle with a ritual that included song, incense, and the ingestion of a special species of mushroom. Her own encounter with these mushrooms shortly thereafter was an initiatory experience. After eating them for several days, she began to have visions and hear their voices. She referred to them as "saint children" and declared that she was their daughter. Her first time using the mushrooms in a curative vigil, or *velada*, however, wasn't until several years after this. When she was in her twenties, her sister became terribly ill. Desperate to save her, María ingested the mushrooms and fed some to her sister, upon which, per her description, "Those saint children gave me advice and I carried it out." She followed their instructions, massaging her sister and chanting the words she received: "I spoke and sang. I felt that I sang beautifully. I said what those children obliged me to say." She then had a vision of wise beings, whom she called the Principal Ones, bestowing her with a giant book: "Then I realized that I was reading the Sacred Book of Language. My Book. The book of the Principal Ones . . . When one takes the *saint children*, one can see the Principal Ones. Otherwise not. And it's because the mushrooms are saints; they give wisdom. Wisdom is Language. Language is in the Book." After this velada, María's sister miraculously recovered, and María began incorporating the mushrooms' healing powers and guidance into her other rituals. Eventually, she found that the book of her visions became part of her memory and she no longer had to refer to it. This "wisdom" poured out of María in the form of chants, which remained a key component of her veladas moving forward.

As María's reputation as a healer grew, so too did her reputation as a singing poet. Eventually word of María's curative gifts and her access to these rare healing mushrooms would spread to the States, through the work of American banker and amateur ethnomycologist R. Gordon Wasson and his wife, Valentina, arguably the first Westerners to participate in María's rituals in 1957. Today, many frame the Wassons' reportage as the worst kind of exploitative colonialism. After lying about their intentions and promising to keep María's ritual private, Wasson wrote an article for *Life* magazine entitled "Seeking the Magic Mushroom," which marked the beginning of a wave of public interest in María. (Her name is changed to "Eva Mendez" in the piece, but there are several photographs of her.) The Wassons also recorded her songs, which were released by Folkways Records under the name "Mushroom Ceremony of the Mazatec Indians of Mexico." Subsequent books and articles by the Wassons and others caused a flood of Westerners to seek out María and her mushrooms. Tragically, this attracted a staggering amount of unwanted attention and strife for María from local police and acrimonious neighbors, and she believed this also caused the saint children to stop speaking to her.

While psychedelic mushrooms have absolutely had positive, even medicinal, effects on countless people both before and since María's involvement with them, it's clear that her particular story is one of betrayal, disrespect, and cultural theft. It's also clear that from María's perspective, the appropriate way to work with the saint children was not only to ingest the mushrooms but to connect with their particular magic through ritual, language, and song. Westerners taking mushrooms without any sense of ceremony or reverence was appalling to her. So too was the idea of people tripping for mere recreation rather than working with the mushrooms exclusively for healing purposes.

Beautiful Spanish and English translations of María's chants have been made available thanks to the work of Álvaro Estrada, Henry Munn, and Jerome Rothenberg. It's clear that her visions are rooted in a combination of animism, Catholicism, ethnobotany, and spiritual self-empowerment. During her chants, she calls on the forces of saints, plants, and animals, and declares her own place among the sacred order. In one of my favorite sections, she states:

> I am the woman Book that is beneath the water, says
> I am the woman of the populous town, says
> I am the shepherdess who is beneath the water, says
> I am the woman who shepherds the immense, says

I'm far from the first person to find María's chants captivating, as poets from Anne Waldman to Juan Gregorio Regino have paid homage to her through their own incantatory writing. As you may recall, the word *enchant* comes from the root words *in*, meaning "upon, into," and *cantare*, meaning "to sing." María was the ultimate enchantress, transforming the material world through her gifts of mycological sacrament and song.

Word Witchery

Language itself has long been considered a magical device, and we see traces of this in some of the very words we use for writing and speech. To *spell* can mean to form a word out of letters, and a spell can involve a string of words that bring about a wondrous shift in circumstance or perception. Likewise, the word for a magical book known as a grimoire is an outgrowth of the word *grammar*. When words are put together with artistry and intention, they have a distinct effect, making us feel stirred, shaken, healed, revealed, put in our place, or carved wide open. They allow us to interface with the invisible and the unknown. As the poet and collagist Helen Adam wrote to her friend and fellow poet Robert Duncan in 1955: "It is so endlessly fascinating this power in words, just the ordinary everyday words of human speech, to suggest when arranged in a certain magical order, something beyond the reach of speech, that hints and breathes of mysteries beyond what is actually said." (Duncan also referred to a poem as "an occult document," which of course I can't resist mentioning here.)

Though any form of writing or speaking may have a magical effect, poetry cleaves closest to spellcraft. It's a concentrated form of communication, with language distilled and energy condensed. In his manifesto, *Projective Verse,* the poet Charles Olson asserts that "a poem is energy transferred from where the poet got it (he will have some several causations), by way of the poem itself to, all the way over to, the reader. OK. Then the poem itself must, at all points, be a high energy-construct and, at all points, an energy-discharge." Poets pay attention not only to what imagery and emotions they convey through description but also to *how* they are conjuring them through sound, rhythm, and vibration (which is why I'd argue the most powerful writing of *any* form has a sense of poetry simmering within). To be sure, there are plenty of poems that work their magic on the page—and indeed the format and visual structure of a poem can be spellbinding in itself. But potent poetry takes on a dynamic new charge when read out loud. A poet performing their work often seems like a witch or magician uttering magic words. In the introduction to her poem collection, *Spells,* Annie Finch writes about poetry as a performative art, stating that it is "patterned language that invites readers to experience words not just in the mind but in the body." When we hear the sounds of the words being spoken, we feel their effect on our physical, sensual selves.

Rhyme has traditionally been a component of spells, poetry, and song. *Incantation* comes from the same singing root word as "enchant," so writing that has a rhythmic musicality to it will often carry a magic-making vibe. A quick online search will lead you to countless spells that have a singsong, rhyming component to them. For example, in a nine knot spell—sometimes known as a witch's ladder spell—the caster envisions what they wish to manifest while reciting a variation of the following as each knot is tied on a single string or piece of rope (this version is from Doreen Valiente's "The Spell of the Cord"):

By the knot of one
The spell's begun.
By the knot of two
It cometh true.
By the knot of three
Thus shall it be.
By the knot of four
'Tis strengthened more.
By the knot of five
So may it thrive.
By the knot of six
The spell we fix.
By the knot of seven
The Stars of Heaven.
By the knot of eight
The hand of fate.
By the knot of nine
The thing is mine.

The "Double, double, toil and trouble; / Fire burn, and cauldron bubble" speech in *Macbeth* is a doubly effective bit of poetic magic in that Shakespeare chooses to abandon his signature iambic pentameter and opt for the more rapid trochaic tetrameter (say that three times fast!) when the witches cast their spell. Interestingly, he employs that same tetrameter in other plays when supernatural beings speak, such as the fairies in *A Midsummer Night's Dream* as well as in some of Ariel's songs in *The Tempest*. Having otherworldly creatures communicate in a more mesmeric meter shows Shakespeare's mastery not only of language but rhythm.

But spells don't always rhyme, and as we know, poetry doesn't have to either. A poem becomes a chant when it makes use of such elements as repetition, looping, intonation, and intent for a change to occur. In *Concerning the Spiritual in Art,* Kandinsky writes, "The apt use of a word (in its poetical meaning), repetition of this word, twice, three times or even more frequently, according to the need of the poem, will not only tend to intensify the inner harmony but also bring to light unsuspected spiritual properties of the word itself." Chanting a repeated sound or mantra is a means of focusing energy and perhaps even harnessing it. When Tibetan monks chant the sound *om,* for example, they are tapping into the primordial energy of the universe, as this syllable is believed to invoke the highest vibration of the cosmos. Doing this is a means of centering and awakening to the divine. Likewise, a mantra such as "Namu Myōhō Renge Kyō," as repeated by practitioners of Nichirin Buddhism, is meant to transform suffering and bring about Buddha nature in oneself and, by extension, the world at large. In her essay "Fast Speaking Woman & The Dakini Principle," poet and legendary en-chant-ress Anne Waldman wrote the following: "Chant is heartbeat. Chant in all cultures is ancient efficacious poetic practice." I love the way she ties heartbeat to efficacy here, making me think that chanting can be literally life-giving—to the chanter and the listener certainly, but perhaps even to the vision that the words carry forth.

Waldman's 1975 poem "Fast Speaking Woman" was inspired in part by the chants of María Sabina. In a litany of lines Waldman describes what sort of woman she is—or perhaps all of the different kinds of women there are that she is honoring and embodying through her invocation. Here's a small segment from it:

> *I'm the woman with the wares*
> *I'm the woman with the whims*
> *I'm the woman with the hems*
> *I'm the woman with the volts*
> *I'M THE POET DREAMING INSIDE HER HOUSE*

Listening to her read it (which I highly recommend you do via recordings online if not in person) feels like witnessing someone cast a spell for awakening creative, feminine power in herself and the world at large.

Chanting allows the poet to wax ecstatic. The Beat Poets would often use this technique to express awe or gratitude, as exemplified in much of Allen Ginsberg's work. In his "Footnote to Howl," the repeated word *holy* is employed like a mantra, gilding everything the poet names—from his typewriter to jazz music to miracles—in a sheen of divinity.

A chant is also a means of manifestation, embodying the poet's desires and enacting their will to bring about some sort of change. Diane di Prima's "Revolutionary Letter #68—Life Chant" can be read as a prayer or spell of planetary protection, as excerpted here:

> *tho the earth seem lost*
> *may it continue*
> *thru exile & silence*
> *may it continue*
> *with cunning & love*
> *may it continue*

Her repeated phrase "may it continue" echoes the common spellcasting phrase "So mote it be," and I believe this is intentional—as is her use of the witchly word *cunning*—for di Prima was a deep student of magical practice and had a library of over a thousand occult books. (And thanks to the work of archivist M. C. Kinniburgh, you can now procure *The Catalog of the Diane di Prima Occult Library* from Granary Books to see what was in her collection.)

Di Prima's friend, the brilliant activist and writer Audre Lorde, also made use of the language of enchantment, most notably in her poetry collection *Black Unicorn*. The book's final poem, "Solstice," reads like an apotropaic incantation with the last stanza repeating the phrase "May I" before her wishes of cultivating safety, bravery, and liberation.

And poet and civil rights activist June Jordan's "Intifada Incantation: Poem #8 for b.b.L." is a chant for change and an ode to romance all rolled up in one.

> *I SAID I LOVED YOU AND I WANTED*
> *GENOCIDE TO STOP*
> *I SAID I LOVED YOU AND I WANTED AFFIRMATIVE*
> *ACTION AND REACTION*
> *I SAID I LOVED YOU AND I WANTED MUSIC*
> *OUT THE WINDOWS*
> *I SAID I LOVED YOU AND I WANTED*
> *NOBODY THIRST AND NOBODY*
> *NOBODY COLD*
> *I SAID I LOVED YOU AND I WANTED I WANTED*
> *JUSTICE UNDER MY NOSE*

MAGIC MAKER

*I SAID I LOVED YOU AND I WANTED
BOUNDARIES TO DISAPPEAR*

As the poem continues, Jordan remarks on how accepting love has made her feel emboldened and, one can assume, reinvigorated in her fight for justice. The repeated phrases—not to mention the all-caps throughout—are charged with a fiery energy that builds as the incantation goes on, ultimately culminating in a stunning declaration of glory: "I AM TASTING MYSELF / IN THE MOUTH OF THE SUN."

When we write or speak with soul-deep conviction, when we make our declarations with care, when we charge our desires with high voltage and express them with considered language, we are spellcasting. We are deploying magic words. In fact, one of the most well-known phrases in the corpus of magic-making alludes to this very phenomenon. According to Craig Conley's delightfully exhaustive book, *Magic Words: A Dictionary*, the word *abracadabra* is often traced backed to a Hebrew-Aramaic exclamation that translates to "I create through my speech" or "I will create as I speak." (By my count, the *abracadabra* entry in Conley's dictionary is the longest in the book, coming in at nineteen pages. The word's continued resonance in culture all these years later from stage magic shows to Lady Gaga's pop megahit is fascinating to mull upon.) Theories abound suggesting that the idea of creating as one speaks is related to the notion of God as creator, for according to the book of Genesis, the very cosmos was created through sacred speech: "And God said, 'Let there be light,' and there was light." As is probably evident by now, I personally find biblical texts to be meaningful when considered from a mythopoetic standpoint rather than a literal one, but either way, it's clear that the idea of speaking something into existence has been with humans for thousands of years.

Still, Conley insists that "if intoned in the proper spirit, any word can be a magic word." As most of us can attest, *how* we make sounds matters as much as the meaning of the words we utter. As I discussed earlier, invocation is related to vocalization, and I've found that using my voice differently in ritual brings about powerful results. In fall 2023, I hosted a group tour of mythical sites in Greece, and it ended up being one of the most profoundly beautiful experiences of my life. We began the trip with a pilgrimage to Brauron, one of the primary sanctuaries devoted to the goddess Artemis. Afterward, I led the group in a seaside ritual to honor Artemis and invoke her lunar magic. Though I was jet-lagged and feeling fatigued, I was able to dig deep and shift into Magician Mode. We set up a makeshift altar on top of a rock, lit our candle, and cast a magic circle there on the beach. Then, using all my might, I called upon Artemis in her guise of the Great Bear, using a modified charm from the *Greek Magical Papyri*. As the spell is written, a list of alternate names and epithets for Artemis is chanted, along with magnificent descriptions of her gifts. I cried out to her with love and conviction, using every bit of energy I could muster, and I asked for her blessings upon our group and our occult odyssey in the week to come. The voice I used during the ritual came from the most central part of my being, and it was forceful and LOUD—it surprised even me. Later, one of the other witches remarked how startled and dazzled the group was that such a booming sound could come out of such a small person; they called it my "god voice." The term reminded me of the Voice that the Bene Gesserit witches use in *Dune*, though for our purposes I would suggest that using a "magical voice," as Janaka Stucky has called it, is not about exerting control over anyone. Rather, it's about electrifying our words with sincere emotion and unbridled imagination. When we do so, magic pours from our mouths.

Magic Markers

Picture a dusty old grimoire in your mind's eye, the kind of book that might be consulted by Merlin or Willow Rosenberg. It is probably full of scrawled incantations, intriguing symbols, and intricate diagrams that glow cryptically by candlelight. These emblems have most likely been drawn by hand, imbuing them with an intimate power. They hint at secret knowledge being passed down from a cabal of wise elders, or else are evidence of a magician's own singular experimentation. Whether drawn or written (and what is putting pen to paper if not an act of drawing at its core?), these are magic markings. Lines made for the purpose of turning desire into outcome.

Letters themselves have long been considered to be magical containers, and many written languages have a history of functioning not as phonetic systems but as a collection of pictographs. For example, aleph (א), the first letter in the Hebrew alphabet, can be traced back to a Phoenician symbol representing an ox or bull. To complicate matters, Hebrew letters can also represent numbers, and Jewish mystics and Kabbalah scholars developed a system called gematria that analyzes the numerological symbolism of the words of the Torah and other sacred texts, adding a whole extra layer of secret meaning on top of their arguably already nebulous semantics. There are also mindfulness practices of meditating upon each Hebrew letter, as well as a divination method called casting lots, which are stones or pieces of paper with each letter painted or carved on them. I also learned there is now a method of t'ai chi called Otiyot Hayyot wherein the practitioner forms the Hebrew letters with their body!

Of course, Hebrew is just one example of a belief in the magic of letters. We now use the word *hieroglyphics* to describe ancient Egyptian writing in particular, but it is derived from *hieroglyphikos*, a Greek word derived from *hieros*, meaning "sacred," and *glyphē*, meaning "carving." And perhaps the most well-known example of magical engagement with letters is that of the Norse-derived divination practice of casting runes. The runes themselves have a long history of magical association. It is said that the Hanged Man or Hanged One tarot card represents Odin, the old Norse father god of wisdom and sorcery. As the myth goes, Odin chooses to sacrifice himself, hanging from Yggdrasil, the World Tree, for nine days and nine nights. In doing so, he receives the runes—magical letters that can be used for spellcasting purposes. (I was positively enchanted to learn that Odin is also referred to as the Great Singer, and that his rune spells are called Songs. The Old Norse word *galdr*, often translated as "magic," actually refers to a specific type of spell that is sung.) The "Hávamál" from the *Poetic Edda* recounts the story of Odin's newfound powers and the eighteen song-spells he has learned. Crucially, the runes for these spells were not only to be uttered but also, at times, inscribed. One section of the epic poem tells of Odin's runic resurrection spell that he casts upon encountering a corpse hanging from a tree: "such spells I write, and paint in runes / that the being descends and speaks."

Other methods of magical mark-making include drawn or written talismans and other protective amulets. These devices seem to exist in all cultures, whether they are written on parchment scrolls, painted on doorposts, or carved in stone or bone. Sometimes they are etched with a ritual knife. Sometimes the very ink or paint the magicians employ to make these marks is created using special ingredients and arcane recipes. In *Grimoires: A History of Magic Books*, Owen Davies describes a practice of writing out a spell in ink or carving it into food, and then literally ingesting the written magic: "In medieval Europe sacred words were written on bread or cheese to be swallowed by the sick. Some medieval religious manuscripts bear the signs of having been rinsed with water so that some of the ink washed off and could therefore be drunk." According to Davies, numerous examples have also been found throughout West Africa where the eating of magical writing was used to cure disease, recover from curses, or undergo an initiation.

As we've established, magical writing is closely linked to magical drawing, and many of the most iconic examples of enchanted symbology employ combinations of letters, numbers, lines, and/or pictograms. Magical glyphs are sometimes used to summon a deity or spirit, such as véve drawings of Vodun that are made to call upon or represent certain lwa. The word *sigil* has been popularized thanks to *The Sandman* comics series and the hit TV show *Game of Thrones*. In a traditional occult context, however, *sigil* refers to a magic symbol that is inscribed for the purpose of summoning a particular spirit. The elaborate, glyph-laden magic circles so often seen in witchy films and horror movies are usually riffing on a specific set of round talismans (called pentacles) taken from much older occult books such as the fifteenth-century *The Greater Key of Solomon* (*Clavicula Salomonis*) and the seventeenth-century *The Lesser Key of Solomon* (*Lemegeton Clavicula Salomonis*). These books have gone through many iterations over time, but they are best known for containing various sigils meant to call forth planetary energies and either conjure or repel demons. It is important to note that these tomes themselves are an example of cultural syncretism at best and cultural appropriation at worst, as the sigils use Hebrew letters and names alongside Greco-Roman systems and others, and they were most likely not derived from Jewish people—though this was rather typical of Renaissance-era magic in general. (Ezra Rose's 2022 zine, *FYMA: A Lesser Key to the Appropriation of Jewish Magic & Mysticism*, is a good primer on this topic if you're curious.)

There are many examples of sigils floating around the internet and in pop culture that purport to be drawn from these Solomonic grimoires but are in fact quite new. For example, there is a Solomonic-style sigil for the goddess Lilith that one can now find on a plethora of gothic T-shirts and witchy jewelry—and which some have no doubt been used in ritual. However, this sigil was designed in 2007 by Robin Artisson, who created it because he felt that Lilith was missing from *The Lesser Key of Solomon*, and he thought she deserved her own pentacle. As he explains in his original LiveJournal entry entitled "We all want a sigil for Lilith":

> Is this sigil ancient? No, it may in fact be the world's newest sigil. But that doesn't matter. Lines, shapes, circles, letters, geometry, creativity ... all these things are ancient and universal aspects of the world-mind and the human mind. Together with intention, they channel, they create changes. Like all self-engineered magical tools or words, any sigil becomes as powerful for you, if you integrate it into your magical worldview, as any sigil ever used in any time or place.

There are those who have taken issue with Artisson's "blasphemy," though I find that to be rather ironic considering that the Solomon books are in themselves idiosyncratic mash-ups of preexisting religious and mystical cultural systems. I'm all for adapting and evolving any tradition, as long as it's done with good intentions and true respect, and from my perspective (and mine alone!), Artisson's sigil is inoffensive to me as both a magical practitioner and a person of Jewish descent. You are certainly entitled to come to your own conclusions. (That said, Lilith is a fierce goddess, so I recommend proceeding with caution should you choose to summon her.)

There is certainly an argument to be made that an outsider "borrowing" the imagery from closed religions such as Judaism or Vodun is problematic, particularly if you don't credit the original group or support the group's current living members (especially if you are from a background that has historically oppressed the people whose work you are "borrowing" from). This is why understanding the principles of how these sigils work is liberating, because you can create your very own versions and charge them with your own personal power rather than appropriating preexisting ones.

In Artisson's Lilith pentacle, he derives his central abstract glyph from a stylized version of the letters *L, T,* and *h,* in the manner of sigil-making developed by the twentieth-century illustrator and occultist Austin Osman Spare. (I'm guessing Artisson opted for a lowercase *h* purely for aesthetic reasons.) Per Spare's method, one begins with a name or short phrase of desire to which the sigil is being dedicated. The letters are then reduced to only their single consonants. And then a glyph is drawn using the shapes of these letters.

For example, if you want to find a new creative partner to collaborate with on a project, you might come up with a phrase such as *NEW CREATIVE PARTNER.* This phrase is then distilled to its consonants (no need to include the repeating ones): *NWCRTVP.* You then create an abstract symbol out of those letters, and voilà, you've designed a sigil that's ready to be activated. For Artisson's Lilith sigil, he chose to also inscribe Lilith's name in capital letters in a ring around the glyph, in keeping with Solomonic pentacle format, though you don't have to use the circle format at all if you don't want to.

A sigil can truly be made of any imagery or symbology you wish, so no need to stick to Spare's method or mimic Solomonic pentacles at all. You are encouraged to be as creative as you can be when crafting your sigil and to make use of your own system of meanings and magical references. It may take several sketches to come up with something that looks and feels right to you. Once you are satisfied with your design, this sigil can then be drawn or etched onto a chosen material, then charged or activated in any number of ways (e.g., doing a visualization, anointing it with oil, sleeping with it under your pillow, burning the paper it's inscribed on, and so on).

To be clear, Artisson created his Lilith sigil to teach his readers how to make their *own* version, not to encourage anyone to copy his. But his pentacle got replicated and meme-ified anyway, which is a good reminder to be very mindful about how your sigils are derived and disseminated. Some sigils are created for specifically communal purposes, and I have been particularly moved by public offerings such as Laura Tempest Zakroff's Sigil for Reproductive Rights, Ketzirah 'haMa'agelet' Lesser's sigil for peace in Gaza, and Ezra Rose's project "We Are Magic: Sigils for Trans Power." Artists such as Leonora Carrington, Harry Smith, Genesis Breyer P-Orridge, Paul Laffoley, Darcílio Lima, Elijah Burgher, and Barry William Hale have also made overt use of sigils in their work. However, sigil-making can be a very private affair, and you are welcome to create yours in secret and embed them clandestinely into your artworks, projects, sacred objects, and rituals, as many Magic Makers do.

Numinous Numbers

Many creative types resist "left brain" approaches to their process, and so you may consider yourself numb to numbers. But there are numerous examples of how mystical math and sacred geometry have been used by Magic Makers in their offerings. As with letters, numbers can be engaged with in a host of enchanting ways, whether as symbolic representations on their own or as a means of magical measurement. Consider experimenting with your own occult calculations.

Intentionally incorporating auspicious numbers into one's process is an obvious but effective way of doing this. Chances are that even your most skeptical friend has a lucky number or makes a wish when a clock reads 11:11. This numerical affinity may spring from sentiment. A child's birth date or the number on a basketball jersey are usually randomly assigned, but they can take on significance in a person's life from that point forward. Beyoncé and Jay-Z have woven the magic of their lucky number 4 into their lives. They were both born on the 4th of their respective birth months, they got married on April 4, 2008 ("eight divided by two is four," Beyoncé explained of the year), and they have the Roman number IV tattooed on their ring fingers. Their daughter Blue was allegedly given the middle name Ivy as a nod to IV as well. And both Beyoncé and Jay-Z have albums named after the number, with Beyoncé's *4* released in 2011 and Jay-Z's *4:44* in 2017.

Taylor Swift's obsession with the number 13 has also been well documented, showing up in her album and video imagery, song lyrics, track list orders, and album release dates. As she explained to Jay Leno in a 2009 appearance on *The Tonight Show*:

> I was born on the thirteenth. I turned thirteen on Friday the thirteenth. My first album went gold in thirteen weeks . . . My first song that ever went number one, it had a thirteen-second intro . . . And every time I've ever won an award at an award show I've either been seated in the thirteenth row or row M, which is the thirteenth letter.

For years she would also draw the number 13 on her hand before she performed, believing it would bring luck to her concerts.

With each of these artists, a lucky number becomes both a talisman and an organizing principle—and it can be a fun Easter egg for listeners as well. BeyHive members and Swifties alike pore over the numerical symbolism of their heroines with cryptological fervor. It's a treasure hunt for meaning, and for further clues that might make these superstars a bit more relatable (or at least slightly better known). And while there are many other factors that have contributed to the success of these particular makers, their lucky numbers have clearly been associated with enough good fortune to merit their continued engagement with them.

As with letters, belief in the magic of numbers seems to extend to the globe's four corners. Certainly any number can be considered lucky, but some seem to have universal appeal. In Chinese culture, the number 8 is considered the luckiest because the Mandarin word for it—*ba* (八)—sounds similar to *fa* (发), the word for prosperity or wealth. One of the most magical symbols in Chinese culture is the bagua diagram, which is made up of eight trigrams representing the forces of the universe being in balance. The octagonal mirror associated with feng shui is based on this symbol. In the aforementioned Jewish system of gematria, *chai* (חי), the Hebrew word for "life," is associated with the number 18. This is why financial gifts for such milestones as bar and bat mitzvahs are often given in multiples of 18. And in Hindu and Buddhist tradition, 108 is considered sacred, and strands of 108 mala beads are used for prayer and meditation. In the Western Arabic numeral system, the figure eight also has the secret magic of becoming an infinity symbol when it's turned horizontally—the Magician's lemniscate.

Numerology used to be known as arithmancy, or divination through numbers. Though some version of it has been practiced by humans since ancient times, it seems to be having a resurgence of late. A quick online search will lead you to an array of websites purporting to help you calculate your "life path number," or expounding on the significance of repeating "angel numbers"—a term popularized by New Age writer Doreen Virtue via her book of the same name in 2005. Much of modern numerology is based on assigning numbers to the letters of someone's name or adding the numbers of their birth date together to discern a person's destiny.

Numbers have also been used for talismanic purposes, most notably in numbered grids known as magic squares in which each row adds up to the same total. Though sometimes these devices were created as arithmetic exercises, occult properties were often assigned to them as well. Early examples of this can be found in the thirteenth-century Arabian grimoire the *Shams al-Ma'arif* (also known as *The Sun of Knowledge* or *The Book of the Sun of Gnosis*), which was written by an Islamic mathematician and Sufi mystic, Ahmad ibn 'Ali al-Buni. In this book, he discusses magic squares of specific letters and numbers that can be used to conjure angelic beings and jinn. In the sixteenth century, German occultist Heinrich Cornelius Agrippa popularized the notion of particular magic squares being associated with planetary energies. For example, his magic square for the planet Mercury is an 8 x 8 grid wherein each row of numbers adds up to 260. (And as an added bonus for our Magic-Making purposes, if you reduce 260 down by adding 2 + 6 + 0, it becomes 8—a nice connection to our Magician / Mercury lemniscate as well!)

Agrippa's *De Occulta Philosophia Libri Tres* or *Three Books of Occult Philosophy* is still considered one of the foremost texts on magic, and his grids, diagrams, and seals have been utilized (and often unknowingly replicated) to this day. Agrippa's magic square for Jupiter is most famously incorporated in Albrecht Dürer's masterful 1514 engraving *Melencolia I*—an interesting and undoubtedly intentional choice, as Jupiter is considered the planet of joy and good fortune. There are those who surmise that Dürer's piece is a sort of spiritual self-portrait, for in the theory of the four humors—or temperaments—melancholy was sometimes ascribed to artists and other sensitive, introspective souls, as well as to the planet Saturn. During the Renaissance, melancholy was also associated with genius, though it was understood that it needed to be balanced out by lighter energies lest the creative person fully succumb to darkness and become what we today might call a tortured artist. In Dürer's piece, the angel of melancholy sits in contemplation surrounded by tools of crafting and measurement, as well as alchemical implements and geometric solids.

Though she has many instruments of creation at her disposal, she doesn't appear to be making anything—at least not yet. Perhaps the Jupiter square above her head is meant as a bit of magic to temper the artist's melancholic tendencies, so that some jovial levity might balance out the gravity of Dürer's colossal creative gifts.

Geometry also has deep magical roots. Like me, you may have first encountered the work of Pythagoras when learning how to calculate the sides of a right triangle via his eponymous theorem. This sixth-century BCE Greek polymath was so much more than a mere mathematician. He is also credited with devising theories of reincarnation or metempsychosis (aka the transmigration of souls), as well as a theory that each planet's movement could be calculated mathematically and therefore was associated with its own musical signature. He surmised that together, these orbits created a silent symphony, which came to be known as musica universalis or "music of the spheres."

The symbol of the pentagram in particular was special to Pythagoras' followers, as it contains the golden ratio, a measurement of harmony and beauty that is seen throughout nature—and which the ancient Greeks and many others aimed to replicate in architecture and fine art for centuries to come. It is apt that one of the most successful contemporary design firms in the world is named Pentagram, and not only because it had five founders. There are those who believe that the pentagram was also used as a secret symbol between members of the Pythagorean brotherhood. (A truly delightful rendition of all this can be seen in the 1959 Disney animated short *Donald in Mathmagic Land*. What it may lack in precise historical accuracy, it makes up for in phantasmagoric beauty.) The ancient Greeks associated the pentagram with Hygeia, the goddess of health and well-being, and invoking her name and her pentagram was a means of blessing someone with wellness and harmony. Pentagrams occur as symbols of balance throughout the world, including the Taoist Wu Xing diagrams depicting the five elements of Fire, Earth, Metal, Water, and Wood. Often misunderstood or mischaracterized as having diabolical associations, the pentagram was used in Germanic folk magic to protect *against* the devil since at least the nineteenth century, as shown in Goethe's 1808 play, *Faust*. Today, the pentagram and the pentacle (the correct term for a pentagram inscribed inside a circle) are associated with modern Pagan practice, including but not exclusive to Wicca, and in this context the five-pointed star represents the five elements of Air, Fire, Water, Earth, and Spirit.

Sacred geometry has been incorporated into the design of many spiritual spaces, from the golden proportions of the Parthenon to the mandala structure of Angkor Wat. The primary symbol of Freemasonry contains a compass and square with the letter *G* inscribed in the center, standing for either *Geometry* or *God*, "the Grand Architect of the Universe." In Islam, it is forbidden to represent Allah figuratively, and so the ingenious and intricate geometric patterns found throughout mosques are meant to give worshippers a sense of the divine without breaking any religious taboos. These tessellating shapes inspired graphic artist M. C. Escher and led him to develop his signature drawing style of repeated forms and gradually shifting symbols. Other modern artists such as Piet Mondrian would come to find geometric abstraction to be a powerful means of representing spiritual forces. Mondrian became famous for his painted grids of black lines and primary color blocks, and though many viewers interpret these pieces as mere exercises in aesthetic simplification, his intentions were far from superficial. Deeply inspired by Theosophy and Rudolf

Steiner's offshoot, Anthroposophy, Mondrian was intending to transmit an expression of divine universality. As he proclaimed in 1914:

> Art is higher than reality and has no direct relation to reality. To approach the spiritual in art, one will make as little use as possible of reality, because reality is opposed to the spiritual. We find ourselves in the presence of an abstract art. Art should be above reality, otherwise it would have no value for man.

Likewise, Canadian American artist Agnes Martin's meticulous, subdued drawings of grids and horizontal bands look at first glance to be quite minimalist. However, she was influenced by Zen Buddhism and meditation, and she intended her pieces to give the viewer a sense of serenity. To do so, she believed she had to be in a peaceful frame of mind when she created each work. As she told *ARTNews* in 1976, "what we make, is what we feel." As with repeated sounds, repeated patterns can have a mesmeric effect, which is why it feels calming not only to view them but to create them, as everyone from sand mandala–making monks to committed knitters can attest.

For self-taught twentieth-century Swiss artist Emma Kunz, her multicolored drawings of radiating lines and kaleidoscopic shapes were meant to be used as healing offerings for herself and others. Her own telepathic and oracular gifts led her to believe that any number of ailments could be healed on the spiritual and energetic levels. The drawings she created were an extension of her research into the relationship between the physical and invisible realms; they were diagnostic devices as well as potential sources of alleviation. The website for the Emma Kunz Center describes her drawings as interdimensional spaces that one may enter in a meditative state, similar to how yantra diagrams are used in Tantric practice:

> She regarded her pictures as holograms, spaces you could walk into, images to be unfolded or collapsed back down again, usually multilayered in their construction. At a primary level, they opened up to her the cryptic answers to numerous questions that interested her. These might be spiritual or philosophical in nature, or they might contain the cause and treatment of an illness, or provide an explanation for a political situation and the resulting consequences.

It brings to mind this statement from shamanic performance artist Joseph Beuys: "Art enters into the person and the person enters into the work of art, no?" And while this principle can certainly be applied to any creative offering, works intentionally derived from sacred geometry put this into clear practice. Magical measurement and the careful ordering of space can shift one's interior landscape and open up new vistas of divinity.

Magical Correspondences

When learning the basics of witchcraft, one will inevitably encounter the concept of *sympathetic magic*. This term was coined by James George Frazer in his groundbreaking comparative magic and religion book, *The Golden Bough* (1889). It refers to the idea that certain magical outcomes can be conjured by working with their associated symbols here in the material world. In other words, if you wish to cast a spell for money, say, you might light a green candle or incorporate some leafy vegetation into your working to represent growth and abundance (and here in the US, our green paper currency). Magic is a living metaphoric language. When we select symbols and maneuver them mindfully, we are communicating with something beyond the limitations of the material world. We speak in signs, signaling to Spirit that we are welcoming its intervention.

I'm of the belief that it is helpful to learn the rules before bending or breaking them. While the language of magic is highly subjective and interpretive, there are some widely adopted symbolic associations that can

MAGICAL CORRESPONDENCES

provide a good jumping-off point. If you want to learn some basics, many foundational witchcraft books and websites contain lists of magical symbols and/or tables of correspondences. These may include traditional associations between gods and goddesses, planets, colors, plants, gemstones, metals, and days of the week.

Following some of the most popular tables, a love spell, for example, might be cast on a Friday, as that is the day associated with the Norse goddess Freya and the Roman goddess Venus, two beloved love goddesses. Going further, one might choose to wear some copper jewelry when casting such a spell, as copper is associated with the planet Venus. Likewise, a book rooted in African diasporic tradition might recommend working with the orisha Oshun, who is associated with love, water, honey, sunflowers, and the color yellow.

Since the Roman god Mercury is the patron deity of this book, I give him extra attention when I'm writing on a Wednesday (as I happen to be today), since in planetary magic practice this is the day of the week that is said to be ruled by him—the French word for Wednesday, *mercredi*, is related to his name. I'm burning incense for him as I write these words and wearing a special pendant that is etched with his sigil.

A belief in symbolic, associative magic has been practiced throughout the world, but the notion of magical correspondence was popularized in Europe by the aforementioned Renaissance occultist, Heinrich Cornelius Agrippa. Drawing on the writings of other magical philosophers before him, Agrippa's *Three Books of Occult Philosophy* is, in part, his attempt to catalog the correspondences between the elements, the seven planets of antiquity, the body, angels, numbers, several alphabets, and various other Kabbalistic (or more accurately Christian Cabalistic) components. Much of this is understood to be for the purpose of conjuration, such as his astrological seals and magic squares, which were intended to invoke the corresponding energies of the planets and deities associated with them.

These magical correspondences were further formalized in the nineteenth and twentieth centuries thanks to the research of Hermetic Order of the Golden Dawn co-founders Samuel Liddell Mathers and William Wynn Westcott. They compiled a manuscript of magical symbol lists that they called *The Book of Correspondences,* though it was only intended to be shared with their most promising occult students and was not originally published. Aleister Crowley expanded upon this work with some of his own research and ideas, and he included a highly detailed table of correspondences in his *Liber 777* of 1909. (His 1929 book, *Magick in Theory and Practice,* also includes some of these tables.) Much of this material would trickle down into Wicca and was eventually brought to a wider readership via such books as Raymond Buckland's *Complete Book of Witchcraft* in 1986 (known affectionately in witchcraft circles as Uncle Bucky's Big Blue Book). Other tables of correspondence one might encounter may include animals, trees, tarot cards, moon phases, seasons, and so on.

If these types of correspondences feel resonant to you, you may want to incorporate them into your creative processes or projects. Some Magic Makers choose to do this overtly. One of my dear friends and all-time favorite visual artists, Jesse Bransford, created a splendid series called The Planets that explored the magic of each of the seven planets of antiquity. Beginning with the sun in 2005 and ending with Saturn in 2013, he created multiple installations, murals, and drawings that incorporated symbols, color palettes, patterns, and magic squares intended to activate the power of each heavenly body and honor its respective deities. Over the years, Jesse and I have had numerous conversations about his work and how it affects him as he makes it and the viewers who are fortunate enough to encounter it in person. When I interviewed him for *Abraxas Journal*, he shared an anecdote about working on Mars ("II MAVORS"), the planet associated with passion, action, and strength, in 2006. He had created a large-scale mural at Germany's Galerie Schmidt Maczollek using the Martian magic square and "red, and fiery" colors that Agrippa ascribed to the planet. In Jesse's words:

> It's very dramatic and is in some ways the "conversion moment" for me in the project . . . In Köln, where I installed Mars I was planning to use an opaque projector that I brought from the states . . . Well, the transformer on the projector I brought was really cut-rate and none of the AC adaptors I brought were doing the trick. The piece in question was a giant cube with Mars's magic square from Agrippa on each of the visible sides, flanked on each side with a column bearing the Olympian seals of Mars from the *Arbatel* [*De Magia Veterum*]. This piece was specifically designed to create an image of convexity in a concave space, an illusion using a little-known quality of perspective. In retrospect it couldn't have been more portal-like. I borrowed an old step-up converter to try to boost the power to the projector, and this worked quite well. Setting the projector at the center point of the composition, I was able to put down the lines that would create the effect I was looking for. Literally, at about midnight the transformer began humming and suddenly exploded in a shower of sparks. The room filled with the smell of ozone and I nearly electrocuted myself unplugging the transformer . . . I've been much more aware of all of my actions since that trip!

Clearly, Jesse learned that playing with fire—particularly of the Martian variety—can have incendiary results, and he's since approached his artworkings with a bit more caution and reverence for the deities in question.

More recently, Jesse has been painting vibrantly colored, glyph-spangled magic circles on gallery floors and walls, as well as in people's homes. Though Agrippa's correspondences are sometimes embedded in them, these circles are constructed using Jesse's own magical lexicon. This has expanded to include a more culturally syncretic (and one might argue, diverse) point of view, as well as his personally developed symbolic associations between deities, colors, and energies. These painted circles are prismatic visual spells, sometimes enhanced with candles, flowers, and other offerings, and activated per Jesse's own occult methods. And while I don't know *how* it works exactly, I can attest that these pieces are the output of a true magician. Stepping inside one of them feels like crossing a threshold or slipping inside a pocket of the sublime. Within the circle, there is a sense of protection and benevolent electricity. There is also an uncanny feeling of *activity*: though the painted imagery is technically stationary, I feel a whirling around me, a whirring inside me, and a drift both away from and further toward myself. It's a sensation of being rewired somehow, as if I'm downloading a program with a consecrated source code.

Your own experiments with magical correspondence can be far less elaborate. A fine entry point into this type of approach is to simply start with color magic. You may be painting a portrait, developing a jewelry line, working on a new fashion collection, or designing a logo. The colors you choose carry energy, and you can apply them in highly intentional ways. I recently interviewed renowned celebrity makeup artist Pati Dubroff on *The Witch Wave*. She explained that being selective about the colors she uses on her clients' faces is its own form of glamour magic (the words *glamour*, *grammar*, and *grimoire* are all etymologically related to the notion of powerful language). Pati has done the makeup for many actors during their press tours, and according to her, the energy shifts depending on the makeup she uses. She told me that getting to use so much pink on Margot Robbie during the 2023 marketing campaign for the film *Barbie* helped conjure a palpable, open-hearted energy amongst crowds of thousands: "It was pulsing with love and joy and pinkness. It was really magic, and it was something we discussed internally about how the power of . . . being amongst all of these people with the right intention can really help manifest for the greater good."

Here is something that is important to keep in mind about magical correspondences, however: these associations are suggestive and *not* prescriptive. Collective belief is a powerful reinforcing agent, so it can be effective to know that you are working with symbols that others believe to have a specific set of meanings. That said, even these collectively reinforced signifiers can shift. We already know this from a cultural perspective, as color meanings vary by region and even morph over time. The color pink was associated with boys in nineteenth-century England, and it wasn't thought of as a "girl color" until the following century. Likewise, in many European and North American countries, the color black is associated with death, while in many Asian countries, white is worn when in mourning. In Hilma af Klint's spiritualist paintings, she associated blue with feminine energy and yellow with masculine energy. Yet in occult painter Ithell Colquhoun's work, she takes an entirely different approach. As Amy Hale writes in her book *Sex Magic: Diagrams of Love, Ithell Colquhoun*, "Male figures are a brilliant blue and females are violet-red or magenta, colors that respectively represent the male sphere of

Chokmah and the female sphere of Binah in the King Scale of the Kabbalistic Tree of Life." There is no one-size-fits-all to symbol systems, and you can certainly adapt or improvise when devising your own magical associations. Remember: the most personal magic is the most potent magic. If you are looking to generate a sweet, loving energy, but the color pink makes you queasy, pop some Pepto-Bismol (on second thought, maybe not) and move on to another color that makes your heart sing.

Often these associations are purely subjective. Picasso's Blue Period is marked by washes of the color he believed best expressed his depression, whereas Alice Neel's signature blue that she used to outline the subjects of her portraits feels like a jolt of liveliness and vigor. One of my very favorite colors is a jeweled, effulgent hue somewhere between fuchsia and grape—the glowing shade of red cabbage, sometimes named in pigment tubes as quinacridone violet. And though many associate the color green with vitality, this radiant purple is my go-to for feeling my most supercharged.

Which colors make you feel bold and which colors subdue you? Which scents conjure sensuality or get you ready to put up a fight? Your own associations may eclipse those that others have developed, so when in doubt, go with your gut. A magical correspondence table may tell you that orange is associated with confidence, but maybe you feel like a badass wearing an altostratus gray. And though it's said that Hecate the goddess of witchcraft is gaga for garlic, perhaps you feel compelled to fix her a bowl of black cherries instead. Preset magical correspondences are helpful guidelines and fascinating tools of inspiration and energetic engagement. But as a Magic Maker, *you* ultimately know best regarding the most significant ingredients to add to your creations. Trust the truth of your own intuition. It will always be a lodestone leading you in the direction of authentic expression and limitless enchantment.

Raising the Dead

It's been said that a rare few have the power to bring the deceased back to life. We may think about the biblical Witch of Endor raising the spirit of Samuel, or Renaissance magician Edward Kelley conferring with a dead man at Walton-le-Dale. Though these stories may be apocryphal, I wholeheartedly believe that the work we make can be resurrective. As Magic Makers, we have the ability to not only communicate with the dead but to prolong their lives through holy acts of memory-keeping. When I cook the same chicken soup that my late great-grandma Fay made, I am increasing the impact she still has in the material realm. She is healing me from across the spectral stovetop with comfort and nutrients, and I am extending the energetic tendrils of her life by making use of her special recipe. In these moments, she is with us once more.

Sometimes I think that punk pioneer and poet Patti Smith is one of the greatest necromancers the world has ever seen. Her moving 1996 album, *Gone Again,* was released after she experienced several devastating losses, including the deaths of her husband Fred "Sonic" Smith and her brother, Todd. It includes songs co-written by Fred—and the elegiac final track, "Farewell Reel," is dedicated to him and includes lines he originally came up with. Smith's stunning 2010 memoir, *Just Kids,* was written about her relationship with photographer and creative soulmate Robert

Mapplethorpe, and it is a profoundly beautiful offering that honors their love and sacralizes his memory. As she recounted on NPR's *Morning Edition*: "I promised Robert the day before he died that I would write our story. And it took me twenty years, but I kept my promise." Though Mapplethorpe may no longer be here in the physical world, it's clear that Smith's relationship with him is still an active and vital one. Her writing deepens her connection to him, and it has helped keep Mapplethorpe's art and life in our collective consciousness. Smith's own photographs, social media feeds, and Substack newsletter are filled with images of gravesites she has visited and odes to her deceased heroes and friends, from Arthur Rimbaud to Kurt Cobain. Though Smith has always been a visionary artist, much of her exquisite work is born from first looking backward, then bringing forth the souls of her beloved dead in a new chariot of song.

When we create in honor of those who are no longer with us, we bestow upon them a kind of immortality. This occurs when we speak about them, certainly, but something powerful happens when we use our gifts to create something that lasts. Public monuments such as Kenzō Tange's *The Flame of Peace* at Hiroshima or Maya Lin's *Vietnam Veterans Memorial* in Washington, D.C., are works of art that simultaneously operate as altars. They are communal places of contemplation, of grieving, of remembrance. Here we are invited to interface with the dead and to ensure they are not forgotten. The makers of these artworks intentionally designed them with a sense of grandeur, elegance, and solemnity, as is fitting for marking losses that occurred on such a mass scale. But we can make these spaces in any medium and for any number of deceased beings with whom we wish to reconnect.

Earlier I wrote about my artistic grandma Sonya, whose lipstick I keep on my altar and whose name I often invoke when I'm calling in ancestral support. But when she was alive, Sonya also created her own ancestral altars, albeit framed ones, incorporating archival family photographs and portraits into many of her artworks. In one of my favorite pieces of hers, black-and-white images of her parents are collaged around a dining room table that's covered in a lacy, ombré-rainbow cloth. The whole tableau feels interdimensional, as her composition plays with perspective in such a way that it seems as if they are floating above a floral rug and wooden floor. Hanging on the wall above her parents is a framed photograph of Sonya's maternal grandparents—a picture within a picture. When I look at this piece, I feel as if I'm transcending time and space, connecting to generations of ancestors through the handcrafted portal of my grandmother's artistic offering. My writing about them now is yet another layer of eternal love and resurrection. It is also an act of divine listening, as I believe they are often murmuring to me and encouraging me to keep their memories alive.

Every now and again, the dead let us know that they appreciate our creative offerings, as my playwright husband, Matthew Freeman, recently learned. Matt doesn't have a distinct magical practice per se, and his spirituality leans more Jedi than Judeo-Christian. But he has loved and lived with a witch for over two decades, and he is open to the mysteries of the invisible world. In 2021, Matt wrote a play called *Silver Spring* about the death of his older brother, Michael. Theirs was a complicated relationship. Michael was born with cognitive impairments that made communicating with him very challenging, and for much of their childhood he lived at Pennsylvania's Camphill School for children with special needs. A couple of years after Michael's passing in 2019, Matt felt compelled to write about the last time they saw each other. This became a gorgeously heartrending family drama about love, regret, and grief. It was also far more autobiographical than Matt had been in his prior work, and though it felt cathartic to write, he grappled with how it would reflect on him and his family and whether he was honoring Michael's memory with grace. Even after *Silver Spring* ended up winning a prestigious playwrighting prize, Matt still felt unsure about the play's potential impact. Was it an OK thing to have written? Would it prove too vulnerable or too exploitative? Did he do his brother justice?

Shortly thereafter, Matt and I found ourselves in a gallery in the Catskills, looking at an art installation by Frances Cape called *A Gathering of Utopian Benches*. These were a series of wooden benches that Cape had carved in the styles of those found in various communal societies, and visitors were welcome to carefully make use of them. We picked up the exhibition pamphlet entitled "We Sit on the Same Bench." Flipping through it, we noticed that one of the benches was modeled after those found in the Camphill community where Michael had spent so much of his young life. Suffice it to say, Matt went and sat on that "same bench" and had an immediate feeling of *knowing* that this was Michael's way of communicating with him. And though Michael's verbal language had been relatively limited when he was still alive, Matt felt certain that this was a nod of approval from him. Now, I realize I may be biased in terms of my assessment of Matt's encounters with the ethereal realm. But as my magically agnostic husband will attest, this experience was an exceptional one, and receiving this message from Michael affirmed for him that his play was received as the loving gesture he intended.

In a prior section of this book, I discussed how spirits can provide us with inspiration. By the same token, we can help their influence endure here amongst the living. Creating work in remembrance of them is a means of closing that loop. It's a way of saying thank you to those who have shared their life force with us, whether in literal terms or spiritual ones. In doing so, we acknowledge what they have given us, and we give them something in return. When we create in memory of someone we care deeply for, we reinforce our bond with them, and we keep their eternal magic alive and circulating.

PART IV

Keeping the Cauldron Lit

Any project has its own particular life cycle, and far be it from me to suggest that there is one universal formula that applies to all creative processes. As any maker can attest, sometimes Creative Force flows quickly, and it's all we can do to try to catch a project by the tail and let it ride. Other projects are slow accretions, dripping their mineral magic ever so slowly with seemingly little progress for years on end, until one day—VOILÀ!—it forms a shimmering stalactite. If you're like me, you work in fits and starts, some days feeling feverish with fecund energy and other days wading through a puddle of sludge.

Any of the above in any combination, I assure you, is normal.

Creativity is an organic, otherworldly, ever-mutating, metamorphosing act of wonder-wrangling. It doesn't adhere to hard-and-fast rules, and it doesn't care who you are or what you're working on as long as you are willing to collaborate with it. It doesn't require fancy materials or a giant worktable or endless resources of space and money and time. All it needs is your open embrace and your ravenous appetite for mystery. Spirit is a relational entity. And as with any relationship, the more faith you have in it and the more you show up for it, the stronger your connection becomes.

That sounds pretty simple, doesn't it? Stay curious? Have faith? Keep showing up? No doubt you've heard it all before.

And yet.

It is so much easier said than done. I'm laughing to myself as I write these very words in this very book, because gods know there have been days— weeks!—when this project has felt daunting, exhausting, and beset by doubts.

This is *also* normal. This is *part of it*. Creative Force thrives with tension and friction—remember the Magician who is the hinge between the celestial and terrestrial realms? It takes an incredible amount of strength to keep your arms spread, to keep your inner and outer eyes and ears peeled, to keep your magic moving. This can be an extremely enjoyable experience—an ecstatic one even. It can also feel like being stretched beyond capacity. In those trying moments, I try to remind myself that creative discomfort is a sign that we're making something worthwhile. An oyster needs grit to make a pearl. Coal needs pressure to become a diamond. There's a reason that katabasis is part of so many heroic journeys: we have to descend into the underworld in order to reemerge with newfound wisdom and renewed perspective.

As that magus David Bowie famously said in Michael Apted's 1997 *Inspirations* documentary:

> If you feel safe in the area that you're working in, you're not working in the right area. Always go a little further into the water than you feel you're capable of being in. Go a little bit out of your depth. And when you don't feel that your feet are quite touching the bottom, you're just about in the right place to do something exciting.

All of these platitudes are well and good, but how can we keep our creative fires burning after that initial flare of inspiration? How do we keep things cooking in the spiritual cauldron not only on our best days but also through periods of stress, stagnation, or disengagement?

How does enchantment endure?

In the following section, we'll talk about the inevitable banes that can show up to thwart your magic, and the bewitching boons that can support you as you press forward on creativity's crooked path. By familiarizing yourself with each, be assured that right in this moment you already have everything you need to keep fanning Spirit's flames.

DEMON SLAYING

Folk tales and horror films are rife with stories about magicians calling upon demons to do their bidding and witches dancing giddily with devils beneath a full moon. In actuality, the magic practitioners I know are far more concerned with casting protective spells and fortifying their spaces and selves to keep such destructive forces away. The word *daemon* or *daimon* originally had a neutral connotation, and it referred to a minor god, magical assistant, or ministering spirit. Over time, this evolved into *demon*, meaning a hellacious fiend or infernal pain in the ass. I would never advise someone to intentionally conjure a *demon*, whether an allegedly literal one or a mythopoetic one. Still, it's helpful to understand how to think about demons so we might be better prepared to deal with them when they arrive to mess with our magic-making.

Belief in demons of one sort or another exists in most cultures, even if only in ancient corners cobwebbed with superstition. In Jewish folk magic tradition, for example, a demon is called a sheyd, and demons plural are called sheydim. It was believed that sheydim are everywhere, surrounding us at all times. As third-century rabbi Rav Huna stated, "Each and every one of us has a thousand demons to his left and ten thousand to his right." Eleven thousand demons is, well, a fuckload of demons! And here you were probably worried about just one or two. Sorry to be the bearer of abominable news. But don't fret, because many modern scholars now interpret these sheydim beliefs as an early attempt at describing germs, disease, and other maladies that vary in threat level. Though Lilith has recently been re-signified as a wrongly maligned feminist icon, before the twentieth century she was widely understood as a mother of demons who caused the death of newborn human babies. This is why many Jewish amulets and incantation bowls (essentially ancient demon traps) are inscribed with spells to protect infants from her power. There's also an outhouse demon named bar Shirika Panda, or the "demon of the privy," who was believed to spread sickness and filth. As someone who detests a Porta Potty, believe me, I get it. Luckily, the Talmud tells us how to best him:

> To be saved from the demon of the bathroom, let him recite as follows: "On the head of a lion and on the nose of a lioness we found the demon named bar Shirika Panda. With a bed of leeks I felled him, and with the jaw of the donkey I struck him.

Leeks and donkeys—got it!

Though the spectrum of sheydim bad behavior goes from irksome to fatal, they are all described as having flying capabilities, a gift for prophecy, and an insatiable hunger for evaporated moisture and fire smoke. My favorite feature of sheydim is that they're all said to have chicken-like feet, which is why if you want to determine if one has been present, it's advised to spread ashes and see if any bird tracks appear. Now you know.

More popular writings about demons include the seventeenth-century Greco-Roman, Judeo-Christian mash-up grimoire *The Lesser Key of Solomon*, particularly the section called "Ars Goetia." It lists seventy-two of these guys, ranked and described with flourish, and at the risk of sounding blasphemous (though let's be honest, that ship has clearly sailed), it's a really fun read. These demons aren't all dastardly. In fact, many of them sound rather amusing if not outright helpful. My personal favorite is Amdusias, whom S. L. MacGregor Mathers describes as such:

DEMON SLAYING

> He is a Duke Great and Strong, appearing at first like a Unicorn, but at the request of the Exorcist he standeth before him in Human Shape, causing Trumpets, and all manner of Musical Instruments to be heard, but not soon or immediately. Also he can cause Trees to bend and incline according to the Exorcist's Will . . .

A cacophonous unicorn demon that communicates with trees? Yes, please. (There is also an astrology demon named Amy, but I digress!)

I tell you all this not only because it delights me but also because I think it's useful to remember that demons can be thought of as anything from silly spirits to personified threats, in the same way that gods can be considered anthropomorphized archetypal energies like Love (e.g., Aphrodite) and Wildness (e.g., Artemis). When we personify entities such as these, we relate to them more easily and are thus better equipped to attract or repel their influence over our lives. We don't have to fear demons, in other words. We just need to be ready to face them if they make their unpleasant presence known.

Now, I can hear you thinking: *Wait just a minute! Weren't those magic circles and all of that other supernatural prep work you mentioned earlier supposed to keep unwanted demons away?* And absolutely, in my experience, those practices are extremely helpful in decreasing their nefarious power. Wearing amulets and casting circles are wonderful demon deterrents, as are banishing rituals and more elaborate counter-magic ceremonies.

But I've also found that spending a bit of time getting to know the particularly relentless demons is equally effective, especially if we learn to recognize them and call them by name. I was reminded of this approach by writer and illustrator Yumi Sakugawa. In her book *Your Illustrated*

Guide to Becoming One with the Universe she tells the reader to "have cake and tea with your demons" (and her accompanying drawing is not to be missed). This phrase is her charming (and far more delicious) summation of a modern Buddhist story that recounts Siddhartha Gautama's battle with the demon Mara. One night, Siddhartha sat meditating beneath the Bodhi Tree. Suddenly, the demon Mara appeared to undermine him, throwing every distraction he could at Siddhartha: lust, greed, thirst, anger, attachment, and so on. After a long struggle, Siddhartha was able to fend off the demon, thus reaching enlightenment and becoming the Buddha. Still, Mara would not leave him be. As the Buddha's message spread throughout the land, Mara would turn up from time to time with his temptations and diversions. Rather than fight the demon again, the Buddha would simply say to him, "I see you, Mara," and then invite him to sit and have some tea. After being given a bit of kindness and attention, Mara would then go on his way.

It's a beautiful allegory about what we can do when hobgoblins of any sort turn up to knock us off course. Rather than trying to suppress negative thoughts, we can befriend them and give them some acknowledgment and a bit of time to be heard. More often than not, this is enough countermagic to keep the demons from taking over and ruining our creative work.

Demons of all sorts can show up during any part of our magic-making. Some are so loud they prevent us from ever getting started, causing us to feel as if we are somehow inadequate and so shouldn't even bother to begin. In my experience, creative demons often get louder the deeper I am into a project. They tell me I'm wasting my time, that I was stupid for thinking I was up to the task, that I should quit now before I really make a fool of myself. "It's not too late to stop," they hiss. "This will never be as good as you want it to be."

DEMON SLAYING

The demons have been with me as I've been writing this book. Lucky for me, I've been through enough creative cycles at this point to expect them and know they appear to everyone who attempts to conjure something new. Demons *hate* new. They would much rather we keep their territory familiar, safe, and small. But creative magic is all about interfacing with mystery. It's about rearranging fantastical furniture and pulling up the carpets to see what's underneath. The demons show up and say, "Whoa whoa WHOA, what are you doing? This room looks nice just how it is! Stop it with the new!" And then they will say anything to keep you from proceeding.

With this current creative project of mine, I suppose I'm doubly lucky because, unbeknownst to them, my demons are also my guinea pigs. Right now I'm not only going to have tea and cake with them, I'm going to study them and catalog them in hopes that this will benefit other makers who are struggling with their creative demons too. And while there may be eleven thousand of them surrounding me at all times, I'm going to focus on the few who tend to be the most obnoxious. Maybe they'll take a break when I'm done with this section so I can write the rest of this book in peace! (Unlikely, but hey, a witch can dream.)

The Demon of Self-Doubt

I would guess that most of us are intimately familiar with this demon. This guy loves to tell us that we simply don't have what it takes to make the work we desire to make. It runs through a litany of the ways in which we're somehow personally lacking: in skill set, character, status, conviction, whatever fill-in-the-blank positive attributes we imagine *real* Magic Makers have. This demon often goes by the moniker *imposter syndrome*, though I love RuPaul's naming of it as "the inner saboteur." Whatever you call it, the dark spell it casts on us is the illusion that we are deeply unworthy of the creative task at hand. It tells us we are ill-equipped at our core, and so trying to make our magic is an exercise in futility.

The trouble with the Demon of Self-Doubt is that it is highly adaptable, and it constantly moves the goalposts of success. While it tries to get us to give up throughout the entire creative cycle (the bastard), I'm here to tell you it also absolutely doesn't give a shit if you prove it wrong! Case in point: I battled constantly with my self-doubt demon while writing my first full-length book, *Waking the Witch*. No matter that I had written countless short-form pieces and had decades of witchly studies under my

THE DEMON OF SELF-DOUBT

belt. This demon loved to tell me that I had bitten off more than I could chew this time, and that an entire book was out of the question! Well, guess what? I did it anyway! I pushed past its fussing and dodged its trapdoors, and ta-da! I wrote the thing. Huzzah! Rejoice! Victory is mine!

Except!

Here I am a few years later, writing another full-length book. I've already proven I am capable of doing this very thing, so you would think this demon would have been put in its place, correct? Wrong! The demon is back, only this time, it likes to tell me that the other book was a lucky fluke. And that this time, I *really* can't do it, because I expended all of my good fortune on that first one. And this one will be even harder because the topic of magic and creativity is so much bigger than the topic of witches alone. And on and on the demon sings. An aria of apprehension.

When I listen to this demon, it tells me that it's worried I'm going to fail. It's trying to protect me from the shame that comes with falling short of a goal. It seems mean, but really, it assures me, it means well. The best way I know to counteract this demon is to thank it for its concern, and then talk back to it. I tell this demon that nothing worth doing has ever been without risk. I say that the work may feel precarious, but the regret I would feel at not attempting it is far more dangerous to my well-being than any regret I might feel having done it. I am kind but firm when I address it, and I let it know who's boss.

Other Magic Makers have used this talk-back technique with success as well. As actor and musician Juliette Lewis explained on Shirley Manson's *The Jump* podcast: "I was really overly self-critical. . . . I had that horrible voice—'Ah you're no good. You're gonna do it like that? That fucking sucks'— that awful, awful voice. . . . Through time and experience and through teachers . . . I could get bigger than that voice."

Drag queen Katya mentioned a similar strategy on an episode of *RuPaul's Drag Race*: "One thing I've been sort of coaching myself with is I sort of name that voice—I call her Brenda—and I just say, 'You know what, Brenda? Shut the fuck up!'"

That oughta do the trick.

But as a magical backup, I'm thrilled to say that recently my mom (a marvelous fine artist herself) made me a literal incantation bowl to trap my self-doubt demon. Here is the spell she inscribed within it:

> May *Shekinah* and her angels spread their light and love around Pamela Grossman to bind and dispel the dark demons of self-doubt, fear, and anxiety. Empower her to embrace her divine talents to create Goodness on Earth. Grant her clarity to recognize and follow the breadcrumbs which help her to walk with confidence and strength toward her unique purpose. May she share her thoughts and words with *chesed** to bring *Tikkun Olam*† into the world.

Yes, my mom is the best.

I keep the incantation bowl in my office to trap the self-doubt demon, and while it doesn't have 100 percent efficacy, it does seem to help. What I appreciate most about this bowl is that when I look at it, I'm reminded that my Demon of Self-Doubt can be contained not only by my own inner fortitude but by the support of those who believe in me and are rooting for me—and who will love me even if I fail.

---

*kindness
†world-healing

The Demon of Distraction

Here's the thing about the Demon of Distraction. It wants us to know that our priorities are all wrong. Who are we to be writing jokes for open mic night or choreographing a calypso dance routine when there is so much else that needs our attention?! Some of these distractions arguably fall under the category of Very Important Tasks. They involve taking our loved ones to doctor's appointments or helping them with homework or providing them with food. There are also Very Important Chores like doing the laundry and buying more AA batteries and fixing the running toilet (damn you, privy demon!). And we're taught that the most Important Distraction of all is working at the job that makes us the money to be able to afford all of the above.

Then there are the less-important-yet-nonetheless-demanding distractions that buffet us from all sides throughout the day. Screens, of course, with their infinite stream of bleak-yet-cozy British detective series and videos of long-haired mini dachshunds in tiny argyle sweater vests. Physically present animals, such as our cat Birthday, who has gotten into the habit of sitting on my hands as I type and purring all the while (the sweetest, softest demon imaginable!). The news. The phone ringing and dinging. Plans with that one friend we haven't seen in months and so *really* shouldn't keep putting off.

The problem with the Demon of Distraction is that it intentionally makes us think that *everything else* is more important or more interesting than tending to our magic is. It also tells us we'll feel better if we just do a couple of things first before we get down to doing our creative work. One more errand, one more video, one more minute of scrolling. It has several infernal accomplices, e.g., the Nixie of Necessity and the Imp of Procrastination. Each operates in their own style of temptation, but they have one thing in common: these creatures feast on time. The longer we delay our hallowed work, the more they gorge.

I've found my own Demon of Distraction responds well to deadlines and structured goals. I've negotiated with this demon over the years, and for this book we've struck a deal: it can distract me and take as much of my time as it wants as long as I hit my monthly word count. My playwright husband thwarts his distraction demon by consistently scheduling readings of his new plays before said plays are finished, then writing like hell to make sure he has something to share with the actors and audience members who have committed their time to him. Accountability to others is a good way to bring focus to your work and create an opposing force to help you resist this demon's temptations. It may have its attention-diverting hooks in you, but the pull of a promise you've made to collaborators and colleagues often proves stronger.

Some makers go to extreme lengths to resist this demon, only writing in windowless rooms with offline computers, for example, or insisting on scribbling by hand rather than risk being distracted by screens at all. In the acknowledgments section of her novel *NW*, Zadie Smith thanks two internet-restricting apps—Freedom and SelfControl—for "creating the time" in which she could write.

You and your own distracting demon might come to different terms, such as self-imposed screen-time limits or waking up a bit earlier to get in an uninterrupted creativity hour. Whatever you decide, know that the Demon of Distraction despises boundaries, and the more you enforce them, the less insistent it will be that everything else is more significant than keeping your creative fire roaring.

The Demon of Inertia

Distraction's demonic cousin is inertia. They are related to each other and look an awful lot alike, so it's easy to confuse the two. But in actuality, they operate from opposite positions. Where the Demon of Distraction comes up with ways to snag your attention and keep you away from your work, the Demon of Inertia makes you fixate on one part of your project and keeps you stuck there. It makes you think that this thing you were so excited about is no longer working, and that it was stupid for you to be excited about it in the first place. With one wave of its spindly finger, this demon makes a thick gray fog descend upon your project, snuffing out your painting's luster or riddling your writing with worn-out clichés. "Why bother?" it asks you. "There's no place to go from here."

The inertia demon really would like everything to slow the fuck down. In fact, it wonders why we don't just stop altogether. It loves stopping. Stopping is predictable. Stopping is safe. Stopping is a guaranteed outcome.

This demon despises surprises, and so it lies and tells you it's seen it

THE DEMON OF INERTIA

all, it already knows how things are going to turn out, and so there's no point in trying to do anything new. This demon *hates* experiments.

Experimentation is where the juice is, though. Novelty is fuel, so the only way to resist this demon's sabotage is to shake things up and keep it moving. Trying a new tactic in your thinking or introducing a seemingly incongruous element into your work can bring revitalizing energy and a freshly polished sheen. But sometimes it's as simple as letting yourself jump to a different section in your project that feels more interesting. When I'm stuck on something I'm writing, rather than obsessing and reworking it to death, I've decided I'm allowed to just move past it and keep going. I tell myself that I can always go back and fix it later, and more often than not, writing my way forward leads me to a clearer vantage point from which to assess that tricky spot later on. I've learned to resist the illusion of stuckness and to follow my own fascinations. The word *fascinate* comes from the Latin *fascinus*, which means "spell" or "witchcraft." By navigating via my project's creative heat map, I go to where the fire is. In other words, I follow the path that feels the most alive and mesmerizing to me, even if that means making a hard left or leaping to an entirely different terrain or topic. I give over to a spellbound state and trust that Spirit is leading our project closer to completion.

John August is an award-winning screenwriter of hit films such as *Big Fish*, *Charlie's Angels*, and *Corpse Bride*, and he also co-hosts the immensely popular screenwriting podcast *Scriptnotes*. He's spoken about how he's learned to stymie his own Demon of Inertia by letting himself work on whatever section of a script he's most excited by at the moment. As he told Mike Birbiglia on the *Working It Out* podcast: "I write out of sequence. And so I'll write whatever scene appeals to me to write on the day, wherever it is in the script . . . If I feel like writing this scene right now I'm gonna write this scene right now because it's interesting to me." Eventually he goes back and figures out how it all fits together, but by first writing whatever is delighting him, he ensures that he keeps things moving. Following his own fascination prevents him from getting stuck.

Sometimes, in the worst moments of the creative process, nothing feels fascinating. That's when you know this demon is really pulling out all the stops. In my experience the best method to bust through this blockade is to get up and *literally* start moving. A *New York Times* profile of R.E.M. frontman Michael Stipe describes how his songwriting process involves intensive periods of movement that help him break through writer's block. As journalist Jon Mooallem describes it: "He knew he'd have to isolate himself in one of the buildings on his property, walk in circles for six or eight or 10 hours at a time, effect a trancelike meditation and wrench out the rest of the lyrics, line by line . . . He turned his body into a fidget spinner so his mind could do the work." I also know of several makers who are runners, including author Haruki Murakami and the witchly illustration duo—and my *What Is a Witch* comic book collaborators—who work under the moniker Tin Can Forest. It is not only healthy for the body to move, it also helps one build up the mental and spiritual endurance to stick with a creative project through times of resistance. As Murakami writes in his book *What I Talk About When I Talk About Running*, "Exerting yourself to the fullest within your individual limits: that's the essence of running, and a metaphor for life—and for me, for writing as well."

I haven't yet tried pacing in circles for hours to battle the inertia demon into submission, and for me and my wonky knees, running feels like a form of torture. But I have learned that other kinds of physical movement are immensely helpful for my creative process. When I'm feel-

THE DEMON OF INERTIA

ing stagnant or just plain stuck, I now take a break, dance to some good music, run a quick errand, stroll through a park or an art museum, or take a meandering hike through glorious Green-Wood Cemetery. I know this may seem antithetical to the idea of productivity, and you might be tempted to think the Demon of Distraction is pulling one of its tricks. But physical movement helps our brains metabolize creative ideas and helps our unconscious problem solve. Furthermore, it opens us up to our augur selves, shifting into a new plane of inspiration. I can't tell you how many times I felt a bit stuck in a project and Spirit delivered me a solution via a lunch with a friend or a spontaneous encounter with a work of art. I just had to leave my apartment to reach it, and to let it reach me.

How can you tell whether stepping away from a project is sabotaging or supportive? When is a creative pause evidence of procrastination à la the Demon of Distraction, rather than your own helpful counterattack upon the Demon of Inertia? Easy. If the "break" leaves you feeling more drained or depressed than before, and you find it difficult to return to work, you'll know you're in the presence of an imp who needs more discipline. But if stepping away for a bit brings you rest, replenishment, and a renewed sense of possibility, you'll know the Demon of Inertia is now blessedly being kept at bay.

The Demon of Scarcity

The Demon of Scarcity is a slippery little bugger. It morphs and twists into terrifying shapes. It wriggles into the soft folds of your mind and implants little seeds of dismay. "If only you had *more*," it murmurs. More time. More space. More money. Better tools. A better education. Better connections. "You will *never* catch up," it says. "You will *never* have enough." And even worse: "Those *other* people have so much more than you do." More talent, better looks, a famous father, a head start, a lucky break.

Have I mentioned that the scarcity demon is a fucking asshole?

It will also suggest that creativity is a kind of race. And that if you don't do something first, if you're not truly original, then you might as well not even bother to try. "There's only so much to go around!" it moans. "There's limited room at the top!" As if the top is a place that Creative Force cares about in the first place.

Let me tell you a story about how my scarcity demon once reared its horrible, horned little head.

In late 2015, I got an email from a writer named Kristen J. Sollée, asking if we could grab dinner. I knew Kristen a little bit, as she had interviewed me for her smart sex-positive blog, *Slutist*. She had also invited me to give a talk on the evolution of the archetype of the witch at an event she had curated earlier that year called *Legacy of the Witch*. (Note to reader: If you are ever invited to give a PowerPoint presentation at a dive bar, absolutely say yes, but also know you will be far less captivating than the burlesque performer before you and the doom metal band after. At least that's what my scarcity demon wants me to tell you!) Now, Kristen was always lovely to me, and was an avid supporter of my work, but at that point we didn't know each other very well.

At our dinner, she shared with me that she was writing a book about how witches have transformed from villainous monstresses into icons of feminism and sexual freedom over time. Not only that, but she already had a book deal and a pub date for said book—and she was hoping to quote me in the book's chapter on witches and art. I tell you, I nearly choked on my tekka maki. What Kristen was describing was not only an idea that I had been lecturing about and writing about for years, but one that I had been dreaming about turning into a book myself.

I am not proud to admit that, internally, I had an awful reaction to this news. My blood ran cold. My heart began racing. And my scarcity demon got REALLY FUCKING LOUD.

"These are YOUR ideas," the demon insisted. "And everyone is going to think they're hers!" As if either of us owns the idea of witches and feminism being related. As if my own work wasn't inspired and informed by the decades of writers and scholars and witchcraft practitioners that came before either of us. As if an idea could be owned at all.

"Her book is going to come out before yours, and so everyone is going to think that *your* book is copying *hers*!" the demon screeched. Never mind the fact that I hadn't even started writing my imaginary witch book, let alone had any book deal to speak of.

"She got there first. No one is going to want another feminist witch book. Maybe you shouldn't write one after all." And on and on the demon went for days. For weeks. I'm embarrassed to say, for *months*.

I lamented about it privately to my husband. I keened about it to a few close friends. I no doubt vented about it to whatever therapist I was seeing at the time. (Nancy, I think. I've had a number of Nancys.) But thank the ever-loving gods I did not express any of my displeasure to Kristen. In the moment she shared her news, I smiled through my seaweed and congratulated her with as much warmth and kindness as I could muster.

In the period that followed, I let myself wrestle with these shadowy feelings in safe and contained conversations. I had enough self-awareness not to bad-mouth Kristen or cut off our burgeoning friendship, and to take ownership over my emotions. In my logical brain, I knew that my dark reaction to Kristen's news was just my Demon of Scarcity doing a really excellent job of being a shitty little panic-inducing prick.

I decided to try to look beneath my jealousy and defensiveness, and there I discovered a far more magical message: I *really* wanted to write *my* witch book. With time and patience, I was able to transmute my scarcity demon's indignation into motivation, its fear into fuel. I didn't have any control over my initial ugly feelings, but I could control how I acted upon them. I could treat Kristen with grace and assume she had the best of intentions and wish her well. And I could write the book that I so clearly longed to write.

Kristen's book, *Witches, Sluts, Feminists*, came out in 2017, and it is wonderful. I was honored to give it a glowing blurb, and I was grateful that she included me in the book as she had originally planned. I also learned a lot from her writing, which only made my own book better—and I quoted and credited her in its pages as such, as she did me.

THE DEMON OF SCARCITY

And guess what? When my book *Waking the Witch* came out two years later, people still wanted to read it! No one accused me of stealing from her as I'd feared. And to the best of my knowledge, no one said, "Another feminist witch book? Who wants it?!" In fact, both of our books, alongside several others that have come out since, have helped grow awareness about the topic and have proven that there are many readers out there who are enthusiastic about defiant, magical women—and who want to read books by and about them. It also affirmed for me that, despite the scarcity demon's protests, there is more than enough interest to go around. After all, no one says, "Uch, *another* book about the Vietnam War?!" "Another book about personal finance, no thank you!" "*Another* book about Abe Lincoln? *You can keep it!*" And there's certainly far more of all of those. May feminist witch books proliferate, I say, and may many more witches be woken!

I also want to offer this experience as a potential alternative to some of the other paradigms of inspiration and creativity that have been going around, namely that if you don't bring a creative idea forth yourself, it will abandon you and go to someone else. This notion has been popularized recently by Elizabeth Gilbert, a writer I do not know personally, but whose work I absolutely adore. (Unbeknownst to her, she has also been giving my scarcity demon an awful lot to talk about lately: "*Your* magical creativity book isn't going to be nearly as good as Liz's! You've never even had your books on the *New York Times* Best Seller list like she has! Why should anyone care about what *you* have to say?!" *Demon, begone!*)

In Gilbert's magnificent book *Big Magic*, she shares an anecdote about a highly detailed idea for novel that she'd been developing but hadn't been able to give her full attention to. Life happens, and she never gets around to fully writing it, but still keeps it simmering on her back burner. Then one day, she learns that her friend Ann Patchett has written a novel that is shockingly similar to the one she had been incubating herself. The two friends share a sort of delighted astonishment about it, and they decide that perhaps the idea had leapt to Ann since Liz hadn't given it enough of her focus. Gilbert recounts this not out of regret—she was happily working on other projects and was at peace with letting this book go to someone else. But she does believe that ideas will find any way they can to be born—if not through you, then through another channel.

I read this anecdote with a dual sense of awe and acute anxiety. How marvelous to know that a writer I admire also believes that ideas come from some other place, are made of their own independent, Spirited stuff. How awful to think that there is an expiration date on inspiration, and that if you don't get to an idea soon enough, it will abandon you forever.

She may be right. She may be wrong. But based on my own somewhat similar experience, I think it would have been just fine if Gilbert had written her own version of that novel, if she'd still felt the fire to! Ideas are expansive, elastic things, and many are big enough that they'll seek multiple outlets. Two Truman Capote films came out within a year of each other (*Capote* in 2005 and *Infamous* in 2006), and I imagine that some Capote-heads couldn't believe their luck. *Studio 60 on the Sunset Strip* and *30 Rock* were both sitcoms about the making of *Saturday Night Live*–style variety shows, and both also came out in 2006. As I write this, there are multiple *Frankenstein* adaptations in the works for film and stage, and as far as I'm concerned, the more love for teen genius Mary Shelley, the better.

My favorite recent example of this involves two musicians I love, Jolie Holland and Buck Meek, who co-wrote a song called "Haunted Mountain." They intentionally each recorded their own version of the song and agreed to release their versions on their respective albums. However, unbeknownst to each other, they both decided to name their entire album after the song! Rather than one artist "winning" and getting to retain this album title, they mutually agreed that they could both put out different albums called *Haunted Mountain* in 2023. First of all, I happen to love both renditions of this song. Meek's is sparkling and upbeat, Holland's is melancholic and sweet and slow as molasses—and each is a thing of beauty. And second, I love that even though they each decided to name their respective albums after the song, they both had the egolessness to decide that releasing different albums with the same name was an absolutely fine thing to do. And I can tell you that as a fan of each musician, I listen to both *Haunted Mountain* albums an equal amount, because they are both wonderful in different ways.

Critics may pit one album against the other or discuss which was "better" or which will stand the test of time. But I really don't think Creative Force gives a fuck about critical success. I believe these ideas wanted to come out, and the makers' jobs were to show up and materialize them as best they could.

And as for my witchly compatriot, Kristen Sollée, I'm overjoyed to report that over the years she has become a dear friend, collaborator, cheerleader, and coven mate. We frequently shout out each other's books, recommend each other for appearances and writing opportunities, and act as sounding boards for each other's work. To be clear, this relationship has as much to do with Kristen's kindness and integrity as it does with my own inner demon slaying. (Kristen also happens to have a deliciously wicked fashion sense, so what's not to love?) I'm grateful I didn't let my demon prevent me from writing the book I was meant to, nor did I allow its scarcity antics to get in the way of cultivating a truly spectacular friendship. Abundance abounds. (And go read Kristen's books! They're really great!)

The Demon of Perfectionism

Oh, what a tease the Demon of Perfectionism is. It hovers just out of grasp, looking so very shiny and pleased with itself. It has no worries, no rough edges, no flaws. If only you could reach it, you would feel so very satisfied! You would feel as if you had really *arrived*.

Trouble is, while this pretty little demon is extremely enticing, it doesn't actually exist, not really. If you get close enough and try to touch it, you'll find it's just a mirage. Even more annoying? After a point, the harder you struggle to reach it, the worse your work gets. Striving for excellence is all well and good, but when we insist on perfection, our creative output ends up feeling sterile and forced.

It can also lose some of the erratic, ecstatic magic that sparked our excitement in the first place, and which makes our creations feel alive. Many are now familiar with the Japanese principle of wabi-sabi, which is difficult to translate precisely into English, but circles around such concepts as imperfection, transience, and the inherent impermanence of the natural world. Often an object is described as wabi-sabi if there is a sense of it being handmade or else being otherwise affected by the passing of time. The

THE DEMON OF PERFECTIONISM

presence of patina, rust, decay, or cracks can give something a wabi-sabi feel, as can thumbprints in a clay pot or a cozy, misshapen shagginess to one's sofa. There is a soulfulness to the wabi-sabi aesthetic. A signal that something has been made or at least enhanced naturally, with all of the unique deviations that *naturalness* implies. Wabi-sabi is the antidote to all things symmetrical, mass-produced, or generated by AI. It has been *crafted* by humans and oxygen and seasons and the cycles of life.

Perfectionism is a false prophet. It promises some sort of gleaming, future triumph while robbing us of the pleasures of the imperfect present.

And here's a secret that the Demon of Perfectionism does *not* want us to know: So-called flaws make us and our work more lovable. Not simply admired or intellectually approved of. But really and truly adored.

Case in point: Patti Smith is one of my all-time heroes. I got hooked on her albums when I was a teen, and then fell in love with her prose and poetry as I grew into adulthood.

A few years ago, I watched a video of Smith performing at the 2016 Nobel Prize ceremony in Stockholm in honor of awardee Bob Dylan. She begins singing Dylan's "A Hard Rain's A-Gonna Fall," with a full orchestra, in front of the king and queen of Sweden and a packed audience of other esteemed attendees. A few lines in, she stumbles over some of the words, seeming to lose her place in the song. "I'm sorry," she says, and asks to start that section again. "I apologize. Sorry, I'm so nervous." The audience breaks into encouraging applause. The music starts back up again and Smith continues the song with a few more slight stumbles, but pushes through with conviction, tenderness, and vulnerable beauty. I have watched this video more times than I can count, and I'm brought to tears each time I do. Not out of stress or schadenfreude, but out of the deepest sense of gratitude. To be shown that even creative legends are human. And to be reminded that perseverance and presence are more important than perfection. Apparently, I was not the only one who was grateful for this flawed-yet-sparkling diamond of a performance. As Smith wrote later in the *New Yorker*:

> In the breakfast room, I was greeted by many of the Nobel scientists. They showed appreciation for my very public struggle. They told me I did a good job. I wish I would have done better, I said. No, no, they replied, none of us wish that. For us, your performance seemed a metaphor for our own struggles.

Sometimes when my Demon of Perfectionism is making me fret about how woolly my words are or how far away my "perfect" final product seems to be, I utter this mantra: "All I can do is my best with the resources that I've been given." It reminds me that my skills, energy, time, and funds are finite, and so my job is to put them to good use rather than lament what I am lacking. Beyond that, it's up to Spirit to do what it sees fit with what I make. It also reminds me that my best will never be perfect, and to try to reframe my work's limitations and aberrations as markers of my own distinct imprint.

I was heartened recently to hear that cello maestro Yo-Yo Ma has come to a similar conclusion. On *Fresh Air*, he explained to Terry Gross how he approaches his own imperfect performances:

> I try and forgive myself because I don't want to be neurotic. I also don't want to fall under the spell of what I call an industrial aesthetic, which is your way of saying perfection, right?

THE DEMON OF PERFECTIONISM

What do we do in industry? You make a million copies of something with the least amount of error. So here's a million copies. Maybe it's six out of a million bad, right? I can't play a million concerts and make—have six bum concerts. You know, that's an unreasonable thing to ask of a human being. What allows me to not be paralyzed is to just say, I'm doing my best. And if it doesn't work, you know my intention is to do the best.

Finally, when this demon is being particularly stubborn, I tell it that even if what I make is dreck, I'm determined to finish whatever it is I'm working on rather than quit because it's not living up to some lofty standard.

And I remind the Demon of Perfectionism that the original meaning of the word *perfect* is not "flawless."

Rather, it means "complete."

The Demon of Suffering

I've made a lot of work when I was in pain. As a teenager, I would stay up late writing reams of poetry and filling canvases with images of weeping eyes and shattered hearts. I once even took a replica of a little red bird and nailed its wings to the thoracic cavity of one particularly maudlin self-portrait. It was a candid depiction, I felt, of my psychological turmoil and suffocating feelings of entrapment. (Subtlety was not my strong suit.)

Creating from a place of pain can absolutely be therapeutic, and I'm grateful that I had a means of converting my aching into art. Externalizing dark feelings and turning them into something tangible can feel like an exorcism of a sort. And if that process begets work that might also heal other people through the act of shared recognition, that's a precious thing indeed.

The trouble is, there is a very dramatic demon who would like us to think that this is the *only* valid method of creation. That our making *must* come out of suffering in order to be great. This demon is responsible for romanticizing such experiences as depression, poverty, hunger, addiction, and self-harm. It tells us stories of writers who wrote superb novels during drug-addled benders and rock stars who recorded lauded albums during weeks-long stints of sleep deprivation and arduous love quadrangles. It insists that masterful makers like Vincent van Gogh,

THE DEMON OF SUFFERING

Diane Arbus, Robin Williams, and Sylvia Plath were brilliant *because* of their mental health struggles, not in spite of them. It heralds tortured artists and sad clowns as the only true geniuses and contends that unhappiness is synonymous with insightfulness.

Like many before me, I had been tricked into thinking that the Demon of Suffering is a necessary companion to my own creativity. I am a highly sensitive soul who has wrestled with anxiety and PTSD for much of my life. I feel the hardships of the world intensely, and I bear the scars of my own battles with a mix of guardedness and pride. I have also long been attracted to shadow-soaked work and artists who are fluent in the language of duende.

Because of this, I was convinced that I needed to lean into pain in order to produce anything of value. That catharsis was the only valid method of creating something great.

As I got older, I realized that I was confusing my subject matter with my own brain matter. I started going to therapy to get support for my emotional strife and slowly learned that things like getting enough sleep and putting nourishing things into my body didn't hinder my creative output as I'd been told they might. In fact, the better I felt, the more productive I was. My focus was sharper, my energy was higher, and the connection to my own magic became deeper and more consistent.

I didn't lose interest in witches and underworldly wonders. I didn't stop telling my personal horror stories, and I didn't stop loving gallows humor, torch songs, and lachrymose poems. But I've learned that I don't have to suffer in order to create or consume them. It is wonderful that we have the ability to morph our suffering into splendor. But it is not the only way to create something of worth.

I also find it reassuring that several of the dark artists I adore have come to the same conclusion.

I've been a PJ Harvey fan since the early 1990s when I fell in love with her scathing noir-rock songs about vengeful women and furious demigoddesses. Though Harvey has had her own share of mental health struggles, she's been adamant that she works better when she's feeling well. As she told *The Times* in 1998: "The tortured artist myth is rampant. People paint me as some kind of black witchcraft-practising devil from hell, that I have to be twisted and dark to do what I am doing. It's a load of rubbish." In a 2004 *FILTER* magazine interview, she doubled down on this, saying, "I firmly disbelieve that one has to be a tortured soul to write good music. I don't buy into that myth at all, the same way I don't buy into the myth that to be a great rock and roller you have to be fucked up on drugs or alcohol."

David Lynch is responsible for some of the most resplendently disturbing films ever made, but his Transcendental Meditation practice taught him that when he felt good, he was able to generate far more of the dark beauty he loves. As he stated in his MasterClass course on creativity and film,

> You don't have to suffer to show suffering. You don't have to be filled with turmoil to show turmoil. Have it in the story . . . A lot of people say "Well, suffering is good for art" . . . Suffering reduces. Negativity is the enemy of creativity. It's common sense. If someone is depressed, they say they don't even feel like getting out of bed, let alone working. If you're sad, or if you're filled with bitter anger, that occupies the mind. Maybe you do angry paintings, so what? You can do angry paintings but be happy in the doing.

I also now make a concerted effort to push back on my own workaholism and my fetishization of stress and extreme striving. The night before the opening for my art exhibition *Language of the Birds: Occult*

THE DEMON OF SUFFERING

and Art, I was in the emergency room due to pain in my left foot that was so excruciating I was certain I had broken it. It turned out to be nerve damage from standing on concrete gallery floors and barely sitting down for weeks on end. And while I was writing my book *Waking the Witch*, I experienced massive acne flare-ups from the intense pressure I put on myself, and then became gaunt and undernourished—and subsequently unfocused—due to cutting out so many so-called inflammatory foods to try to clear my skin.

When I began writing this book, I struck a bargain with my gods and guides. I promised them that I would do my very best and would work hard to bring their message through, but that I have set the intention *not to suffer for it*. During this writing process, I've been careful to take breaks, eat well, get enough sleep, and consistently allow myself delightful little indulgences that help sustain my body and my spirit. And though there have been inevitable moments of stress here and there, both as I've been writing and in my life overall, I can say that working on this book has been a far more easeful experience than any of my prior projects have been, and these words are getting on the page far more fluidly *without* the excess pressure and deprivation I submitted myself to in the past.

Making things is challenging work, no question. Most of the time it isn't easy, and it certainly isn't effortless. Much as we might try to manifest the perfect circumstances for our making, it also doesn't take place in a vacuum: no matter how committed we are to our creativity, other tough parts of being human may encroach via disturbances with our health, our homes, and our communities at large. Life happens.

But we can set an intention to take as excellent care of ourselves as we possibly can throughout the entire creative process, and not fall prey to the Demon of Suffering's anguished allure.

The Demon of Judgment
(Demon of All Demons)

The thing about demons is they feed on fear. And for me, the number one thing I am most afraid of in my creative life is Other People's Opinions. I hate admitting this, and I hate that it is true. But when I'm focused on how my work will be received by the outside world, it knocks me out of Magician Mode and into a sort of Pseudo-Psychic Crisis Mode.

Here is how this usually goes.

First, I start envisioning all of the possible criticism that could come my way once I release my misshapen monster of a creation into the world. I picture the shitty reviews and snarky comments that are sure to be waiting in the wings, ready to strike the moment I let my monster loose. I see an avalanche of bad press, dismal ratings, and single stars. I imagine being called out or canceled, berated and humiliated, and roundly rejected by the general population—and particularly by the people I most admire.

Then, I stop whatever I'm working on and immediately start strategizing about how I can get ahead of this inevitable barrage of repudiation: "Maybe if I tweak this or modify that now, no one will possibly say

THE DEMON OF JUDGMENT

anything negative about it!" This is a problem that *must be solved posthaste*, you see, and the only way to solve it is to make changes right away, so that I might please my future detractors.

It doesn't stop there though. Oh no! Because then I feel foolish for worrying so much about what those future disapproving people will think, because I should be so lucky to be noticed by them at all! Because nothing is worse than being ignored, right? At least if people hate my monster, it will have mattered enough to have left an impression! And so I feel ridiculous for even assuming that anyone will give a shit about what I've made in the first place! 'Cause chances are, no one will even care at all!

And then I really start to panic. Because if no one cares about what I make, how will I survive? My very livelihood is tied to my creative output, isn't it? And if no one pays attention to it, or if they deem it unworthy, then how, pray tell, am I supposed to pay my rent, keep the lights on, buy groceries . . . I might *starve*, for fuck's sake! I might die a penniless pariah!

And you know what? *I'll deserve it*. Because who was I to have thought that I was a Creator at all? Who was I to have imagined that anything I make would have value? Oh what a fool I was/am/will always be!

Before I know it, the Demon of Judgment has gorged on my fear, made a feast of my future-tripping. Worst of all, it's brought my creativity to a grinding, paralytic halt. It's made me grip my hands tightly in an attempt to control how my work will be received instead of keeping them open to the flow of Creative Force as I am working. It's made me focus on how I will be perceived rather than the present pleasure of producing. It's inflamed my ego and blocked my immediate experience of enchantment.

This demon got between me and Spirit, and it interfered with my creative crosscurrents of inspiration and intention. It made me forget the whole point of making things, which is to reflect and reshape the material world using the divine power of our imagination. To create an offering to something greater than oneself: Humanity. Divinity. Love.

The Demon of Judgment is not a loving entity. It might tell you it has your best interests at heart, that it is protecting you from failure. Do not believe it. Its only mission is to stop you from creating. And it knows that its flood of nightmare and daymare scenarios will scare you stiff. It doesn't have to do much more after that, because it also knows you will tie yourself in knots trying to "fix" your work today so that it pleases the proverbial masses tomorrow. Or better yet, you'll just quit on your creative magic altogether!

It's not always easy to wade into wonder, to merge with mystery. It is tempting to overthink, overcomplicate, to distance, to hedge, to hesitate. But the unknown is the only destination for any maker, and one must pursue it with faith and enchanted abandon.

How will other people judge your work? What will they say about the results of your creative quest? It's really not for you to question at this stage—if ever. Your job as a creative being is simply to create, and to do so from a place of authenticity, curiosity, and openness.

As experimental filmmaker and poet James Broughton writes in his cinematic manifesto, *Making Light of It*: "It is easier to be pretentious than to be at ease. It is easier to make great confusion than it is to create a simple complicated truth. One asks merely for a little magic. If the magician's act turns out to be Great Art, that part of it will not be his concern. The unforgettable films remain those conceived with the sturdiest poetic imagination."

The same can be said for any painting or play, any business proposal or potential bio-tech development. When we offer Spirit our poetic imaginations with sturdiness, we are rewarded by getting to work with Creative Force. That, and only that, is the exchange. And while I know it is so much easier said than done, this means that we must suspend our desire for acceptance and adulation—for outstandingness and outcome—and focus solely on letting generative energy flow through us. As modern dance innovator Martha Graham famously told choreographer Agnes de Mille about this force, "It is not your business to determine how good it is nor how valuable nor how it compares with other expressions. It is your business to keep it yours clearly and directly, to keep the channel open. You do not even have to believe in yourself or your work. You have to keep yourself open and aware to the urges that motivate you. Keep the channel open."

There are ways to try to outsmart the Demon of Judgment. You may decide to never look at any online comments about your work. You can refuse to read reviews. Or you can take the advice that filmmaking iconoclast John Waters shared in *LitHub*: "Read the bad ones once, the good ones twice, and put them all away and never look at them again." Do whatever you have to do to maintain the conviction to keep going—to create for the sake of creating and to flow past the fear. There are no guarantees that what you make will be celebrated in your lifetime, or even in the years following your mortal demise. There is no way to control how anyone will react to your offerings.

Human approval is unpredictable and fickle as fuck.

One way I've learned to break the Demon of Judgment's curse—at least momentarily—is to actively shift my attention from what I call low frequency concerns to high frequency intentions. It's normal to desire things like approval, critical success, money, and praise, and there's nothing wrong with entertaining those material, lower vibration urges in moderation. But when I find myself fixating on such things and getting anxious about whether or not I'll achieve these ego-driven outcomes, I now take a beat and focus on being present to the higher energies surrounding my work. I remind myself that I'm creating to forge connection, to honor Spirit, and to live my true purpose. What I make is an expression of my love. And making is ultimately about giving, not getting.

Fear of other people's opinions is a demonic delicacy, and unfortunately, I've thus far found it impossible to starve my judgment demon entirely. (And hey, a demon's gotta eat.) But I've met it enough times on my path to now not be totally cowed by the encounter. I say, "Hello again," with a sigh and a smile, then toss some trepidation treats its way and let it nosh on some toothsome doom for a while.

But while that dude is nibbling, I take extra care to also nourish my relationship to Spirit. I remind myself that the artistic elixir I've been brewing is being created for the sole purpose of feeding *that* magical connection here and now. I tell myself that if I can be just 1 percent more excited and curious and awe-led than I am fearful—just 1 percent more focused on spiritual service rather than on trying to impress—then that's all I need to keep my cauldron of Creative Force on a nice, steady simmer.

And I know that the divine finds my attempts to be highly appetizing, and that anything I create in the present moment is enough to please its spectral palette. I'm a chef to the celestial, and my very making is a banquet for the gods.

MYSTIC GIFTS

There's no question that the act of making can be a challenge, and some may argue that if creativity were easy, it wouldn't be worth doing in the first place. Maybe so. But if we only focus on the travails and frustrations of the creative process, we risk relinquishing our delight and becoming untethered from our magic. Our work becomes labored and depleting if we allow our demons to run the show, and this can cause us to succumb to paranoia and a stance of permanent defensiveness. It's far more pleasurable—not to mention productive—to reframe our making as a net-positive experience, and to assume that Creative Source wants us to have a good time while we do it. I take inspiration from astrologer and author Rob Brezsny, who wrote a book called *Pronoia Is the Antidote for Paranoia: How the Whole World Is Conspiring to Shower You with Blessings*. As Brezsny writes, "The actual term 'pronoia' was coined in 1976 by Grateful Dead lyricist John Perry Barlow, who defined it as 'the suspicion that the universe is a conspiracy on your behalf.'"

Lucky for us, there truly are as many boons that one may encounter as there are banes in the Land of Magic-Making. These are great, mystic gifts that we may make use of whenever we wish. It is my belief that Spirit does not want us to be miserable in our making. And so it has been sure to provide us with plenty of support to lighten our load, encourage our imaginative enterprises, and buoy beauty.

In his groundbreaking book *The Hero with a Thousand Faces*, mythologist Joseph Campbell writes about "supernatural aid" that the hero may receive on their journey. Campbell says that often this assistance is bestowed by an older, wiser being like a crone, a fairy godmother, a wizard, or a hermetically inclined hermit. There are endless examples of this: Obi-Wan Kenobi giving Luke Skywalker his lightsaber in *Star Wars*. Oz's good witch Glinda gifting Dorothy the ruby slippers. In *The Fellowship of the Ring*, Galadriel heaps the titular fellows with a veritable treasure trove including an Elfstone, Elven cloaks, brooches, belts, a rope, a bow, and a silver nut from a sacred tree. Sometimes the mystic gift is given by a beloved, such as Vasilisa the Beautiful receiving a magic doll of protection from her dying mother or Theseus being gifted his lover Ariadne's a-maze-ing thread.

I am very fortunate to have people in my life who have given me some rather supernaturally supportive gifts. On my primary altar are beeswax candles from my friends Ben and Sochi, an Artemis statue given to me by my parents, a carved wooden owl from my friend and mentor Susan, and a bottle of sand collected from around the world that I received from a lovely reader during my last book tour. My walls are festooned with painted magic sigils gifted to me by my friend Jesse and my bookshelf is now watched over by a clay golem from Prague that was given to me by my friend William Kiesel, one of the world's foremost experts on grimoires.

I have also given myself innumerable mystic gifts, often in the form of talismanic jewelry or splendid garments that bring out the Magician in me. Today as I write these words, I'm wearing a skeleton key pendant with the word *MYSTERY* carved into its stem. It reminds me to embrace the unfamiliar and the uncharted as I venture forth.

In each of the aforementioned cases, the objects in question may have pragmatic functions as weapons or tools of a sort, but they also represent an intangible yet infinitely powerful gift: encouragement. The word *courage* comes from the Latin *cor*, meaning "heart." In receiving these gifts, we heroes are assured that someone believes in us, and that we don't have to face the unknown alone. We are helped, and we are *heartened*.

And so, when considering our own magic-making, I think it is crucial to not only take demonic attendance but to also become intimately aware of the eleven-thousand-or-so divine gifts that are always present and ready to come to our creative aid—though for the purposes of page count, we'll be focusing on seven. Perhaps they have been sent by those multi-eyed, message-bringing angels, or by that mystical messenger Mercury himself. Or maybe you prefer to picture each gift being bestowed upon you like a magic jewel from a wizened hag's hand. Wherever they come from, just know that they are available for you to call upon and incorporate into your magical practice, now and forever.

You may use these mystic gifts as armor against any demons that appear, of course. They can be a sort of supernal subterfuge against the dark arts of doubt, distraction, and despair. But I recommend you try using them proactively, mindfully applying those that feel supportive to your current creative mission.

May you receive each gift without hesitation, and may you take heart in knowing the spirits are on your side.

The Gift of Play

One might assume that I'm a fan of lots of witchcraft podcasts since I'm the maker of one myself. In actuality, most of what I listen to in my downtime are comedy podcasts: *Las Culturistas, Conan O'Brien Needs a Friend, The Bald and the Beautiful with Trixie and Katya, Blocks w/ Neal Brennan* . . . the list goes on. I may not be a comedian, but I'm a diehard *Saturday Night Live* fan and appreciate any sketch show or stand-up special that makes me laugh my ass off. I also love learning about wit-craft. It's fascinating to hear about the art of constructing jokes, and I'm inspired by how great comedians can alchemize fear and discomfort and vulnerability into a golden laughter tonic for the audience to imbibe. As someone who can get stuck in her head a lot, I'm also grateful for anything that helps me take myself less seriously. Conan O'Brien is fond of saying, "I worship at the altar of silliness." I realize he's saying this metaphorically, but actively embracing the playful, silly side of Spirit has made my creativity flow more easefully and has made my life better overall.

There is a misconception that the act of creativity must always be a solemn pursuit. One pictures the scientist working into the wee hours in their laboratory, the playwright grinding away at their script, the robed priestess leading ritual in resolute, booming tones. But while it's true that there is hard work involved in making things, often the most profound creations are the result of playfulness, spontaneity, and the embrace of happy "accidents." The most magical makers I know often employ an approach of what I call reverent irreverence—a paradoxical attitude of caring deeply while not taking stuff too seriously. In his 1957 essay "Experimental Music," John Cage wrote that when he composes, he aims to have "a purposeful purposelessness or a purposeless play." By relinquishing some measure of control, we keep our imaginations supple, we welcome the unpredictable, and our work is more adaptable to the unknown. Striking a balance of seriousness and playfulness is one of the many ways the Magician balances opposite energies with grace and turns them into something exciting and new.

Like many children of the 1980s, I'm a lifelong Jim Henson fan. I consider him to be a sort of bodhisattva of the fantastical, and I believe his many creations to be sacred in their absurdity. Between his groundbreaking work on *Sesame Street* and his tremendous creation of the Muppets and *Fraggle Rock* (not to mention two of my favorite films, *The Dark Crystal* and *Labyrinth*), Henson was an enormously prolific Magic Maker by any measure. He certainly had to have exceptionally high levels of ambition to turn his homemade puppets into an entertainment empire. But he truly loved his work, and he believed one of the secrets to his success was that through it all, he maintained his childlike sense of wonder. In his own words: "The most sophisticated people I know—inside they're all children . . . We never really lose a certain sense we had when we were kids." It's the blending of these two forces—hard work and unfettered play—that makes marvelous things happen. Muppeteer Jerry Juhl de-

THE GIFT OF PLAY

scribed Henson as having had "a whim of steel," and I can think of no better words to describe the steadfast playfulness that is such a boon to the creative process.

Play is magic. It gives our work a spaciousness, providing a landing pad for the weird and wondrous. By surrendering our need for perfection (which, as we've established, is a demonic illusion anyway), our edges soften, our rigidity loosens, and so our capacity to receive expands. It also helps stave off negativity. One of my favorite pieces of magical advice I've ever gotten is that the best way to get rid of an unwanted ghost is to flash it and laugh. Laughter is a warding spell—it protects us from harm and attracts good energy.

Likewise, embracing "mistakes" can be a form of glitch witchery, because these unplanned occurrences can take us in new creative directions. In 1943, chemical engineer James Wright was trying to invent a replacement for rubber when he mixed boric acid with silicone oil. He tossed the resulting gooey substance onto the floor and discovered that it bounced—and toy sensation Silly Putty, as it came to be called, was born. Similarly, when David Lynch was filming a scene of his 1990 TV show *Twin Peaks*, the reflection of set dresser Frank Silva accidentally showed up in a mirror. Rather than nixing the shot, Lynch liked Silva's look so much that he ended up creating an entire menacing character named Bob out of the moment, and he included Silva in subsequent episodes. Bob became one of the most iconically terrifying elements of the show, and *Rolling Stone* would eventually rank him as number five in their "40 Greatest TV Villains of All Time" list. Wright could have thrown his bouncy putty away and Lynch could have left Silva's accidental mirror apparition on the cutting room floor. Instead, they were open to the magic of spontaneity and recognized its strange gifts. Staying loose and playful while we work shifts us from a state of What Is to What If.

If you've ever taken an improvisational comedy class, then you'll be familiar with the notion of "yes and." In her book *Bossypants*, Tina Fey explains this concept:

> The first rule of improvisation is AGREE. Always agree and SAY YES. When you're improvising, this means you are required to agree with whatever your partner has created. So if we're improvising and I say, "Freeze, I have a gun," and you say, "That's not a gun. It's your finger. You're pointing your finger at me," our improvised scene has ground to a halt. But if I say, "Freeze, I have a gun!" and you say, "The gun I gave you for Christmas! You bastard!" then we have started a scene because we have AGREED that my finger is in fact a Christmas gun.
>
> Now, obviously in real life you're not always going to agree with everything everyone says. But the Rule of Agreement reminds you to "respect what your partner has created" and to at least start from an open-minded place. Start with a YES and see where that takes you.

By just going with the scene as it spontaneously unfolds and ping-ponging off each other's ideas, improvisational actors often manage to conjure an experience that is entertaining for the audience, though largely unplanned.

Many of the most lauded sketch comedians have a background in improv. Though they may have been naturally funny growing up, they became great artists through learning the art of deep, collaborative play. And many of them were part of such Chicago improv institutions as the Second City and ImprovOlympic (today known as iO), the latter of which was co-run by Del Close and Charna Halpern.

THE GIFT OF PLAY

Comedy nerds will recognize Del Close as the teacher of a staggering list of sketch comedy icons that includes John Belushi, Bill Murray, Dan Aykroyd, Gilda Radner, Mike Myers, Chris Farley, Tina Fey, Amy Poehler, Bob Odenkirk, Amy Sedaris, and Stephen Colbert. In 1980 and 1981, he had two stints as the *Saturday Night Live* "house metaphysician," a term that encompasses the philosophical coaching style he brought to the cast. But at his core, he believed that improv was an art unto itself and not merely a means for ideating scripted comedy, which was how many were using it during his time. He is perhaps best known for "The Harold," a long-form style of improv he developed with Halpern, and which made use of various improvisational exercises to build an entire show on the spot.

What many don't know about Close is that he was a practicing Wiccan, and he incorporated several of the magical techniques he learned from his Toronto coven into his comedic craft. By his account, the coven also helped him kick his cocaine habit via a banishing ritual, and its efficacy left a big impression on him. As he told *Chicago* magazine in 1987:

> Whatever you want to banish from your life, you symbolize; it's this rock in one hand and a candle in the other; and you use the energy of the group to imprint on these objects . . . So it was not a matter of witchcraft works, ooga booga. I had accepted the images of the universe of the pagans, to the point I was allowing [them] to work in me.

On Halloween 1982, Close did a public ritual at a downtown Chicago art gallery during which he cast a magic circle and then led the audience in an invocation to an imaginary god. Halpern was in attendance, and they didn't hit it off at first, as Halpern admonished Close for not doing enough to protect the attendees against evil spirits. However, the following year she would invite him to teach a workshop at ImprovOlympic, which she was then running. He decided to try to stick it to her by teaching his invocation to the students, but this time Halpern was impressed with the results. "The Invocation" is considered one of Close's signature improv exercises. Halpern, Close, and Kim "Howard" Johnson's improv bible, *Truth in Comedy*, describes it as "an exercise where students invoke a 'god' that they create themselves from their own group vision . . . This god and his or her characteristics, then influences the scenes which follow." In "The Invocation," the group first describes the god, then talks directly to it, and then worships it, using improvised statements that address the god through a series of "It" then "You" then "Thou" statements (one wonders if Close was a fan of Martin Buber's). In some versions, the players take things a step further and become the god, using "I" statements thereafter. The idea here is that by riffing on an idea and approaching it playfully from different perspectives, it can materialize into something real.

Clearly with this exercise, Close has taken reverentially irreverent liberties with the magical language he learned from his coven. But I'm certain that Wicca's forefather Gerald Gardner wouldn't have minded: in *Witchcraft Today* he writes, "witches are consummate leg-pullers; they are taught it as part of their stock-in-trade." Some may debate whether Close truly believed in witchcraft or simply found it to be an effective means of accessing the state of openness that improv demands. We do know that "he would take out his little pentagram and put it on his chest before he performed because he said the stage was a sacred space," as Stephen Colbert relayed on *Mike Birbiglia's Working It Out* podcast. We also know that he had a Pagan priest and priestess do the Ritual of the Four Ele-

THE GIFT OF PLAY

ments as part of the send-off celebration that his friends arranged for him during his final days at Illinois Masonic Hospital in February 1999. But more importantly, we know of the incredible impact Close's teachings left on his students, and on the world at large. In *The Funniest One in the Room: The Lives and Legends of Del Close*, Kim "Howard" Johnson includes actor Howard Hesseman's eulogy:

> All the great Masters can make you see with your ears and hear with your eyes and stuff like that, but Del makes you speak with your skin. He takes you into a space—THE Space—where you, all of you, all of your being, your history, your dreams, your neural impulses—can work all at once, without fear of contradiction. And no matter what comes out, no matter how scary it gets, you feel safe. No matter what happens, no matter how confused it feels, no matter how crazy it gets, no matter how wrong it seems, no matter how little sense it makes . . . Relax. Del Close has been there and back, and taught us everything he could. Relax. Follow your impulse. Del will always support you. Thanks, Del.

Certainly, Close was a special being. He was a gifted teacher who made his students feel brave enough and safe enough to enter a state of creative free fall on stage, and to become their boldest artistic selves. But that freedom is something that anyone can access. I believe that Spirit has a sense of humor. It doesn't want us to be joyless, inflexible, or bored. And so I try to remember that in my own nobly foolish attempts to create.

For what it's worth, the Gift of Play has also proven to be one of the most powerful means of protest and activism. In a 2021 *Slate* article titled "Don't Fight the Fascists. Laugh at Them," Sophia A. McClennen and Srdja Popovic write, "The best counter to the aggressive and delusional anger of the right is creative, playful, often humorous counterprotests. Strange as it may seem, there is a lot of evidence that proves that the lighthearted, fun-loving, ironic challenges to Nazis are more effective than anger." In their book, *Pranksters vs. Autocrats*, Popovic and McClennen detail how "laughtivism"—or intentionally funny protest actions such as clowning, using giant puppets, or chanting silly slogans—has been an effective means of helping to deflate authoritarian regimes. In my favorite example, they write about the 2007 Burmese "Panties for Peace" campaign against a military junta known for its violence against women. After a particularly brutal crackdown against the Saffron Revolution protests, activists in Burma (now Myanmar) took a new tactic that played upon the Burmese superstition that female undergarments can curse men and drain them of their power. For nearly a year, Burmese women and other sympathizers around the world mailed their panties to local embassies and military members. Though it seemed silly, it was highly effective: "With no clear answer to the creative provocation of these 'laughtivists,' the Burmese ruling generals *just abstained from reacting*." The usually retaliatory, violent regime became paralyzed, whether due to their genuine belief in the panties' nefarious nether-regional powers or just as an attempt to save face by ignoring the debasing gesture. Regardless of why it worked, the result was that the activists become more confident, their momentum grew, and their movement expanded.

Playfulness is deceptively powerful. It might feel goofy at times, but it's a fruitful goofiness. If we remember to stop taking shit so seriously, we just might find ourselves conjuring some seriously magical stuff. When my work is feeling stagnant or uninspired, I summon the spirit of

THE GIFT OF PLAY

silliness to my circle. I ask it to take the reins for a while and follow whatever impulses feel fun and frisky. Calling upon the Gift of Play invites in sacred trickery and reckless splendor. It reminds us that at our core, we are all just children playing make-believe, which is a ridiculous, magnificent notion. Make. Believe. Make a mess. Make it up as you go along. Tickle your own funny bone. Amuse the muses.

Crack up the cosmos, and you'll break through your creative blocks.

The Gift of Collaboration

Another myth about creativity is that it is always a solitary activity. This book has been written by me and my name is on the cover of it. And it's true that I've needed a great deal of time by myself to work on it. In that sense, putting these words on these pages has been done by me "alone," though as we've well established, I've been getting much assistance from the nonphysical world as well. By the time this book finds its way to you, however, it will have been refined by my collaborations with an entire creative coven. Its contents will have shape-shifted based on feedback and notes from my editor and copy editors and several other readers besides, and it will be a different book than if I'd shown it to no one and published it myself. Furthermore, many of the ideas I've teased out here are the fruiting bodies of years of collaborations between friends, mentors, colleagues, and teachers, not to mention the work of all the Magic Makers this book seeks to be in dialogue with. So while I believe we must celebrate our own enchanted efforts, it's equally important to acknowledge and credit those who have influenced our crafting.

THE GIFT OF COLLABORATION

Sometimes the Gift of Collaboration is more like cross-pollination, as it can form a web of like-minded people exchanging inspirations and influences, whether directly or by proxy. Musician Brian Eno coined the term "scenius" to counteract the idea of the solitary genius. As Eno describes it, a scenius is a collective intelligence that bubbles up between creative people who inspire and influence each other. They needn't be working in the same medium. For example, some proclaim Johnny Rotten as the genius who kicked off the punk movement of the 1970s. But not only was he collaborating with his Sex Pistols bandmates, they all drew inspiration from fashion designer Vivienne Westwood and her London boutique, which she co-owned with Sex Pistols band manager Malcolm McLaren. Furthermore, the Sex Pistols' impactful collaged album art was created by Jaime Reid, a Pagan activist artist who referred to himself as a "socialist druid." And, of course, the Sex Pistols were also crossing streams with many other punk musicians during the time, including the Clash, the Buzzcocks, the Ramones, Patti Smith, MC5, and Iggy and the Stooges. While any of the individual artists in the scene may be heralded as geniuses, the collective scenius created punk overall. As writer Austin Kleon puts it, "Genius is an *egosystem*, scenius is an *ecosystem*."

There is, however, a truly magical thing that happens when two or more people intentionally choose to collaborate on a specific project. When there is enough trust and unguardedness between them, the separation between their consciousnesses begins to evaporate, and their creation becomes greater than the sum of its parts. Their individual egos slide aside for a bit, and the makers seem to temporarily operate as one. In the aforementioned improv book *Truth in Comedy*, Halpern, Close, and Johnson refer to this as "the group mind":

When a team of improvisors pays close attention to each other, hearing and remembering everything, and respecting all that they hear, a group mind forms . . . [W]hen a group mind is achieved, its members have a very strong sense of the group as an entity of its own, and connects with its feelings and requirements.

They go on to discuss the phenomenological capabilities that their improv group has experienced when all members are perfectly present and in sync:

Scenes created have turned out to be prophetic, and ESP has actually occurred on stage. Players are able to speak simultaneously, at a normal rate of speed, saying the exact same thing, word for word. Some teams became oracles on stage, answering the great questions of the universe, one word at a time, leaving audiences chilled and astonished.

In occult and art circles this phenomenon is sometimes referred to as "The Third Mind," popularized by the writer William S. Burroughs and the artist Brion Gysin via their 1977 book of the same name. This book collected many of the collaborative collages, texts, and graphics they created using their signature cut-up technique, and so "third mind" is a term many people think originated with them. They were, in fact, borrowing the language from early twentieth-century self-help writer Napoleon Hill's 1937 book, *Think and Grow Rich*. In it, Hill writes about the "Master Mind" principle, which is his idea that collaboration between the right combination of people can create magnificent things that none of them could have come up with alone. He encourages readers to form a

THE GIFT OF COLLABORATION

Master Mind alliance with someone or several someones, and in the original text, he describes the Master Mind as "the coordination of knowledge and effort, in a spirit of harmony, between two or more people, for the attainment of a definite purpose." Hill also writes: "No two minds ever come together without, thereby, creating a third, invisible, intangible force which may be likened to a third mind."

Paul McCartney and John Lennon are a prime example of this. During the decade they worked together as the Beatles, they created some of the most brilliant music ever written (along with bandmates George Harrison and Ringo Starr, of course). Though music-making is perhaps the clearest example of divine collaboration, this gift extends into many other fields as well. Biologists James Watson, Francis Crick, and the shamefully overlooked Rosalind Franklin together discovered the double helix structure of DNA. Chicago Bulls teammates Michael Jordan and Scottie Pippen developed an almost uncanny way of supporting each other's plays during their legendary games. Comedic duos from Abbott and Costello to *Broad City*'s Ilana Glazer and Abbi Jacobson exemplify this particular alchemy; Bowen Yang and Matt Rogers have referred to how they become "one mind" when they collaborate on their podcast and other projects. And the Wachowski siblings and the Coen brothers are responsible for creating some of the most riveting films of all time (and filmmaking in general is one of the most collaborative art forms there is). When kindred spirits mingle their attention and point it toward the same goal, the work that results seems to come from a separate entity altogether.

I'm particularly interested in visual artists who collaborate on the same artworks, such as Gilbert & George, Hilma's Ghost, and Ryan M. Pfeiffer + Rebecca Walz. When viewing pieces rendered by these duos, it is impossible to tell who contributed what, as the art they've created together has its own aesthetic sensibility. In 2023, I interviewed painters Tino Rodriguez and Virgo Paraiso on *The Witch Wave*. They both have thriving solo careers, but their romantic partnership and mutual interest in mystical imagery evolved into a shared art practice as well. Together they create paintings of winged hybrid beings and intricately detailed Surrealist skulls that seem to be made of a dizzying flurry of flora and fauna. I asked them what it felt like to collaborate on the same piece, and Paraiso told me, "Part of the awareness is that we are all the same energy, and two energies together create a greater energy." Rodriguez agreed, interjecting, "We create a third artist, and it's really exciting . . . It's like our conversation love piece. Yeah, it's a lot of fun. Also, it's half the work that I have to do on a piece, so it's great!" Paraiso responds, "It's great, because we get it done—half as difficult and twice as beautiful so what could be better than that?"

Melding your mind with another's can magnify the magic in more ways than one.

The Gift of Divine Timing

Time is a mystery, elastic and electric. Depending on what we are doing, some hours feel like entire years, and some seem to whiz by in mere seconds. When we are in creative flow, time seems to both stop and stretch on infinitely, almost as if it expands to contain the right amount of energy we need to materialize our magic into something concrete. We may fantasize about having endless time to work, but the vast majority of us are fitting our most sacred creative acts between the other more mundane demands of our lives. It can feel overwhelming when our demons of distraction and scarcity trick us into thinking we'll never be able to focus on our work or bring it to completion. This is when the Gift of Divine Timing can be a great ally.

Across the globe, the way most of us now organize time is linear, following the twelve-month Gregorian calendar. This has certainly been useful for scheduling purposes, as well as for structuring such capitalist-driven goals as labor organization and profit generation. However, this dating system is rather arbitrary, and it is now a palimpsest of relatively recent religious and civic holidays mapped on top of a much older planetary clock. Many pre-Christian calendars were and are lunar-based, including those devised by Jewish and Hindu peoples and those followed throughout East Asia. And many holy days followed an agrarian calendar, marking the sun's placement in the sky and the seasonal growth cycles. People across the world have long considered these shifts of heavenly bodies sacred, worthy of attention and celebration. Incorporating this sense of divine timing into my magic-making life has been profound for me, as it connects me to a far more natural—and supernatural—rhythm.

As someone who was raised Jewish and is now also a practicing Pagan, I find it liberating to follow my own calendars coiled within the "universal" calendar. I celebrate the "new year" multiple times over the 365¼ days we're allotted annually on this planet, each with its own significance. There's January 1 to be marked, of course, but then the Jewish New Year of Rosh Hashana in early fall, followed by Samhain—or Witches' New Year—at the end of October. I also love celebrating the early winter Lunar New Year festival with my Asian friends and neighbors. Though each New Year holiday has its own specific history and cultural context, these moments also present an opportunity for a clean slate and to begin anew.

In modern Pagan practice, we celebrate eight sabbats, or seasonal holidays, per the Wheel of the Year. Though some think this calendar follows ancient Celtic agrarian holidays, it is in fact a postmodern mash-up of several European, pre-Christian seasonal holidays as well as solstice and equinox celebrations. Even the naming of the Pagan holidays Litha, Ostara, and Mabon wasn't done until 1974 by Wiccan writer Aidan Kelly. Names aside, the practice of pausing to celebrate seasonal shifts and take note of the cycles of birth, growth, death, and rebirth has helped

THE GIFT OF DIVINE TIMING

me redefine my relationship to the planet and honor my own creative cycles in turn.

There are those who believe that one must write every single day or publish a book a year. If you are one of those people and that works for you, that's fabulous! No need to change a thing. However, I've come to learn that my creativity has its own seasonality, just as the earth does. There are periods of potential, when I'm jotting down lots of inspiring fragments and planting seeds for possible new projects to see what sprouts. There are periods of joyful fertility, when I'm gestating those ideas and then providing creative water and sunlight so their tender shoots can flourish (as well as pulling out any invasive demon weeds before they ruin my crop!). The harvesting period is often a satisfying one, as I'm able to gather up what I've grown in a big bouquet and, in some instances, offer it to others in hopes that they'll find pleasure in it too. And then there are the inevitable and oh-so-important fallow periods. These are necessary times of rest and rejuvenation, which many mistake for creative blocks. Just as the land needs time to replenish its nutrients, we need time to replenish our magic. Following the Wheel of the Year in my spiritual life has helped me be far less anxious about the so-called inconsistent rhythms of my creative work. I now recognize that each part of the cycle has its purpose and so there needn't be any self-flagellation during bouts of low-to-no output. It's *all* productive time, divinely guided by the spinning of celestial orbs.

Still, I realize we don't always have the luxury of being driven by our individual time engines. Whether we need to be accountable to an external force, like an impending art opening, or an internal one, like a self-imposed drop date for an album or zine, certain types of work require a measure of planning. In these instances, I find it helpful to align project milestones with the solar holy days when possible, such as doing a fiery brainstorming session on Imbolc to honor Brigid, the Celtic goddess of the creative flame. I know other Magic Makers who choose specific dates for project deadlines or releases based on preferred planetary correspondences, benefic astrological days, dates with personal numerological significance, or the feast day of a favorite deity. There are those who refuse to release a project during a Mercury retrograde period, though in the context of creation, I've been taught that this is a good time for reflecting on/revising a current project or revisiting/resurrecting an old or historically relevant one, and not an overall ill-fated time as some people misconstrue it. We can also combine different divine timing modalities and engage with the spiritual energy that collects around civic holidays. In one of my recent Occult Office Hours sessions, my client planned to finish the first draft of a manuscript on Juneteenth of the following year since her book is about reparations and ancestral healing from racism, and the holiday had spiritual resonance for her. We can conjure our own calendars and sanctify our own schedules.

That said, creative occultification isn't only an annual affair. There is plenty of monthly magic to be made. I like to remind myself that the words *month* and *moon* are ancient relatives, and working with the monthly lunar phases has been a game changer for me. In modern witchcraft we believe that the moon is not only a mirror for sunlight but a signal booster for our inner energies as well. Just as the oceanic tides ebb and flow with the moon's pull, so too do our magical tides. Therefore, specific magical activities have become associated with each part of a lunation.

The new moon is believed to be a time of setting new intentions, beginning projects, making a fresh start.

THE GIFT OF DIVINE TIMING

The waxing phase is a time of growth and cultivation. Just as witches cast spells for things they want to manifest and increase during a waxing phase, Magic Makers may choose to focus on adding to their mural, movie, or model during this time.

The full moon is often considered a moment of completion and release, thus an ideal time to send off a final draft or schedule a public reading, screening, or project launch.

The waning moon is associated with decreasing and turning inward, and thus is a good time for editing or refining a project—or for banishing a specific demon that's been tripping us up.

And the dark moon is a phase of turning inward, doing any sort of shadow work that can help bring about healing, or simply taking time to rest.

One may choose to work on a project, or a certain aspect of a project, from new moon to full moon, or even for an entire lunation when appropriate. I tend to work with a lunar phase when it feels most spiritually supportive and most relevant for my craft and my Craft.

In her book *Daily Magic*, Judika Illes writes, "The year is filled with magical dates, if only we know when and how to celebrate them. Rather than feeling oppressed for time, let's savor it, and maximize the blessings and opportunities afforded by these days of power." By working with the Gift of Divine Timing, we see that any day, any phase, and any season is a potentially powerful one that can aid us in our making.

The Gift of Place

Humans have long believed certain sites are imbued with holiness, and many have gone to great lengths to visit these places. Some of the most famous pilgrimages include the annual Hajj that Muslims make to Mecca, the Catholic Camino de Santiago trail in Spain, and Japan's Shikoku route of eighty-eight Buddhist temples. Trips to sacred sites like the Giza pyramids or Jerusalem's Wailing Wall are at the top of many bucket lists, whether visitors are seeking an architectural marvel, a memorial of historical events, an experience of spiritual transcendence, or some combination thereof. Places call to us. They stir us from our everyday environments and invite us to engage with the world in an altered state.

Though marquee destinations like those mentioned above get a lot of attention, a pilgrimage can be made to any place on the planet. It can be to a temple at the top of a misty mountain, or to an empty barn down the road whose beams creak with secrets. And unless there's an imposed dress code at a specific site, you can usually come as you are and wear whatever you feel comfortable in. Pilgrims don't only wear buckled hats

THE GIFT OF PLACE

or white robes, and they don't need to follow any particular religion. Etymologically, the word *pilgrim* means "stranger" or "foreigner," but it traces back to the Latin *peregre* or "from abroad," whose root words mean "beyond country," or "beyond the field." Any of us can go beyond the field of the familiar by simply stepping outside our domiciles and into a realm of discovery. Doing so can deeply influence our creative magic by heightening our senses and our extrasensory perception. Whether our wanders lead us to man-made marvels or ones sculpted by nature's hand, we come face-to-face with the unusual. We may be strangers when we arrive, but we leave having made the acquaintance of awe.

Sometimes these journeys start off with a pragmatic intention. A trip to a place of interest can be massively helpful for research purposes, as my excursions to Salem, Edinburgh, and the Witchcraft Collection at Cornell University were when I was writing my witch-centric books. But these pilgrimages operate on another level if you let them: spirits begin to whisper in your ears, telling you stories and revealing secret signs. The augury skills you've honed will be put to good use as you suddenly decide to pop into a beckoning shop with sun-stained curtains or make an unplanned visit to a local grave. If you feel like a place is inviting you to spend some time there, go. These are destinations of desire, of destiny. You owe it to yourself and to Spirit to step away from your usual spaces and find out what the Gift of Place would like to show you. The only rule is to treat these trips and these places with respect.

Many makers have taken inspiration from the places they have traveled to and through. Jack Kerouac's *On the Road*, John Steinbeck's *Travels with Charley*, Cheryl Strayed's *Wild*, and other trip-centric tales can be read as travelogues and spiritual memoirs—and these are often interchangeable taxonomies. Musician Tori Amos has long used travel as a means for song-seeking. As she told *The New York Times* in 2012, "There are ways to stimulate being prolific, and part of that is making pilgrimages, and being open to listening, changing up the routine." One of her cross-country expeditions turned into the 2002 album *Scarlet's Walk*, which Amos refers to as a "sonic novel," and is about a woman who travels to all fifty states to excavate the soul of America post-9/11. In a 2002 radio interview on *The Kevin & Bean Show*, she explained, "[T]here was a seed that was planted after the eleventh, which was that people started seeing America as a soul, as a being . . . She was a being, as the Native Americans have always thought of her, she's a living essence who has a past that goes back before, you know, the colonists."

Setting forth on a creative expedition is a wonderful way to collaborate with the Gift of Place, provided you tread lightly on this new-to-you territory. You are not there to stake your claim on it, but rather to learn what magic it may decide to share with you if you are lucky. You may be an intrepid explorer indeed, but you must also always remain a gentle guest.

All of that said, there is a great tradition of makers who don't stray very far to find the Gift of Place. In 1996, shamanic poet, John "Crow" Constable had a vision wherein a goose revealed to him the secret history of his neighborhood of Southwark, London. Much of this vision centered around Crossbones Graveyard, which had been a burial ground for medieval prostitutes who were known as the Winchester Geese. There are also bodies of an estimated fifteen thousand paupers and other people of "ill-repute" deemed unworthy to be buried in hallowed church grounds. Constable's vision from the goose led him to write a cycle of poems, plays, and stories known as *The Southwark Mysteries*, and to hold a series of vigils for these and other "outcast dead" at seven p.m. on the twenty-third of every month. These vigils have been performed continuously

THE GIFT OF PLACE

since June 2004, and I had the honor of attending one in October 2024. It was one of the most profoundly moving and magical evenings of incantation and ritual that I've ever been part of, and if you have the chance to experience it yourself, do not hesitate. Thanks to the work of Constable, his collaborators, and the Bankside Open Spaces Trust, Crossbones Graveyard has been turned into a living shrine and a lovely community garden of remembrance—and it has even been blessed by the Dean of Southwark Cathedral. By being open to the local magic surrounding him, Constable not only generated a gorgeous body of work and a ritualized performance series, but he helped transmute a site of neglect and rejection into a space of beauty, sanctuary, and intergenerational healing.

Alan Moore has also found deep inspiration very close to home. Though he has written such fantastical graphic novel masterpieces as *Watchmen* and *From Hell*, he has focused his more recent novels *Voice of the Fire* and *Jerusalem* on his hometown of Northampton, England, where he was born and still lives. Each novel spans centuries, a veritable layer cake of lore and historical imaginings. As a self-declared magician, Moore is intimately aware of the interlacing of the immaterial and material realms. He's cited philosopher Guy Debord's idea of "psychogeography" as an inspiration for this work, which Debord defined as "the study of the precise laws and specific effects of the geographical environment, consciously organized or not, on the emotions and behavior of individuals." Moore describes it with his signature magical bent in a 2017 interview in *World Literature Today*:

> Psychogeography would be the understanding that in our experience of any place, it is the associations, the dreams, the imaginings, the history—it is all the information that is relevant to that place

which is what we experience when we talk about a place. *That* is what we're talking about. We're not actually talking about the hard bricks and mortar.

In other words, psychogeography posits that a place is a basin of energies and ideas that collect over time, a stratum of ghosts. It's interesting to consider this in light of so many different cultural beliefs in local spirits such as the Shinto kami, Indigenous American land spirits, and the Old Nordic landvættir. Ancient Romans also believed that every place had a guardian spirit, or *genius loci,* and an altar would be built to honor it and petition it for its protective powers.

The Gift of Place can also be found hyperlocally. As a Magic Maker, you have license to haunt your own house. By attuning yourself to be more sensitive to the energies of your home, you will likely find much magic tucked under its roof and draw strength from its spaces. One of my favorite magic power couples, the poet Robert Duncan and collagist Jess Collins (usually known simply as Jess), lived together for decades in San Francisco's Mission District. Though they occasionally collaborated on illustrated poetry pamphlets and the like, their old Victorian house was their true shared project. Inside they each had their own work spaces, room for guests, shelves stuffed with books, and walls teeming with art. Their poet friend Jack Spicer described his visits to their home in a letter (a copy of which I have hanging on our refrigerator): "Their house is built mainly of Oz books, a grate to burn wood, a second story for guests, paintings, poems, and miscellaneous objects of kindly magic. Cats." And he goes on to write: "It is possible if you have the humility to create a household and the sense to tread on all pieces of bad magic as soon as they appear."

THE GIFT OF PLACE

Duncan referred to his practice of intentional place-making as being a "householder" and wrote, "The household Jess and I have made I have seen as a lone holding in an alien forest-world, as a campfire about which we gatherd [sic] in an era of cold and night—a made-up thing in which participating we have had the medium of a life together." Surely we could all use homes that protect us from "bad magic," but as a queer couple living in mid-twentieth-century America, Duncan and Jess had double the incentive to create a sanctuary for themselves, so they could make their work, host their circle of mystical bohemian friends, and love in peace. Though they traveled on occasion for work and otherwise, their house was central to their respective art practices, as it was to the visitors who were fortunate enough to be welcomed into it.

There's no need to lament if you don't have the means or inclination to travel to distant destinations. Franz Kafka reminds us in his *Zürau Aphorisms* (1917–1918): "You do not need to leave your room. Remain sitting at your table and listen. Do not even listen, simply wait, be quiet, still and solitary. The world will freely offer itself to you to be unmasked, it has no choice, it will roll in ecstasy at your feet." The default state of *all* ground is hallowed.

Our surroundings directly affect our inner worlds. By getting to know their energies, spirits, and stories, we can generate work that honors them, and we can map new skeins of meaning upon them.

Go out. Go inward. The Gift of Place will be happy to meet you, wherever you happen to be.

The Gift of Handcraft

The prefix *chiro* means "hand," hence the art of palm reading being called *chiromancy* and *chiropractic* referring to a medical practice done with the hands. In Greek mythology, the centaur Chiron is a healer and teacher of medicine, herbalism, music, and archery, and his name roughly translates to "skilled with hands." Perhaps this is why in astrology, our Chiron placement is said to show us the parts of our lives where we have the most opportunity for healing. The Gift of Handcraft is a gift that shapes and transforms. It transmits subtle forces through the power of touch and tactility. It reminds us that in this so-called digital age, we rarely use our actual digits to make things. This gift beckons us away from our screens and asks us to make something, anything, using the power our hands hold within them.

The women in my maternal line are said to have magic in their hands. My great-grandma Fay, an immigrant from Chortkiv, Poland (now Ukraine), worked as a practical nurse at New York's Rockland State Hospital (the same psychiatric institution Allen Ginsberg references in his poem "Howl"). I'm told her hands had healing powers that she applied to her cooking, embroidery, gardening, and furniture building, and I like to imagine she used them to soothe her patients as well. When I was little, my grandma Trudy would rub her self-declared "healing hands" vigorously before placing them gently on my scrapes and headaches to ease the pain. My mom trained in Reiki to learn how to direct her own healing powers with more precision, and I sense that she applies this to her radiant paintings as well.

Belief in the magic of hands proliferates throughout the world, from various "laying on of hands" healing modalities to the many hand-shaped charms that people hang in their homes, cars, and around their necks for protection. A hand of Fatima, or hamsa, is a popular amulet derived from Middle Eastern and North African folk magic traditions that is believed to ward off the evil eye. I have a purple ceramic hamsa facing upward in our apartment, a stop sign to prevent negativity and harm from entering our space. Some choose to hang theirs pointing down to welcome abundance, and come to think of it, hanging a second one in the opposite direction would be a beautiful gesture—and an excellent way to symbolize the Magician's upward and downward hands as well. The Italian mano cornuta ("horned hand") and manu fica ("fig hand") are also worn to protect against negative energy. As gesticulations, these symbols today are sometimes considered rude or lewd, but in their original ancient Roman and Greek contexts, they were meant to distract and divert evil spirits.

Other historical examples of enchanted hand imagery span from the alchemical Hand of the Philosopher emblem to the macabre Hand of Glory spell of Western European folk magic—the latter being a hand severed from a hanged criminal that was then turned into a candle and was believed to either stop interlopers in their tracks or open any door, depending on the telling. In Martin Duffy's book on magical adornment, *The Devil's Raiments,* he writes the following about hands and gloves:

> In folk magic both the amuletic outstretched hand as in "five, the symbol at your door O" and the pentagram are considered protective. In particular the five points of the pentagram are assigned to the five fingers, thereby denoting the round of life, birth, maternity, wisdom and death; the hand becomes a mnemonic, enciphering the pentad as an expression of the natural cycles. Accordingly does the glove and the hand it fits, like the scabbard sheathing the sword, become symbolic of the generative organs and the feminine mysteries connected with the tides of creation and destruction. In this manner are hands a vehicle of "action" through which things may be shaped, moulded and crafted into being or broken apart in accordance with the design seen in the "minds eye," that is to say they are directed by head and heart.

Whenever I speak with craftspeople on my podcast, they inevitably talk about how doing work by hand takes more time, and how that slowing down is part of the magic. In an interview with esoteric embroidery artist Tessa Perlow, she described to me how even though stitching her meticulous beadwork is labor-intensive, she also finds it deeply soothing and meditative. When I look at her embroidered hoops shimmering with sigils, or her jaw-dropping decorative gloves fit for a High Priestess of the most flamboyant order, I know that I'm witnessing not only beauty but bewitchment. She was in a mesmeric state when she made them, and they are mesmerizing to behold.

The Gift of Handcraft is on offer for any maker, no matter if the bulk

THE GIFT OF HANDCRAFT

of your work is done with software, hardware, or another type of machinery. A lot of my writing is done on a laptop these days, but keeping notebooks is a crucial part of my practice. I find that writing by hand is effective when I'm first figuring out my piece's intentions or when I want to be in a more dreamy state of receptivity. This is especially helpful whenever I get stuck and feel my engagement waning. In these moments, I pull out a piece of paper and let myself trance out, jotting down any word fragments or images that float my way. I am also a compulsive doodler, and I have always found that drawing marginalia as I'm taking notes actually helps me focus more in classes or during meetings. Science has backed me up on this: in a 2009 University of Plymouth study on the link between doodling and memory recall, they found that doodlers performed 29 percent better than non-doodlers. Cartoonist Lynda Barry is evangelical about the direct connection between the brain and the hand, and as previously mentioned, she tells her students to simply doodle or write the alphabet when they get stuck. She also breaks through her own blocks by using a "decoy page." This is her name for a separate page she uses in tandem with the main page she's working on where she can doodle freely until more ideas arrive.

I also know of several makers whose primary work is analogue, yet who still like to pick up another handcraft on the side as a hobby, from knitting to whittling to weaving to baking. Tarot illustrator Cat Willett does stained glass just for fun, and my brilliant actor friend, Moira Stone, has fallen in love with pottery. Occult filmmaker and ethnomusicologist Harry Smith was obsessed with both the creation and collecting of cat's cradles and other forms of string art. I've recently rekindled my childhood love of paper marbling (thank you, Grandma Sonya), and I turn to it whenever I'm in need of using my hands for no other purpose than feeling the pleasure of swirling something into being that was not there before. The "success" of such practices is beside the point. Hands are made for making.

The Gift of Handcraft is an excellent Demon of Inertia repellent. Using the magic of our hands also heals us from our addiction to flawlessness by kicking the Demon of Perfectionism to the curb. Hands are not factories; they pulse with genuine mercurial power. As poet Diane di Prima recited on her outgoing answering machine message: "Let the hand shake. The line is a living thing."

A creative charge pours from our palms and flows from our fingertips. The secret of this Gift of Handcraft is that you receive it by giving it away.

The Gift of Eternity

It is very easy to get caught up in wanting immediate recognition for the things we create. The ego insists that who we are and what we make matters, and it searches everywhere for evidence to prove that it's right. This hunger is further catalyzed by our current age of instantaneous clicks, likes, viral videos, and meme-able sound bites. And for those of us whose incomes are, at least in part, tied to our creativity, the pressure to stay relevant can feel crushing. It makes us believe that it is terribly important to get attention and adulation now, *now*, NOW OR ELSE!

These moments of sweaty fretting are precisely when the Gift of Eternity can be summoned to reassure our creative selves that it's all going to be OK, because it *is* OK, and it always was. As far as gifts go, this one is quite difficult to describe, for it's as dense as a pinball and as ephemeral as a cloud of spun sugar. This gift is always with us, reminding us that we truly have no control over how our creations are received by the world, or when, or by whom. And it brings forth the Möbius strip of time, an infinite loop of magic like the one that crowns the Magician's head. "Time is not linear," it tells us. "Time is a construct. You can engage with it at any point you wish." (This gift sounds like it rather enjoys psychotropic substances, but hey, so might you.) Everything is happening always and all whens.

That's all well and good, you may be thinking, *but what does this actually MEAN, for gods' sakes?!*

It means that we can create with the knowledge that our work will absolutely affect the world somehow or *somewhen*, and so we can choose to direct our attention to other points on the timeline beyond just today.

Let me give you an example. Though I'm currently in my forties, I sometimes jokingly refer to myself as a Teen Crone. I like this phrase not only because its two components average out to my actual middle age, but because it speaks to the fact that I have always felt rather ageless. Or perhaps panphasic is more apt, because I have felt all ages at all times. When I was young, I was often described as an old soul due to my bookish nature and penchant for asking Big Questions, though as I grow older, I cleave more closely to the whimsy of my childhood self. My inner teen is never far behind me, all smirk and slouch and sparkle. And I see my senior self before me, moon-haired and cackling, full of stories and scars and celebration.

There's a photograph of me that's considered legendary in our family lore: I'm three years old, standing in front of a mirror and singing intently to my reflection, using my mom's curling iron as a microphone. I'm wearing purple Velcro shoes, blue jeans with a rainbow belt, a white shirt with red trim, and multicolored ribbon barrettes streaming through my hair. I am completely engrossed, seemingly unaware of the camera, lost in the deep concentration of entertaining nobody but myself and any Spirit watching.

I have always loved this photo, not only for my undeniable sense of style, but because it shows me in a pure moment of making for its own sake. Though I thankfully have a digital copy, for many years I lamented that I had lost the original, and I periodically sifted through storage boxes and drawers to try to relocate it. Then one day in April 2023—just as I was preparing an outline for this book, the photograph fluttered out from the pages of an old notebook, reminding me who I am and who I will always be: a maker of magic using whatever I can fashion into a wand. Even more uncanny, I noticed for the first time that in the background of the photo is a wicker love seat, and at the bottom of it, the wood is twisted into a sideways figure eight. I immediately placed the picture on my altar, thanking the Gift of Eternity for reminding me that one of the people I'm making things for is three-year-old, rainbow-spangled me, a tiny magician singing my heart out for no purpose but the pleasure of it.

I sometimes think that my job is to make my younger self excited and my crone self proud. I want their approval more than any other human's. They are my eternal inner audience, and I hope they enjoy my awestricken attempts at making artful work.

The Gift of Eternity has more to offer than our own self-satisfaction, though. It also lets us communicate with those who have passed and others who are yet to come. Creativity enables us to be in conversation with a possible contemporary audience, but also with those whose future lives we can only imagine. Our museums and libraries are full of works written by people from the past who couldn't have conceived of the impact their creations are still having on us, long after their worldly departure. Some of them enjoyed critical success in their time and some were excoriated. Some remained unknown or were otherwise roundly ignored. And in some cases, makers have chosen not to have their work released until after they were dead, believing the world needed time to catch up to their prescient ideas. Hilma af Klint stipulated that her Spirit-led abstract paintings were not to be shared until twenty years after her passing (they weren't shown publicly until several more decades after that). No matter if they experienced acknowledgment during their own lifetimes, the stellar aspirations of our creative predecessors live on in the present via their inventions, their writings, their paintings, their visions. Their magic-making extends far beyond their own brief moments of skeletal dwelling. As the poet H.D. writes in her collection *The Walls Do Not Fall*, our creative work is everlasting, because it is "magic, indelibly stamped."

I know this may feel like small comfort for those of us striving for acknowledgment, income, or survival in the here and now. But Spirit does not owe us comfort. Still, with the Gift of Eternity in our pockets, we might find motivation in knowing that our work will find the right audience at the right time if it is meant to, even if we are no longer around to witness it. What we make is for the ages, and it is useful to picture it being lovingly received by someone who has yet to be born.

This is true in the opposite direction as well. Experimental musician and artist Laurie Anderson told *The New York Times*, "Books are the way the dead talk to the living." I would add that any act of making is also a way that the living may talk to the dead. Our own creative actions can dialogue with any preexisting person whose work we may revere, question, or vehemently rail against. And they can also allow us to communicate with those who have passed, and offer them respect, love, and even retroactive healing. During the pandemic, I fell down a genealogy rabbit hole and learned a great deal more about my family history. This led me to doing more research into the rich history of Jewish folk magic and mythology that has been obscured from mainstream culture due to the multistrand effects of assimilation, antisemitism, and intergenerational trauma. Incorporating the magic of my people has profoundly influenced both my spiritual practice and creative work, and I believe it is also healing for my ancestors as well. They could only dream that their stories, suffering, loves, and losses could bear a fruiting metaphysical legacy many years after their own embodied existence. I sense that when they are remembered, and when the gossamer threads of their lives are woven into new creations, their souls are somehow both revivified and more at rest.

I get that same feeling when I invoke the names of my chosen and spiritual ancestors, from my favorite painter, Remedios Varo, to my favorite shape-shifter, David Bowie, to my favorite teacher, the poet Lois Hirshkowitz. Mentioning them here and in my other writing adds in some small way to their respective legacies. But they also live on in me and their many other admirers simply by having inspired us with their own work. Their creative magic manifested more creativity. Their lives have begotten more life.

I especially love when a maker's work becomes a kind of ancestor altar honoring those who have guided them in direct and indirect ways. Sometimes these altars are quite literal in form. When I view the altar installations of artist Amalia Mesa-Bains, it's clear that these works are not only for those of us lucky enough to visit them in the present but for her spiritual kin and kindred heroes across the veil. Her piece *Circle of Ancestors* is a prime example: it consists of seven chairs facing each other in a ring around a group of candles. Each seatback contains a portrait of someone meaningful to the artist, including her grandmother Mariana Escobedo Mesa; the pioneering twentieth-century Latina artist Judith F. Baca; and the seventeenth-century Mexican poet, composer, and nun Sor Juana Inés de la Cruz. There is also a chair for the artist herself. Mesa-Bains describes the piece as "a woman's circle. You can imagine it as a group of women sitting together, across time and distance, having a conversation, about what we went through. . . . it is also a private conversation, and you are an observer at best." Other pieces that blur the line between altar and artwork include Judy Chicago's *The Dinner Party* (1974–79) with its thirty-nine triangulated place settings for feminist spirits both mythical and historical, and Edgar Fabián Frías's *3 of Cups* (*Tatéi Neixa*) (2023), a fluorescent multimedia merging of tarot imagery and elements honoring the rain ceremony of their Wixárika ancestors.

But an art altar doesn't need to be crafted from solid objects. Rita Dove's 1980 poem "This Life" can be read as a verbal altar to her grandmother, told through the aphorisms and ideals she passed down to the poet. And Van Morrison's 1983 song "Rave On, John Donne" is a litany of creative ancestors he feels an artistic kinship to, including ecstatic poets William Butler Yeats, Walt Whitman, Omar Khayyam, and Kahlil Gibran. Works such as these are time machines. They allow spirit, maker, and receiver to slide between the signposts of Then and Now, and coexist in a Forever Realm.

This gift makes me think of such time-keeping triple deities as the Norse Norns, the Greek Moirai, and the Hindu Trimurti of Brahma, Vishnu, and Shiva. Each of these triads represents the impermanence of life, and the ways in which all stages in the growth cycle are happening at once. And I think of two-faced Janus, the Roman god of gateways, doorways, and new beginnings, from whom the word *January* is derived. As the god of transitions, he looks at what's behind and what's ahead at the exact same time, in a state of eternal enchantment.

I welcome the Gift of Eternity whenever I'm feeling anxious about any feedback my work might be subject to, or when my Demon of Judgment pops by for a visit. It reminds me how miniscule I am in the grand scheme of things, and how our relationships with other human beings extend far beyond the borders of our own short time on earth. It suggests that I focus on making work that honors my past beloveds, including my past selves. And it encourages me to commune with the friendly occupants of a gently unfurling future.

The Gift of Devotion

Many people will tell you that if you want to live the life of a maker, you have to be disciplined. They will insist that you need to stick to a daily routine no matter what, that you must show up even on those days when you are bone-tired and uninspired and lost in the slurry of your own making. They will use imposing words like *stringent* and *strict* and the sternest one of all, *sacrifice*. They will utter phrases like "no pain, no gain" and the ever-so-unpleasant "keep your nose to the grindstone." I suspect many of these folks are spellbound by the Demon of Suffering. They've internalized the grueling language of punishment and developed an internal taskmaster to keep themselves on point.

This framing can be highly effective for some people, and if you're one of them, then don't let me stop you. Show those muses what you're made of and grind away, my darling!

However, if you're like me, you may respond poorly to threats of penalty and expectations of progress at all costs. For instance, I am not the most athletic sort (shocker), so I've gone as far as swapping out the word *exercise* with *movement*, as the latter makes me feel far less pressure. I work out just as hard no matter what I call it, but thinking about moving my body feels joyful and additive, whereas for me, a chronic Presidential Fitness Test failure, thinking about exercising feels like a drag. By reframing this activity, I'm far more likely to actually do it.

My relationship to my work has also undergone a semantic shift. Instead of thinking of my writing as an act of discipline, I now think of it as an act of devotion. This means that I'm not typing away right now merely because *I better hit my word count OR ELSE*. Rather, I'm here writing as an expression of my devotion to this book, to my craft, and to Spirit. I'm engaged in an act of love.

This doesn't necessarily make doing the work easier per se, as my demons still sometimes rudely appear to make me feel resistance and dismay. It also doesn't ensure that what I make will be any good or get lots of fanfare once it's public. But it does make stepping into my office and opening up my laptop feel far less daunting. The Gift of Devotion tells me that my work is an offering to something far bigger and more important than my own little ego-driven goals. And it says that when we love something, we show up for it, even on the days when that feels really hard to do.

In an Occult Office Hours session, my client told me she wanted to start a podcast, but she was finding aspects of it to be a complete pain in the ass (relatable!). She wasn't sure if she should keep going with it: while she was still fired up by the idea of the show, the actual logistics of making it were proving to be far less inspiring. She felt her motivation starting to stutter, and she asked me for ways that magic could help her be more disciplined in seeing the project through.

As she was telling me this, a little Bichon terrier kept head-butting her foot to try to get some attention. This dog was persistent I tell you: nudge

THE GIFT OF DEVOTION

nudge nudge. "Oh, that's Otto," she said. "He's a needy little pest, but we love him anyway." And she then proceeded to launch into a list of Otto's challenging behaviors. After telling me about everything from Otto's tiny bladder to his bouts of car sickness to his predilection for nibbling on her Nikes, she sighed with a smile and said, "He really is the sweetest, though, and he makes life so much more fun."

"Well listen," I said. "You clearly love Otto even though he can be annoying sometimes. And I also bet there are days when it's pouring buckets out, and you really don't want to take him for a walk. But you keep showing up for him and taking care of him anyway because you are devoted to this being. And I bet the cold walks and queasy car trips don't feel so hard when you think about how much you adore him, right?" She agreed.

I told her it can be the same with her podcast, or with any other project that requires our attention over an extended period of time. You do it because you have devoted yourself to it, and to the Creative Force that initially arrived to get you excited about it in the first place.

The word *devotion* is related to the word *vow*. When we devote ourselves to something, it means that we are fulfilling a sacred promise that we have chosen to make.

The Gift of Devotion would like me to remind you that it really doesn't matter to whom or to what you have made this promise. At the beginning of this book, I listed various honorifics one might choose to use, like Creative Force or Source or Spirit. You are welcome to switch up the phrasing as often as you like. Each project of yours might be devoted to a specific ancestor or friend or deity, or you may prefer to use a more general term for the recipient of your creative devotion: Art. Curiosity. Perhaps Love itself.

My musician father is one of the most devoted people I have ever known, not only to his family, but to his own craft. He is now in his seventies and he still practices clarinet for two hours a day (and my parents' dog, Avi, is devoted to being his yowling accompanist). Though he's technically retired, he still performs with various chamber music groups and orchestras for the pleasure of it, and he is still committed to becoming a better player. When he was seventy-one, he got an opportunity to play Respighi's "Pines of Rome," which has one of the most notoriously challenging clarinet solos ever written. He practiced and practiced, determined to hit the piece's notorious sustained high A. He could pull it off during rehearsal, but as the concert drew nearer, he found himself getting a bit anxious about the performance. It was one thing to play the piece well at home, but would he be able to hit and hold the note in front of a packed house?

Then he had a revelation. He realized that this wasn't a contest and that his love of playing wasn't about trying to impress an audience. Rather, he played to bring them joy and because he was excited to share his love of this particular piece with them. When he shifted into an energy of offering rather than impressing or achieving, he felt an immediate sense of ease. And as you may have guessed, he played the piece beautifully, and completely nailed the high note. My dad is devoted to Music, and to connecting other people with its beauty and emotional power.

You can invent your own term to refer to the receiver of your devotion, and I quite enjoy hearing about those who have done so. Filmmaker James Broughton called cinema his "duty to the Lords of Creation," and Ralph Waldo Emerson wrote of "authorities of the universe" who he believed assigned each of us a specific purpose we must work to fulfill. Alan

THE GIFT OF DEVOTION

Moore came up with a demigoddess of creativity and magic named Promethea, who he brings to life in the thirty-two-issue comic book series of the same name that he made with artist J. H. Williams III. (And since it happens to be one of my favorite works of all time, Promethea is represented throughout my home, and, indeed, on my altar.)

And in 1962, Robert Duncan and Jess bestowed artist and friend George Herms with the "Servant of Holy Beauty Award," which came with a hand-drawn certificate and twenty-five dollars. I can think of no better higher power to devote oneself to than Holy Beauty, and I hereby proclaim that we must continue to give out this award to deserving Magic Makers today!

The Gift of Devotion doesn't make demands. It is not punitive, nor does it ask that you make yourself miserable to generate your magic. All it requires is that you honor your loving commitment to it and keep turning up to do your work on its behalf.

So go on: Offer your skills to the friendliest force you can imagine and stay by its side with a glad and devoted heart. Take an oath to always tend to your flames and fascinations. Swear yourself into the Sacred Order of the Magic Maker.

Vow that your life will forever be in service of Holy Beauty.

Keep your promise.

PART V
Complete Magic

When I told my art mage friend Jesse about my idea for this book and explained how the Magician is its guiding mascot, he was very encouraging. Sitting at his dining room table, I struck Magician's Pose, stretching my hands upward and downward while expounding about being a bridge between realms and using magic to materialize the immaterial. He nodded along vigorously.

"That's great!" he said, and he proceeded to tell me how excited he was about my writing. Then he paused. I could sense that he had more to say but didn't want to overstep.

Jesse is one of my most trusted collaborators, a trust we've built up over fifteen years of conversation around art and the occult, as well as through many studio visits, early reads of each other's writings, and countless brainstorming sessions. He's the rare person I welcome feedback from during a project's nascent phases.

"Go ahead," I said. "Tell me what you're thinking."

"Well, there's this," he said, mirroring my Magician's Pose, "but there's also this," and he proceeded to extend one arm behind him, reaching backward, and one arm in front, reaching forward. He explained: "There is magic when the work is being made, and there can *also* be magic that gets shared with others when the work is complete."

Now it's fair to say that as both an internationally exhibiting painter and a fine arts professor at a large university, Jesse's creative life is community-oriented on a relatively large scale. And while not all Magic Makers will find themselves in such a rarified position, I thought he made an excellent point.

And so this begs the question: How can magic assist us once a project is finished?

And furthermore: How can we enchant the sharing of our work?

This book is primarily focused on the making of things, and the magic that can support us during that process. By now we're familiar with methods to help us shift into Magician Mode so that we can ready ourselves to create. We've learned ways to receive Spirit-led, inspired input, as well as how to direct our enchanted output with intentionality. And we're also well aware of the demons that will inevitably stop by for a visit when we are working and of the mystic gifts that can sustain us and keep our creative fires burning. There are instances when all of these tools are enough on their own and we are satisfied to make for making's sake. Some work is meant to be kept private, secreted away from those who might bruise the fruits of our labor with their assessment and opinions. Sometimes we are conjuring ideas and individual components that don't feel fully ripe, or which may or may not become part of a larger magnum opus down the road. We may choose to keep such work curtained close in our innermost chambers, at least for a time. This doesn't make it any less valuable. All magic-making is meaningful and worthwhile, whether or not it is intended for public consumption.

But sometimes there is work we feel compelled to share. Releasing what we've made into the world and telling people about it is an aspect of the creative process I call shoutput. As a Magic Maker, I have developed ways to ensure that my shoutput stage is as magically considered as my input and output stages. This isn't merely a matter of self-promotion, though that is a necessary part of my livelihood these days. It's also about how I collaborate with Spirit to offer what I've made to the world with integrity, intention, and hopeful direction.

COMPLETE MAGIC

It can feel jarring to release our creative manifestations into the public arena. It takes such a long time to make something and a far, far shorter time for that thing to be consumed. A meal that takes hours to prepare can be devoured in five minutes. A play that has taken years to develop can be watched in a mere few hours. We pour so much life force and Spirit force into our making that it is daunting to think that someone can not only ingest it but form an opinion about it in moments. This is why aphorisms like "It's not the destination, it's the journey" help refocus our perspective. What we make, why we made it, and how we ourselves are divinely transformed in the making of it—this is what matters most. This is the Great Work the alchemists spoke of and illuminated in their symbol-laden manuscripts. Materializing the immaterial changes us. As we create, we are re-created with Spirit's gold-tipped wand.

Still, Spirit thrives in a system of interconnection. It wants the things we make to reach others, and to inspire those others to make new things in turn—whether as an homage, a mutation, or even a rejection of what has come before. It has given each of us a unique suite of desires, curiosities, and talents. And when we use these gifts to create something new, it sparks others to use theirs to create more new things.

We don't know when this chain reaction will occur (as the Gift of Eternity reminds us). And we may only choose to share some of what we make with a select group, rather than trying to reach a global audience. But if you feel called to show the results of your spellcraft, magic is there to take you by the upward/downward/backward/forward hands.

RITUALS FOR RELEASING

Whether or not one releases their creations into the material world during one's lifetime, it is powerful to release them in the spiritual realm. This means that we are signaling to Spirit that we have reached a moment of ending in our work, and that we are offering it up to the celestial layers of the universe to do what it will with it. Perhaps a certain project's time has not yet come, and it is destined to remain obscured until future generations discover it. Or maybe there are already plans in place for a more public reveal, and so we must ready our offering to find its way to those who will benefit from its message the most. How the work is received isn't up to us, but we can do our best to let it exit our creative cauldron with magic and grace.

What follows are some recommendations for ways to ritualize the completion of your work as well as methods to help you intentionally propel it from your magic circle to the outer cosmos.

As ever, these suggestions are magically modular. There is no correct order you must do them in, and there are some aspects you may spend more time on than others, depending on what you intuit will best serve you and your offering. But each of these recommendations has supported me as I've prepared to turn my gaze outward and shift into shout-put gear.

Revel

In my family, we are celebrators. After every dance recital, soccer game, or good report card, my sister and I were taken to our local Friendly's to celebrate with towering Reese's Peanut Butter Cup sundaes that we ate with extra-long spoons. Birthdays were a big deal too, as were wedding anniversaries, retirements, and other such milestones, each marked with a party at our house or a meal at a favorite restaurant. I grew up thinking this was normal, completely unaware that plenty of families don't do this, whether due to economic or emotional constraints. It wasn't until I became an adult that I learned that my own father wasn't given any birthday parties as a child, as his parents were anxious about having a lot of people in their home. Celebrating was a skill he had to acquire, and my boisterous mom and her family saw to it that he did.

Rites of passage are built into every culture for good reason. They are threshold crossings, marking the end of one phase and the beginning of another. They help initiate transition into a new state of being—psychologically, spiritually, and sometimes physically. When we celebrate the ending of something, we're not only being given a pat on the back for reaching a specific stage of life, but we are also readying ourselves for whatever adventures await beyond the border of becoming. The same is true in our creative lives. Taking time to say "I fucking *did* that" helps us metabolize our experience of magic-making and gives us a pause to take pleasure in our work. I think of creative revelry after the completion of a project as a kind of mini harvest festival. It's when I reflect on what I've accomplished and reward myself for a job done as well as I could do it.

A celebration doesn't need to cost money, nor does it have to involve a big group of people. As I've gotten older, I've become more aware that I'm an introvert with an extrovert's candy-coated shell, and that parties aren't always my favorite. But I do love good food enjoyed with a few select people or sensuous treats like handmade soap or a bouquet of dark purple calla lilies. I've also been known to buy myself a special piece of jewelry upon finishing a writing project, or draw myself a beautiful bath after teaching a workshop. And my number one way of celebrating that's quick and not too expensive is to treat myself to a slice of a nearby restaurant's incredible chocolate peanut butter bomb cake. (Come to think of it, this is the grown-up version of my Friendly's sundae! Old habits die hard.)

Turning something from ether into enchanted material is difficult business, and it's important for our bodies and souls to stop and take stock of what they've done. When you finish something, make space to revel in the finishing in whatever way feels good to you. Watch a great movie. Take a trip. Buy yourself a Very Good Candle. Celebrate the milestone of having made something. Spirit will revel right alongside you.

Request

Another release ritual I recommend incorporating into your practice is to thoughtfully petition the spirits to help your work find its best way forward. I realize you may have asked them for plenty of assistance already when you invoked the guiding Forces of your choosing at the beginning of your process. But releasing your work into the world is an appropriate time to engage in sacred supplication. Your ask can be as simple as saying:

> Dear Spirit: May what I have made reach whomever
> it is meant to so that it may do the most good in the world.
> May it be worthy of you, and may it help generate more
> positive magic, more imaginative energy, and
> more love in all realms. So mote it be!

You can make your own request as elaborate or specific as you wish. Creating a full ceremony with candles and other occult accoutrements is absolutely appropriate here. This can happen anytime it feels right to you, though if you are having trouble choosing, remember a full moon is associated with the magic of releasing and completion.

It is worth noting that some of our projects may come to a stopping point before we feel they are "done." Sometimes this is due to external factors, like a contract ending earlier than expected or a creative plan being canceled due to budgetary or time constraints. And sometimes, for whatever the reason, the initial spark that ignited our excitement just feels like it might never become the creative conflagration we envisioned. In these instances, ritual can help you release your focus on it and, best of all, allow it to become something even better than you pictured. Personally, I don't believe in "failed" projects, as I've learned that so many of my own half-baked attempts and premature endings are actually just compost for far more fecund future work. I regularly turn back to old notebooks of mine and revisit dormant early drafts, and I'm often delighted to find that they contain precisely the turn of phrase or bit of research I'm in need of right now. Sometimes an early "failure" is just an idea that's ahead of its time! Because of this, I'm not a proponent of releasing incomplete work back into the universe. Rather, I think these moments are opportunities to ask Spirit to assist you in peacefully stepping away from your project for the time being, and to help these ideas ripen or transmute as they're meant to. In my experience, the excess debris has a tendency to simply dissipate on its own.

When I do feel I'm at a point of completion, another habit I've picked up is to place my finished project, or a symbol thereof, on my altar for a time. I've kept a copy of my book *Waking the Witch* on one of my altars for years now, to request that the spirits help give it a signal boost so that it may have the most positive impact it can. My friend Peter Bebergal also gifted me a magic square upon that book's release, to help curry favor with Jupiter, the Roman god of good luck. And when I'm done with

REQUEST

this manuscript, I will be placing it on my book altar to charge it up before sending it off to my editor. I'll be doing the same once I receive the published copy of this book, a physicalized request to my guardian spirits to bless it as they see fit. You can also put a photograph or printout of an image that represents your project on your altar, or place one in a moonlit window to bathe it with celestial blessings.

The night before my husband's play *The Ask* opened in Manhattan in the fall of 2024, we asked Dionysus, god of theater, for his blessings on the production. We lit candles and did our ritual, leaving an open bottle of wine on my altar (Bacchus label, of course), since that is Dionysus's beverage of choice. The next day I poured some of the wine as a libation offering into an empty patch of dirt inside the community garden across the street from where the play was being performed. With Matt's permission, I also hid a tiny, magically charged Dionysus mask inside one of the props on set. I'm happy to report the play was a wild success, primarily due to the brilliant script, performances, and hard work done by Matt and the entire cast and crew. But I have a feeling that having Dionysus on our side didn't hurt either.

Other methods of petitioning include writing down your request in a journal or on a piece of paper that you burn or sleep with under your pillow. Science fiction author Octavia E. Butler was a steady practitioner of spiritual requests and manifestation magic, not only for her projects but her career overall. In her journals, she would write lists of specific things she desired. One 1988 entry reads:

> My books will be read by millions of people!
> I will buy a beautiful home in an excellent neighborhood
> I will send poor black youngsters to Clarion or other writer's wkshops [*sic*]

I will help poor black youngsters to broaden their horizons
I will help poor black youngsters go to college
I will get the best of health care for my mother and myself
I will hire a car whenever I want or need to
I will travel whenever or wherever in the world that I choose
My books will be <u>read</u> by <u>millions</u> <u>of</u> <u>people</u>!
So be it! See to it!

Butler was very interested in the power of the mind to manifest desired outcomes, and her journals are peppered with quotes from Ralph Waldo Emerson as well as self-help books such as Napoleon Hill's *Think and Grow Rich* and Jim Rohn's *Seven Strategies for Wealth and Happiness*. In another note to herself, she writes, "Every day in every way I am researching and writing my award-winning books and short stories." This is her spin on psychologist Émile Coué's famous affirmation, "Every day, in every way, I'm getting better and better."

To be clear, Butler was critical of organized religion, and the relationship between the individual and the divine was a theme explored throughout her body of work: in *Parable of the Talents* she writes, "To shape God, shape Self." I don't know if she was addressing her journaled wishes to a specific deity, to her own psyche, or to some hybrid of the two. Regardless, it's clear that writing down her requests and desires was a key part of how she kept herself motivated and spiritually sustained. Some may point to her publication of fourteen books and her MacArthur "Genius Grant" as evidence that her manifestations came true. Certainly, her brilliant, prescient writing has lasted far beyond her own life, and it continues to impact the lives of millions of others today.

Respect

Asking for supernatural assistance is a well-established part of many spiritual paths, whether through petition, prayer, or more elaborate spellcraft actions. And yet it surprises me that once Spirit has intervened, some folks skip the simple act of giving thanks afterward for whatever magic has occurred. Having an attitude of gratitude is a way of absorbing the blessings that we have received and integrating them into our finished work. And to state the obvious: it is simply good magical manners! If someone or Someone has given you a gift, saying thank you is a gesture of appreciation and respect. It also means that they are far more likely to help next time you come knocking.

Some people prefer to give their thanks to the spirit world publicly, as evidenced by the many Oscar recipients who thank God in their acceptance speeches. I don't believe one has to be quite so conspicuous with their ethereal acknowledgment, though I confess I got a special thrill out of hearing *Transparent* director Joey Soloway thanking the Goddess in their 2015 Emmy acceptance speech, as well as from watching footage of Cybill Shepherd's 1996 Golden Globes win for Best Actress, during which she says, "In particular thanks to the great Goddess in all her guises. May she bring us peace, joy, and righteous anger. Blessed be." And when Jinkx Monsoon claimed her 2022 *RuPaul's Drag Race All Stars* win "in the name of Hecate, Mother of Witches!" my delighted screams no doubt startled the neighbors. If thanking your deities and ancestors in your own acceptance speeches, show programs, and album liner notes feels right to you, by all means go for it.

But if you're on the more reserved side when it comes to the prospect of exposing your magical collaborators, I assure you that thanking them privately is just as appreciated. Leaving an offering of flowers or food for your guides is perfectly appropriate, as is doing a simple gratitude ritual with candles, incense, or libations. You may even choose to tailor your thanks to the ancestors or gods who were particularly helpful during your creative process, and do a special ceremony or pilgrimage of thanks just for them. Since Mercury has been such a guiding force for this book, when it's done, I plan to visit the sculpture of him that's over the entrance of Grand Central Terminal. My friend the occult scholar Mitch Horowitz taught me to say "Hail Mercury" whenever I pass by or beneath this mercurial clock during my midtown wanderings, but I will likely add a bit more oomph this time and sneak him a more substantial gift that reflects his vast involvement.

Even the most solitary Magic Maker is never alone, thank the gods. So have humility and gratitude—and thank the gods!

Reveal

Curtains up. Ribbon cut. The entrance sign flips to "Open." The mic switches on. The moment you've anticipated has arrived, and it's time to show the world what you and your magic have made.

This might happen via an in-person reveal, like a presentation, art opening, listening party, or performance. It might be hitting the "Publish" button on your article or clicking "Share" on your (fingers crossed) viral video. You are probably feeling nervous or filled with the butterflies that visibility brings. Well, you are in luck! Many of the techniques in this book can charge your shoutput with an extra bolt of divine lightning, as they are applicable not only in the crafting stage but in the staging stage as well.

Casting a magic circle, lighting up your altar, or otherwise asking your unearthly buddies for some backup are all appropriate here. Magical correspondences are also your friend. I've been known to coordinate my book release outfits to conjure specific energies through color, and to wear certain amulets whenever I'm doing work on camera or in front of a live audience. (My Artemis socks are reserved for extra-special occasions like these, and you just might catch them peeking out from my Doc Martens if you look real close.) And when I'm able to choose the dates of an announcement or public appearance, certain moon phases, Pagan holy days, and other such moments in my stellar schedule are given careful preference.

But what I want to impart to you regarding self-revelation is this: There is no shame in wanting to share your work. Doing so honors the myriad gifts you've been given by your ancestors as well as the divine ones or One of which you are a materialized extension. What we create is a message in a cosmic bottle, sent out on a sea of mystery to reach those whose lives it's meant to touch in ways that may be intentional and yet ever-so-impossible to predict. We create to honor Spirit. And we create to connect with other people—community members, kindred strangers, humans of an unknowable future. We make things to alter perception and to propose new possibilities. Our deepest wish is that others will be catalyzed by our creations, as we have been stirred awake by the makings of those Magicians who have lit up our own lives. It is a noble undertaking to craft the inspiring prima materia you have received into something that can be looked at or listened to or felt by other beings here on earth. You have molded subtle forces into desired shapes. You have collaborated intimately with ineffable entities, and together you have brought forth a sparkling bit of magic where one didn't exist before.

Showing what we have made to someone else is a vulnerable undertaking, but it is one of the primary ways we can ignite new and vital embers of enchantment in the world.

So stand tall in your magic-making. You, with your head crowned with wonder, with your hands spinning spells and spanning realms.

Step into the spotlight, into the starlight. Let your work become a beacon. When you do, it helps others find the path.

Be unabashed in your sharing, and blaze bright.

Return

So. Here we are, at The End.

This is your moment of departure from your making. But it is also a moment of arrival.

You have come to a stopping point in your Great Work, or, if you prefer, an interlude in your enchanted experiments. You have released what you have made into the vast unknown, or at least into a drawer to be reflected upon at a later date. Regardless of the results of your esoteric operations and exoteric expressions, you have finished something. You have met the call to create as best you were able, and you sense it is now time to move on to a new chapter of transfiguration.

How do you mark this moment of completion? And what, in Mercury's name, happens next?

From a ceremonial standpoint, it is important to demarcate the end of a working, and to leave the crucible of creation empty of any lingering energetic residue. If you have cast a magic circle, now is when you should open the circle back up, setting the energies free to find other containers, to assist other intrepid Magic Makers. We do this by thanking and dismissing each of the elements and/or guides in the reverse order that we called them in. Here are some lines of mine you may use to help you do this, but of course your own words will be just as effective, if not more so.

Thank you, Spirit of the Center, for your gifts of
Mystery and Artful Crafting.

Blessed be.

Thank you, Spirit of Above, for your gifts of
Illumination and Celestial Inspiration.

Blessed be.

Thank you, Spirit of Below, for your gifts of
Rootedness and Wise Guidance.

Blessed be.

Thank you, Spirit of Earth in the North, for your gifts of
Growth and Abundant Beauty.

Blessed be.

Thank you, Spirit of Water in the West, for your gifts of
Replenishment and Supple Shape-shifting.

Blessed be.

Thank you, Spirit of Fire in the South, for your gifts of
Incandescence and Star-fueled Desire.

Blessed be.

Thank you, Spirit of Air in the East, for your gifts of
Incantation and Spellbinding Song.

Blessed be.

The circle is open, yet unbroken.

Merry meet, merry part, and merry meet again.

RETURN

The circle is open, *yet unbroken*. These are the words I was taught to say at the end of any magical gathering. I love this idea of unbrokenness. It implies that this dissipation of divine power is a temporary state. Just as vapor can be collected once more into a shining pool of water, we can conjure our circle again whenever the desire arises. The ring of creation is always with us: a lemniscate twisting above the head in a hallowed halo. A rainbow ouroboros snaking around one's waist. A hoop of wobbling potential hoping to be called into form.

Until then, we rest, we quest, we let mundane demands rush in. We allow any feelings of grief that may show up to flow through us, as so often happens at the end of any great voyage. There is always loss in letting go, after all.

But so too is there a sense of crackling excitement, because we know that *right now* there is an infinite field of Creative Force at the ready.

In time, you will spread your arms wide to embrace the opposite poles of possibility.

Soon Spirit will summon you, and together you'll start to craft something numinous and new.

And so you will begin again.

Begin again.

BEHOLD!

Your magic is waiting to meet you, merrily so.

Afterword

A MAGICIAN IMAGINES

As I write these words, our planet dangles on a precipice. There are so many problems in need of fixing, so many wounds that need mending and medicine. It can feel daunting to face such mammoth challenges as environmental pillaging, democratic fragility, wealth hoarding, war, and the rampant inequality and division between so many factions of our earthly family. I don't have the solutions to make it all better, and I'm thankful no one is asking me to come up with them.

What I do know is this: the only way we humans have ever improved our circumstances is by imagining courageous alternatives to the current way of being. The world is shaped and reshaped by those with the vastest imaginations and the valiance to bring their visions forth and make them material. Speeches, structures, software, songs—they all originate in the imaginal realm. Learning how to actualize them with intention is the great lesson of the Magic Maker. Magicians create change. The imagination is their most precious weapon.

This is why Ursula K. Le Guin writes, "The exercise of imagination is dangerous to those who profit from the way things are because it has the power to show that the way things are is not permanent, not universal, not necessary."

This is why bell hooks writes, "Imagination is one of the most powerful modes of resistance that oppressed and exploited folks can do and use."

This is why Diane di Prima's poem "Rant" declares:

MAGIC MAKER

THE ONLY WAR THAT MATTERS IS THE WAR AGAINST
THE IMAGINATION
ALL OTHER WARS ARE SUBSUMED IN IT

The dismantling of worn-out old frameworks is a necessary part of any life cycle, but it takes imagination to begin to build something better or to resurrect a wiser, more ancient practice in its place. Imagination is survival, creativity is sustenance. These are the magic wands that conjure true and lasting abundance from which all beings benefit.

There are cowards who stockpile their own power by stoking fear and acrimony. They are convinced that only a select few can be well-resourced and free, and they inject this poison into their followers while pretending it's a remedy. Condemning this tyranny is important, but our work can't end there.

Tori Amos once said, "You can't beat a bully at his own games. And I'm not talking about one particular bully here; it's energy. You have to out-create the destruction—it's the only way."

Now is the time for each of us to fulfill our highest potential and use our Spirit-given gifts to contribute to the project of collective flourishment. We must out-imagine oppression and out-create harm. It is not enough to curse unworthy ways of being. We must manifest hope-driven visions and bless each other with radically radiant care.

I believe that together, we can make a new reality.

I believe in the power of images and incantations, elbow grease and electricity, deft strategy and starlit destiny.

I believe in trusting the truth of my own desires.

I believe in the possibility of soft tomorrows and generous legacies.

I believe in my heart of hearts that better days are on the way.

A MAGICIAN IMAGINES

I believe in my deities, my guides, and myself.
I believe in magic.
And I believe in you.

May you know your own limitlessness.

May you be guided by the gods of imagination.

May your creations be portals for enchantment.

May your life be a love spell cast in all realms.

No one can transform the world alone, but each of us can do our part and heed the call of the Great Creatrix.

She reaches out a hand to yours.

She chants your name.

Acknowledgments

Many Magicians helped me conjure *Magic Maker* into existence, and I'm grateful to each of them.

I feel so very fortunate to have found a home at Glass Literary Agency. Alex Glass, you are a dream agent who possesses a rare combination of kindness, encouragement, patience, and acumen. Thank you for being a tremendous partner in bringing my books into being. (And thank you to Rick Pascocello, who first brought me into the fold.)

Deep thanks to my editor, Amy Sun, whose belief in this book and enthusiasm for my work overall has been such a guiding light. Your skill, intuition, friendship, and utterly delightful marginalia comments are all so appreciated by me. You are the living embodiment of your name.

Many other brilliant people at Penguin Life touched this book with their magic wands, including Brian Tart, Meg Leder, Isabelle Alexander, Nick Michal, Lavina Lee, Tess Espinoza, Katelyn Mackenzie, Megan Gerrity, L. J. Young, Jason Ramirez, Alexis Sulaimani, Kate Stark, Mary Stone, Rebecca Marsh, Yuleza Negron, and Anna Brill. Thanks to each of you for being so good at what you do and such a pleasure to collaborate with. Extra thanks to designer Lynn Buckley for conjuring such a splendid cover. The team at Hay House UK also added their stardust along the

ACKNOWLEDGMENTS

way: thank you to Amy Kiberd, Jo Burgess, Katherine O'Brien, Michelle Pilley, Portia Chauhan, Diane Hill, and Tom Cole.

Several of the ideas found within these pages were developed during the workshops on creativity and magic I've taught over the years both online and in person. My collaborator and co-teacher in many of these, Janaka Stucky, has been a great inspiration and a gracious friend. Thank you for giving me your blessing on this book, Janaka, and for being such a blessing in my life overall. And many thanks to the students who have attended these classes and given such heartening feedback on them.

I'm grateful to all of the inspiring Magic Makers who have been guests on *The Witch Wave* podcast, and to my listeners, Patreon backers, and supporters of the show. Thank you to Josh Wilcox and the rest of the Brooklyn Podcasting Studio team for years of happy sonic partnership.

Jesse Bransford and Susan Aberth continue to be two of my biggest influences and champions. May I never stop learning from each of you and basking in your magic. Thank you for being the dearest of friends and the brightest of beacons. Special thanks to Jesse for bringing me back into NYU's lecture halls via our Occult Humanities Conference, and for being so generous with your octagonal sanctuary, which has been a warm incubator for so much shared magic and conviviality.

Love and gratitude to the members of the Queenright Coven and the 2023 Grecian Coven. May we continue to merry meet in new iterations, as sabbats and stars align.

There are so many other supportive compatriots in the occulture community that I fear I'll never be able to name them all; many of them are woven throughout this book already. However, I would be remiss if I didn't mention the following whose friendship and work have been particularly buoying over these last few years of writing: Peter Bebergal,

ACKNOWLEDGMENTS

Judika Illes, Kristen Sollée, Simon Costin and the Museum of Witchcraft and Magic, Steven Intermill and the Buckland Museum of Witchcraft & Magick, Christina Oakley Harrington and Treadwell's Books, Erica Feldmann and HausWitch, Amy Hale, S. Elizabeth, Phyllis Curott, Rachel Pollack (may she rest in heresy), Jessica Hundley and the Library of Esoterica team, Robert Shehu-Ansell and Fulgur Press, Mitch Horowitz, Brian Cotnoir, William Kiesel and Ouroboros Press, Ben Warfield and Sochi Lynne of Mithras Candle, Frances F. Denny, Mallory Lance, Kristin Fayne-Mulroy, Liza Fenster, Liv Swenson, Bri Luna, Chelsea Wolfe, Jinkx Monsoon, Kenneth Friend, Nicholas Favia, Alex Hertzberg, Jodi Wille, Pati Dubroff, Amber King, Jen Ziegler, and Lakshmi Ramgopal of Lykanthea, thank you all.

Huge gratitude to my Occult Office Hours regulars who teach me as much as I try and teach them. And bouquets of thanks to other early readers and champions of this book, including Dylan Thuras, Austin Kleon, and Yumi Sakugawa. Many thanks to Jewitch makers and teachers Dori Midnight, Ezra Rose, Ketzirah 'haMa'agelet' Lesser, Deatra Cohen, and Adam Siegel, whose work has deepened my own ancestral spiritual practice and connection to Jewish folk magic. Thank you to James North and Ronald Hutton for Dion Fortune detective work, Ian Gould for Shakespearean assistance, Kristi Showers and Jeff Freeman for help with German translation, and David Freeman for sending me such thoughtful books (a few of which snuck their way into this one).

Thank you to my teachers, Robin Rose Bennett on this side of the veil and Lois Hirshkowitz on the other. May my offerings honor the mystic gifts and lessons you've imparted to me.

I have two very wonderful Laras in my life who support me in different (though occasionally similar) ways. To my therapist Lara Goodman, I am

ACKNOWLEDGMENTS

so very grateful to you for the magical healing container you create for me each week. Thank you for your acceptance and care, and for helping me remember my Magnificent Beast. To my part-time assistant and full-time friend (and illustrious artist in her own right), Lara Antal, thank you for all you do to make my life better, including the myriad occult outings, heart-to-hearts, post office runs, and cardamom-infused treats.

To my beloved friends Megha Ramaswamy, Lauren Schreibstein, and Shiwani Srivastava, thank you for making me feel so very wealthy in love and for being such steadfast companions in all things sacred, mundane, and profane. Thank you to the Pomerantzes, Wilsons, Freemans, Baar-Bittmans, and LeClairs for being my official and exceptionally lovely extended family, and to Moira Stone and Robert Honeywell, Suzannah Murray, Melly Hawks, the DelGrossos, the Trumbulls, and the Baldwin-Ancowitzes for feeling like you are.

Feline familiars, Monday and Birthday: thank you for being the silliest silkworms, and for providing me with the softest possible company as I wrote this tome. Albee and Remedios "Remy" Varo, thank you for your purring protective presence and love from on high.

Emily, you are not only my literal sister but a sister on the enchanted path of writing and spiritual seeking. I know that we are connected at the highest frequency, and I love you dearly.

Mom and Dad, I'm lucky to have grown up watching you each make your own creative magic, and I can't thank you enough for always encouraging me to make mine. I'm grateful for your love, and for your devotion to leading lives steered by compassion, generosity, and beauty.

Matt Freeman: Husband. Hero. Heart. Thank you for inspiring me infinitely with your artistic audacity, and for cheering the loudest when I lean into mine. You have taught me the true meaning of devotion, and

ACKNOWLEDGMENTS

I thank the gods, graces, and great Forces that brought us together to share such love.

Thank you to Mercury, thank you to Artemis, thank you to Iris.

Thank you to my ancestors, familial and spiritual.

Thank you to Spirit for collaborating with me on this book, and for helping it make its way to *you*, dear reader.

And thank you very much for reading it, and for sharing the magic of your attention with me.

Blessed be.

Index

Abbott and Costello, 269
Aberth, Susan, 67
abracadabra, 184
Abramelin oil, 74–75
Abramović, Marina, 82–83
Abraxas Journal, 203
Abstract and Abstract Expressionist art, 22–25, 115, 197–99
Adam, 95, 96
Adam, Helen, 178
adornment/anointment, 74–84
Adorno, Theodor, 7
advisors, spiritual, 113–18
Aether, 59
affusion, 52–53
af Klint, Hilma, 20, 22, 115, 205, 289
age, 288
Age of Enlightenment, 8
Agrippa, Heinrich Cornelius, 195, 201–4
air, 58–59
   baths, 80
   as cleansing method, 48–50
   magic circle and, 58, 61
alchemy, 34, 54
aleatory methods, 138–39
aleph, 30, 37, 186
Alexander, Christopher, 107
Allah, 197
Allure, 98
altars, 72–73, 114, 280
   ancestral, 208–9, 291
   artwork and, 291–92
   invocation/altar-cation, 67–73
   public monuments as, 208
   releasing work and, 312–13, 317
alter egos and personas, 87–90, 93, 98

Amaterasu, 87
Amdusias, 218–19
Ame-no-Uzume, 87
American Magazine, 115
Amos, Tori, 3, 277–78, 326
amulets, 84, 164, 218, 219, 317
   drawn or written, 187–88
   hamsa, 283
ancestors, 54, 60, 70, 113–14, 118, 208–9, 290–91
Anderson, Laurie, 138, 290
Angel Cards, 128–29
Angelou, Maya, 70
angels, 59, 60, 68
Anger, Kenneth, 145
Angkor Wat, 197
animistic systems, 48
anointment/adornment, 74–84
Anthroposophy, 198
Aphrodite, 219
Apollinaire, Guillaume, 22
Apollo, 36, 110
apophenia, 12
apotheosis, 32, 87
apotropaic magic, 159
Apted, Michael, 214
Aradia, Gospel of Witches (Leland), 79
Arbus, Diane, 243
Argento, Dario, 169
Aristotle, 58–59
Aristotle's "Doctrine of the Mean," 35
arithmancy, 194
art, xix–xx
   Abstract and Abstract Expressionist, 22–25, 115, 197–99
   altars and, 291–92

INDEX

art (*cont.*)
  collaborative, 269–70
  Dada, 91, 138–39
  magic and, 17–18
  modern, 21, 22
  occult and, 19–27
  Spiritualist, 20
  Surrealist, xviii, 5, 17, 22–23, 36–37, 89, 94, 120–21, 125, 128, 129, 270
Artemis, 4, 35–36, 71, 83, 148, 185, 219, 254, 317
Arthur magazine, 160
Artisson, Robin, 189–91
L'Art magique (Breton), 17, 121
ARTNews, 198
Art of Synthesis, The (Leo), 171
Asawa, Ruth, 134
Ascent magazine, 161
Asclepius, 151–52
Ashkenazi Herbalism (Cohen and Siegel), 124–25
Ask, The (Freeman), 313
aspersion, 52–53
assistance, requesting, 67–69
associations and correspondences, 200–206
astrology, 9, 171, 282
Auden, W. H., 117
audience, 287, 289–90, 296
augury, 144–49, 277
August, John, 229–30
automatic writing, 119–22
Avalon, Arthur, 75
awen, 15
ayahuasca, 174–75
Aztecs, 54–55

Baca, Judith F., 291
Bacon, Francis, 8
bagua, 194
Baker, Norma Jean, 89
Banksy, 94
Baphomet, 30–31
baptism, 52–53
Barbie, 205
Barlow, John Perry, 253
Barry, Lynda, 122, 125, 285
Bash, The, 85
bathing, 52
Baubo, 87

Baum, L. Frank, 21–22
Bax, Clifford, 170–71
Baynes, Cary F., 137
Beastie Boys, 76
Beatles, 88, 150, 269
Bebergal, Peter, 312
Beckett, Samuel, 70
Beiles, Sinclair, 139
Beltane, 50
Bennett, Robin Rose, 58
Besant, Annie, 22
betwixt-and-betweenness, 62–63
Beuys, Joseph, 199
Beyoncé, 87–88, 90, 98, 192–93
Bible, 184, 207
  David in, 172–73
  divination through, 132
  Exodus, 74
  Genesis, 36, 96, 184
  Torah, 95, 186
bibliomancy, 132–35, 142
Bighorn Medicine Wheel, 58
Big Magic (Gilbert), 235–36
binary pairs, 33–34, 36
Birbiglia, Mike, 229, 262
birds, 146
Birth of Tragedy, The (Nietzsche), 36
Bisttram, Emil, 72
Björk, 3, 164, 172
Black Ark, 75–76
Black Mountain Poems (Creasy, ed.), 134, 135
Black Unicorn (Lorde), 183
Blake, William, 120
Blavatsky, Helena, 21
Blount, Herman Poole, 93
Bono, 88
Book of Changes (I Ching), 136–38, 140, 142
Book of Correspondences, The (Mathers and Westcott), 202
Book of the Sun of Gnosis, The, 195
Book of Thoth, The (Crowley), 20–21
books, divination through, 132–35, 142
Bossypants (Fey), 260
Bowie, David, 68, 89–90, 140, 141, 214, 291
Bransford, Jesse, xxii, 18, 202–4, 254, 301
Brauner, Victor, 23, 36, 121
Brauron, 185
breath, 48–50, 167
Breton, André, 17, 22, 120–21
Brezsny, Rob, 253

INDEX

Brigid, 274
Broad City, 269
Brooks, Garth, 88–89
Broughton, James, xx, 248, 296
Brouk, Joanna, 173
Brownstein, Carrie, 174
Buber, Martin, 69, 262
Buckland, Raymond, 202
Buckland Museum of Witchcraft and Magic, 27
Buddhism, 31, 138, 181, 194, 198, 220
al-Buni, Ahamad ibn 'Ali, 195
Buñuel, Luis, 23
Burgher, Elijah, 191
Burma, 264
Burroughs, William S., 18, 139–40, 268
Butler, Octavia E., 313–14
Butler, W. E., 16
Butterworth, Jez, 167

CAConrad, 114
Cage, John, 134, 137–38, 140, 258
calendar, 271–72
Caliban and the Witch (Federici), 8–9
Calliope, 67
Calvino, Italo, 130
Campbell, Joseph, 253–54
candles, 50
Cantor, Georg, 9
Cape, Frances, 210
capitalism, 8–9
Capote, 236
Capote, Truman, 236
Caravaggio, 70
carnelian, 84
Carrington, Leonora, 23, 34–36, 121, 128, 191
cartomancy, 126–31
   see also tarot
Casale, Gerald "Jerry," 81–82
Cassel, Anna, 20, 115
casting circles, *see* magic circles
casting lots, 187
casting runes, 123, 142, 187
Castle of Crossed Destinies, The (Calvino), 130
Catching the Big Fish (Lynch), 65
Cat in the Hat, The (Seuss), 83
Cave, Nick, 102
celebration, 309–10
Celts, 15, 63, 274
centering/circling, 57–66
   see also magic circles

Centering in Pottery, Poetry, and the Person (Richards), 63–64, 135
Ceridwen, 15
ceromancy, 124–25
chakras, 75
Chakras, The (Leadbeater), 75
Champs magnétiques, Les (Breton and Soupault), 120
chance operations, 137–38
Changing Light at Sandover, The (Merrill), 118
channels, 109–12
chanting, 166, 175, 177, 181–85
chi, 15
Chicago, 261
Chicago, Judy, 291–92
Chinese culture, 15, 59, 116, 174, 194
   I Ching, 136–38, 140, 142
Chiron, 282
Chiuri, Maria Grazia, 84
Christian, Heather, 167
Christianity, 52–53, 59, 96, 143
   Pentecostal, 111
Christie, Agatha, 94
chwal, 111
circling/centering, 57–66
   see also magic circles
Clarke, Arthur C., 12
Clash, the, 76
cleansing/clearing, 47–56, 57
Clemente, Francesco, 127
Clifton, Lucille, 118
Close, Del, 260–63, 267–68
clothing, 76–84, 98, 254
clutter, 47–48
Cobain, Kurt, 141
Coen brothers, 269
Cohen, Deatra, 124–25
Cohen, Leonard, 102, 172–73
coin tosses, 137–38
Colbert, Stephen, 261, 262
collaboration, 266–70
collective belief, 205
collective effervescence, 166
Collins, Jess (Jess), 280–81, 297
color, 204–6, 317
Colquhoun, Ithell, 121, 128, 205
Coltrane, Alice, 161–62
Coltrane, John, 161–63, 170
comedy, 257, 260–61, 269

339

INDEX

Concerning the Spiritual in Art (Kandinsky), 22, 181
Conkel, Joshua, 130
Conley, Craig, 184–85
Connors, Kathleen, 116
Conrad, CA, 114
consciousness, 16–18, 19, 57, 93
Constable, John "Crow," 278–79
Contemporary Artists (Naylor and P-Orridge, eds.), 18
control, 258
correspondences, 200–206
Corso, Gregory, 139
Cotnoir, Brian, 34
Coué, Émile, 314
coulage, 125
courage, 255
Court de Gébelin, Antoine, 126
craft, 101, 104, 155
    handcraft, 282–86
Craft, The, 58
Creative Force, 14–15, 17, 39, 102–3, 152, 157, 213, 232, 237, 295, 321
    automatic writing and, 122
    candle lighting and, 50
    centering and, 65
    circle and, 57
    as current, 33
    judgment and, 247–50
    sex and, 167
    signs and, 146
creativity, xv–xxv, 3–4, 12, 30, 121, 213, 326
    collaboration and, 266
    cycles of, 29
    energy in, 33
    flow in, 271
    magic and, 17
    as magnet, 103
    occult and, 19–20
    scarcity and, 232
    seasonality of, 273
Creem magazine, 49
Crick, Francis, 269
Crispin, Jessa, 130
criticism, 246–50
Crossbones Graveyard, 278–79
Crowley, Aleister, 16, 20–21, 74, 96, 202
crystals, 52, 56, 84

Curott, Phyllis, 50
cut-up technique, 139–41, 268

Dada, 91, 138–39
Daily Express, 90
Daily Magic (Illes), 275
Dalí, Salvador, 23, 37, 128
dance, 86–87, 165–66, 169
David, 172–73
Davies, Owen, 188
Debord, Guy, 279
decalcomania, 125
deceased, 20, 60, 207–10
    ancestors, 54, 60, 70, 113–14, 118, 208–9, 290–91
    communication with, 289, 290
    mediums and, 107, 109, 116, 120
    Spiritualist movement and, 20, 115, 116
de Chirico, Giorgio, 23
Delphi, Oracle of, 110
Demeter, 87
de Mille, Agnes, 249
demons, 217–21, 253, 255, 273, 294, 302
    of Distraction, 225–27, 228, 231, 271
    of Inertia, 228–31, 286
    of Judgment, 246–50, 292
    of Perfectionism, 238–41, 259, 286
    of Scarcity, 232–37, 271
    of Self-Doubt, 222–24
    of Suffering, 242–45, 293
De Occulta Philosophia Libri Tres (*Three Books of Occult Philosophy*) (Agrippa), 195, 201
Deren, Maya, 117
desire, 156, 157, 159, 161, 184, 186, 190
devil, 197
Devil's Raiments, The (Duffy), 79, 284
Devo, 81–82
devotion, 293–97
Dick, Philip K., 137
Dionysus, 36, 86, 313
Dior, Christian, 83–84
di Prima, Diane, 182–83, 286, 325–26
directions, seven, 31, 58, 60, 70
discipline, 293, 294
disenchantment, 8–9
distraction, 225–27, 228, 231, 271
Divine Comedies (Merrill), 117

INDEX

divination, 23, 114, 123–25, 131, 132, 152
   arithmancy, 194
   bibliomancy, 132–35
   cartomancy, 126–31; *see also* tarot
   casting lots, 187
   I Ching, 136–38, 140, 142
   non-dominant hand in, 142–43
   oracle decks, 128–31
   runes, 123, 142, 187
DNA, 269
Dogma and Ritual of High Magic (Lévi), 30
Donald in Mathmagic Land, 196
Donne, John, 292
doodling, 285
Doolittle, Hilda (H.D.), xx, 290
Dore, Jessica, 16–17
Dove, Rita, 292
Down Below (Carrington), 34–35
drag, 92–93
Drake, Joy, 128–29
drawing, 187–88, 285
Drawing Down the Moon, 32
dreams, 150–52
drumming, 166–67
Dub (Veal), 75–76
Dubroff, Pati, 204–5
Duchamp, Marcel, 91
duende, 68, 243
Duffy, Martin, 79, 284
Duncan, Robert, 134, 178, 280–81, 297
dunce caps, 81
Dune, 185
Du Noyer, Paul, 90
Duns Scotus, John, 81
Dupin, Amantine-Lucile-Aurore, 94
Dürer, Albrecht, 195–96
Durkheim, Émile, 166
Dylan, Bob, 94, 127, 140, 239

earth, 58–59, 197
   as cleansing method, 54–56
   magic circle and, 58, 61
Edison, Thomas, 115
eggs, 124
ego, 65, 267, 287
Egypt, 15, 54, 95, 187
Einstein, Albert, 12
ekphrasis, xix–xx

elements, 58–59, 65, 197
   see also air; earth; fire; water
Eliot, T. S., 127
Elvira, 89
Emerson, Ralph Waldo, 296, 314
Eminem, 88
Empedocles, 58–59
Empress, 128
enchantment, 66, 177, 179, 214, 292
   disenchantment, 8–9
encouragement, 254–55
Ende, Michael, 96
energy, in spells, 165–68
Eno, Brian, 130–31, 267
entheogenic plants, 174–77
enthusiasm, 72
Enya, 173
Erev, Rebekah, 129
Ernst, Max, 23, 89, 121, 125
Escher, M. C., 197
Escobedo Mesa, Mariana, 291
Estrada, Álvaro, 177
eternity, 287–92, 303
ethereal realm, 107
Etteilla, 126
Eve, 143
exercise, 294
Exodus, 74
experimentation, 229

"failed" projects, 312
Farr, Florence, 20
Fatima, 283
Faust (Goethe), 197
Federici, Silvia, 8–9
Fellowship of the Ring, The (Tolkien), 254
feminism, 233–35
feng shui, 194
Fey, Tina, 260, 261
figure 8 (infinity symbol; lemniscate), 29, 194, 195, 287, 289, 321
FILTER magazine, 244
Finch, Annie, 179
Fini, Leonor, 23
fire, 58–59, 197
   as cleansing method, 50–51
   magic circle and, 58, 61
500 Hats of Bartholomew Cubbins, The (Seuss), 83

INDEX

Flame of Peace, The (Tange), 208
flashlight vision, 35
flaws, 239, 241
forest bathing, 56
Forest of Symbols, The (Turner), 62–63
Fortune, Dion, 16
Foucher, Adèle, 80
Fragoso, Sam, 112
Frankenstein (Shelley), 236
Franklin, Benjamin, 79–80
Franklin, Rosalind, 269
Frazer, James George, 200
free association, 119
Freeman, Matthew (husband of author), 209–10, 226, 234, 313
Freemasons, 19–20, 25–26, 197
Fresh Air, 60, 240
Freud, Sigmund, 121, 151
Freya, 201
Frías, Edgar Fabián, 292
Frith, Michael, 83
Fuller, Buckminster, 134
fumage, 125
Funniest One in the Room, The (Johnson), 263
FYMA, 189

Gabriel, 59
Gao Yuan, 173–74
García Lorca, Federico, 68
Gardner, Gerald, 16, 25, 26, 79, 262
Gathering of Utopian Benches, A (Cape), 210
Geiger, John, 140
Geisel, Theodor, 83
gematria, 186, 194
gender, 90–93
Genesis, 36, 96, 184
genius, 267
Gentle Art of Swedish Death Cleaning, The (Magnusson), 47
geometry, 196–99
Ghost, 109–10
Giardino dei Tarocchi, Il, 127–28
Gibran, Kahlil, 292
gifts, 253–55
    of collaboration, 266–70
    of devotion, 293–97
    of divine timing, 271–75
    of eternity, 287–92, 303
    of handcraft, 282–86

    of place, 276–81
    of play, 257–65
Gilbert, Elizabeth, 235–36
Gilbert & George, 269
Ginsberg, Allen, 137, 182, 282
glamour magic, 205
Glass Beams, 86
Glazer, Ilana, 269
glossolalia, 111
glyphs, 166, 190–91, 204
God, Goddess, 14, 32, 36, 197, 314
gods, deities, 14, 113, 219
    apotheosis and, 32, 87
    triple, 292
    see also Greek mythology; Roman mythology
Goethe, Johann Wolfgang von, 197
Golden Bough, The (Frazer), 200
Golden Dawn, 20, 120, 126–27, 202
golden ratio, 196
Gorey, Edward, 94–95
Graham, Martha, 249
grammar, 178, 205
Granderson Lewis, Mari, 133–34
gratitude, 315–16, 320
Graves, Robert, 112
Greater Key of Solomon, 188–90
Greece, 185
Greece, ancient, 159, 185, 189
    dance in, 166
    drama in, 36, 86
    mantis role in, 123
    Oracle of Delphi in, 110
    pentagram in, 196–97
    Sanctuary of Asclepius in, 151–52
    temenos in, 73
Greek Magical Papyri, 185
Greek mythology, 283, 292
    Apollo, 36, 110
    Artemis, 4, 35–36, 71, 83, 148, 185, 219, 254, 317
    Chiron, 282
    Dionysus, 36, 86, 313
    Hermes, 32, 70–71
    Hygeia, 196–97
    Iris, 71–72
    muses, 67
grief, 321
grimoires, 178, 186, 189, 195, 205, 218, 254
Key of Solomon, 188–90

INDEX

Grimoires (Davies), 188
Gross, Terry, 60, 240
grounding, 55
groups
    collective belief, 205
    collective effervescence, 166
    group mind, 267–68
Guadagnino, Luca, 169
GuRu (RuPaul), 92–93
Gustav Holst (Holst), 171–72
Gysin, Brion, 18, 139–40, 268

Haitian Vodou, 111, 117
Hale, Amy, 205–6
Hale, Barry William, 191
Halloween, 86, 113
Halpern, Charna, 260–62, 267–68
hamsa, 283
handcraft, 282–86
hands, 142–43, 282–84
    healing and, 283
    writing and, 285
Hanged Man, 187
Harahel, 133
Harris, Lady Frieda, 20
Harrison, George, 269
Harvey, PJ, 3, 244
hats, 80–83
H.D., xx, 290
healing
    hands and, 283
    music and, 173–74
Hebrew, 59, 186–87, 189, 194
Hecate, 206, 316
Heinrich von Ofterdingen (Novalis), 36
help, asking for, 67–69
Henson, Jim, 258–59
Heraclitus, 35
herbs, 51, 52
Herman, Pee-wee, 89
Hermaphrodite, The (Khunrath), 31
Hermes, 32, 70–71
Hermetic Order of the Golden Dawn, 20, 120, 126–27, 202
Herms, George, 297
Herochiel, 133
Hero with a Thousand Faces, The (Campbell), 253–54
Hesseman, Howard, 263
hexes, 160

hieroglyphics, 187
Hildegard von Bingen, 15
Hill, Napoleon, 268–69, 314
Hilma's Ghost, 269
Hinduism, 15, 75, 113, 170, 194, 272, 292
Hiroshima Peace Memorial Park, 208
Hirshkowitz, Lois, 291
holidays
    Beltane, 50
    Halloween, 86, 113
    New Year, 272
    sabbats, 272–73
    Samhain, 113–14, 272
Holland, Jolie, 236–37
Hollywood Reporter, 169
Holst, Gustav, 170–72
Holst, Imogen, 171–72
home, 280–81
    cleaning of, 47–48, 52
Hoodoo, 118
hooks, bell, 325
Horowitz, Mitch, 316
Houghton, Georgiana, 20, 115
How to Read a Poem . . . and Start a Poetry Circle (Peacock), 163–64
How To with John Wilson, 146
Hughes, Ted, 116–17
Hugo, Victor, 80
Hunchback of Notre-Dame, The (Hugo), 80
Hyde-Lees, Georgie "George," 120
Hygeia, 196–97

I and Thou (Buber), 69, 262
icaros, 175
I Ching, 136–38, 140, 142
Ideal Suggestions (Saterstrom), 152
I Have Nothing to Say and I Am Saying It, 138
Illes, Judika, 275
imagery, 125, 191
imagination, 325–26
immersion, 52–54
imposter syndrome, 222
improvisation, 260–62, 268
ImprovOlympic (iO), 260, 262
incantation, 179
incantation bowls, 218, 224
incense, 51
Indigenous peoples, 51, 96, 166, 174, 278, 280
inertia, 228–31, 286
Infamous, 236

INDEX

infinity symbol (figure 8; lemniscate), 29, 194, 195, 287, 289, 321
inspiration, 49, 101–2, 104, 108, 210, 214, 236, 302
   muses and, 67, 68
Inspirations, 214
intentions, 159–64, 302
interconnection, 303
intuition, 206
invocation, and vocalization, 69, 185
invocation/altar-cation, 67–73
Iris, 71–72
Isis, 95–96
Islam, 197

Jackson, David, 117
Jacobson, Abbi, 269
Janus, 292
Japanese culture, 53, 113
   kagura, 86–87
   shinrin-yoku, 56
   Shinto, 48, 87, 280
   wabi-sabi, 238–39
Jay-Z, 87, 192–93
Jericho, Chris, 85
Jerusalem (Butterworth), 167
Jerusalem (Moore), 279
Jess, 280–81, 297
Jesus, 143
jewelry, 83, 254
Jewish traditions, 53–54, 59, 166, 189, 190, 290
   Abramelin oil, 74
   calendar in, 272
   ceromancy, 124–25
   demons in, 217–18
   gematria, 186, 194
   Judenhut, 81
   Kabbalah, 30, 133, 186, 201
   names in, 95
   Talmud, 95, 218
   Torah, 95, 186
   Yizkor, 113
Jobs, Steve, 77, 78
Johnson, Kim "Howard," 262, 263, 267–68
Jones, Suranne, 150–51
Jordan, June, 183–84
Jordan, Michael, 269
Juana Inés de la Cruz (Sor Juana), 291

Judge, William Quan, 21
judgment, 246–50, 292
Juhl, Jerry, 258–59
Jump, The (podcast), 223
Jung, Carl, 73
Jupiter, 312
Just Kids (Smith), 207–8

ka, 15
Kabbalah, 30, 133, 186, 201
Kafka, Franz, 281
kagura, 86–87
Kahl, Matilda, 77, 78
kami, 48, 280
Kandinsky, Wassily, 22, 181
Karcher, Stephen, 136
Katya, 224
Kekulé, August, 151
Kelley, Edward, 207
Kelly, Aidan, 272
Kelly, Ellsworth, 72
Kerouac, Jack, 277
Kevin & Bean Show, The, 278
Key of Solomon, 188–90
Khan, Natasha, 129
Khayyam, Omar, 292
Khunrath, Heinrich, 31
Kiesel, William, 254
Kimmerer, Robin Wall, 9
King, Stephen, 94
Kinniburgh, M. C., 183
Kleon, Austin, 35, 267
Knife, the, 86
Kobrin, Ed, 138
Kofsky, Frank, 162
Kondo, Marie, 47, 48
Krans, Kim, 129
Kunz, Emma, 198–99

Lady Gaga, 91–92, 184
Laffoley, Paul, 191
language, 177, 181, 184, 205
   letters, 97, 186–88, 190–91, 195
   poetry, 178–84
   words, 178–85
Language of Birds, The (Pendell), 123–24
Language of the Birds: Occult and Art (exhibition), xxii, 244–45
lapis lazuli, 84
Laraaji, 173

344

INDEX

Lasky, Dorothea, 101
laughter, 259
Leadbeater, C. W., 22, 75
Leary, Timothy, 40
left-handedness, 142–43
Left-Hand Path, 143
Le Guin, Ursula K., 95, 325
Leikeli47, 86
Leland, Charles Godfrey, 79
Leland, Kurt, 75
lemniscate (infinity symbol; figure 8), 29, 194, 195, 287, 289, 321
Lennon, John, 269
Leno, Jay, 193
Leo, Alan, 171
Lesser, Kohenet Ketzirah 'haMa'agelet', 129, 191
Lesser Key of Solomon, 188–90, 218
letters, 97, 186–88, 190–91, 195
Lévi, Éliphas, 16, 30–31, 126
Lewis, Juliette, 223
Liber 777 (Crowley), 202
Lieberman, Rachel, 129
Life, 176
Life-Changing Magic of Tidying Up, The (Kondo), 47
Lilith, 95, 189–91, 217–18
Lima, Darcílio, 191
liminality, 63
limpia con huevo, 124
Lin, Maya, 208
Lincoln, Abraham and Mary Todd, 115
Listening to the Golden Boomerang Return (Conrad), 114
LitHub, 249
Lorde, Audre, 183
Louis, Morris, xix–xx
love, 58, 65
  spells for, 201
lucha libre (Mexican wrestling), 85, 98
Lunar New Year, 272
lunar phases, 274–75
lwa, 111, 188
Lykanthea, 65–66
Lynch, David, 64–65, 244, 259

Ma, Yo-Yo, 240–41
Macbeth (Shakespeare), 180
Machen, Arthur, 20

magic, xv–xxv, 3–4, 5–13
  art and, 17–18
  Breton on, 121
  creativity and, 17
  defining, 14–18
  derivation of word, 15–16
  negative, 143
  spelling of word, 15
  stage, 15
Magic (Butler), 16
Magical Universe of William S. Burroughs, The (Stevens), 140
"Magic and the Arts" (Seligmann), 37
magic circles, 57, 70, 73, 168, 188, 204, 219, 261–62, 317
  opening, 319–21
Magician, 28–37, 39, 63, 213–14, 301
  binary pairs and, 33–34
  lemniscate over head of, 29, 194, 195, 287
  pose of, 32–33, 66, 103, 155, 157, 283, 301
Magician Mode, 43–46, 57, 98, 108, 163, 302
  adornment and, 78
  music and, 65
  personas and, 87–90, 93
Magick in Theory and Practice (Crowley), 16, 21, 202
magic squares, 194–95, 312
Magic Words (Conley), 184–85
Magloire, Marina, 118
Magnetic Fields, The (Breton and Soupault), 120
Magnusson, Margareta, 47
Magritte, René, 23
makeup, 78, 86, 204–5
Making Light of It (Broughton), xx, 248
mandalas, 198
Man in the High Castle, The (Dick), 137
mano cornuta, 283
Man Ray, 91
Manson, Shirley, 223
mantis, 123
mantras, 181, 182
manu fica, 283
Mapplethorpe, Robert, 207–8
Mara, 220
markings, 186–91
Maron, Marc, 146
Martin, Agnes, 198
MaryLand, 150–51
masks, 85–87, 93, 98

INDEX

Masons, 19–20, 25–26, 197
Master Mind, 268–69
materialist worldview, 7
Mather, Cotton, 124
Mathers, Samuel Liddell MacGregor, 74, 202, 218–19
Mavis on 4, 11
māyā, 93
McCartney, Paul, 76, 150, 269
McClennen, Sophia A., 264
McLaren, Malcolm, 267
meditation, 63–65, 198
    Transcendental Meditation, 64–65, 244
Meditations on the Tarot (1980), 17
mediums, 107, 109, 116, 120
Meek, Buck, 236–37
melancholy, 195–96
mental health issues, 111
Mercury (god), 32, 70–71, 201, 316
Mercury (planet), 274
meridian points, 75
Merrill, James, 117–18
Mesa-Bains, Amalia, 291
metal, 59, 197
Mexican wrestling, 85, 98
Michael, 59
Midsummer Night's Dream, A (Shakespeare), 180
Mike Birbiglia's Working It Out (podcast), 229, 262
mikvah, 53–54
Minutes to Go (Burroughs et al.), 139
Mirror of Magic, The (Seligmann), 37
mistakes, 259
Miyazaki, Hayao, 103
Monáe, Janelle, 88
Mondrian, Piet, 22, 197–98
Monroe, Marilyn, 89
Monsoon, Jinkx, 92, 93, 316
monuments, public, 208
Mooallem, Jon, 230
moon, 274–75
Moore, Alan, 18, 160, 279–80, 296–97
Moore, Justin Patrick, 133
Morning Edition, 208
Morrison, Simon, 173
Morrison, Toni, 11
Morrison, Van, 292
Morrissey, 116

Moses, 74
Moss-Bachrach, Ebon, 112
MotherWitch Oracle, 129
movement, 230–31, 294
    dance, 86–87, 165–66, 169
Mumler, William H., 115
Munn, Henry, 177
Murakami, Haruki, 230
Muse, muses, 67, 68
Museum of Witchcraft and Magic, 27
museums, xix–xx
mushrooms, psychedelic, 174–77
music, 65–66, 168, 169–77, 179, 269
    of the spheres, 196
Myanmar, 264
Mysterio, Rey, 85, 98

nakedness, 79–80
namaste, 69
name-taking/shape-shifting, 85–98
Native Americans, 51, 96, 166, 278, 280
nature walks, 56
Neel, Alice, 206
NeverEnding Story, The (Ende), 96
Newman, Barnett, 23–24
Newman, Sandra, 98
Newton, Isaac, 9
New Year celebrations, 272
New Yorker magazine, 174, 240
New York Review of Books, 136
New York Times, The, 83, 230, 278, 290
New York University, xxii
Nichirin Buddhism, 181
Nicks, Stevie, 49–50
Nietzsche, Friedrich, 36
nine knot spell, 179–80
Noh theater, 87
non-duality, 63
Norse, 201, 292
Nosworthy, Helen Peters, 116
Nothing Is True Everything Is Permitted (Geiger), 140
Notre-Dame de Paris (Hugo), 80
Novalis, 36
nudism, 79–80
numbers, numerology, 97, 186, 188, 192–99
NW (Smith), 226–27

Obama, Barack, 77, 78
Oblique Strategies, 131

INDEX

O'Brien, Conan, 257
occult, xxii, 6, 7, 18, 19
    art and, 19–27
Occult Humanities Conference, xxii
Odin, 187
Olcott, Henry Steel, 21
Oliveros, Pauline, 173
Olson, Charles, 179
om, 181
On Alchemy (Cotnoir), 34
On Feeble Love and Bitter Love (Tzara), 139
On the Road (Kerouac), 277
oomancy, 124
Oppenheim, Méret, 23
opshprekherin, 124–25
Oracle of Delphi, 110
oracles, *see* divination
Ordo Templi Orientis (OTO), 20
orgone, 81
Orphic Hymns, The, 72
Oshun, 201
Ouija board, 115–18, 140

Paganism, 25, 50–51, 97, 166, 197, 261, 262, 272
    holidays in, 113–14, 272–73
pain, 242–45
Panties for Peace, 264
Parable of the Talents (Butler), 314
Paraiso, Virgo, 270
pareidolia, 11–12
Parris, Betty, 124
Parthenon, 197
Patchett, Ann, 235–36
Paz, Octavio, 137
Peacock, Molly, 163–64
Peck, Orville, 86
Péladan, Joséphin, 22
Pendell, Dale, 123–24
pentacles, 75, 188, 190, 191, 197
pentagrams, 59, 196–97, 284
Pentecostal Christians, 111
perfectionism, 238–41, 259, 286
Perlow, Tessa, 284
Perry, Lee "Scratch," 75–76
Persephone, 87
personas and alter egos, 87–90, 93, 98
Peterson, Cassandra, 89
peyote, 174–75
Pfeiffer, Ryan M., 269

phytoncides, 56
Picasso, Pablo, 206
pilgrimages, xx, 55, 276–78
Pippen, Scottie, 269
places, 276–81
    thin, 63
planets, 195, 196, 202–4
plants, 56
    entheogenic, 174–77
    herbs, 51, 52
Plasmic Image, The (Newman), 24
Plath, Otto, 117
Plath, Sylvia, 116–17, 243
play, 257–65
Poetic Edda, 187
poetry, 178–84
Pollack, Rachel, 15, 31, 127, 130
Pollock, Jackson, 23
Pop, Iggy, 140
Popovic, Srdja, 264
P-Orridge, Genesis Breyer, 141, 191
Portrait of a Lady on Fire (Sciamma), 167
potato battery, 33
Potter, Sarah, 130
prana, 15
Pranksters vs. Autocrats (Popovic and McClennen), 264
prayer, bedtime, 59
preparation, 43, 107–8
    anointment/adornment, 74–84
    circling/centering, 57–66
    cleansing/clearing, 47–56, 57
    invocation/altar-cation, 67–73
    shape-shifting/name-taking, 85–98
Primordial Sound Meditation, 64
Prince, 91
procrastination, 226, 231
Projective Verse (Olson), 179
Promethea (Moore and Williams), 297
Pronoia Is the Antidote for Paranoia (Brezsny), 253
protective guides, 59–60
pseudonyms, 94, 97
psilocybin, 174–75
psychedelic mushrooms, 174–77
psychogeography, 279–80
psychology, 121
psychopomp, 32
punk movement, 267
Puritans, 124

INDEX

Purple, 172
Pythagoras, 196

qi, 15
quantum physics, 12
quartz, 56
Quest, 172
Quintessence, 59

Ra, 95–96
Rainbow Body (Leland), 75
Raphael, 59
rationalism, 7–9, 12
Rav Huna, 217
Regino, Juan Gregorio, 177
Reich, Wilhelm, 81
Reid, Jaime, 267
release rituals, 302–3, 307
   request, 311–12
   respect, 315–16
   return, 319–21
   reveal, 317–18
   revel, 309–10
religion, 6–7, 9, 10, 21, 26
R.E.M., 230
Respighi, Ottorino, 296
respiration, 49
Reubens, Paul, 89
reverent irreverence, 258
rhyme, 179–81
rhythm, 166–68, 169, 179, 181
Richards, M. C., 63–65, 134, 135
Richman, Jonathan, 148
Rider-Waite-Smith tarot, 20, 28–30, 126–27
right-handedness, 142–43
Right-Hand Path, 143
rites of passage, 309–10
rituals, 174–77
Roberts, Nora, 94
Roberts, Ty, 140, 141
Rod of Asclepius, 151
Rodriguez, Tino, 270
Rogers, Matt, 269
Rohn, Jim, 314
Rolling Stone magazine, 259
Roman mythology, 146, 283
   Janus, 292
   Jupiter, 312

   Mercury, 32, 70–71, 201, 316
   Venus, 201
Rose, Ezra, 189, 191
Rosicrucians, 22
Rothenberg, Jerome, 177
Rothko, Mark, 23–25
Rotten, Johnny, 267
Rubin, Rick, 47
Rule of Agreement, 260
runes, 123, 142, 187
running, 230
RuPaul, 92–93, 222
RuPaul's Drag Race, 92, 224, 316

Saar, Betye, 144–45
Sabat Magazine, 128
Sabbatic Goat, 30–31
sabbats, 272–73
Sabina, María, 175–77, 181
sacrifice, 293
Saffron Revolution, 264
Sagan, Carl, 156
sage, 51
Saint Phalle, Niki de, 127–28
Sakugawa, Yumi, 219–20
Salem witch trials, 124
Salon de la Rose + Croix, 22
Samhain, 113–14, 272
Sanctuary of Asclepius, 151–52
Sand, George, 94
Santuario de Chimayo, 55
Saterstrom, Selah, 152
satire, 160
Saturday Night Live, 236, 257, 261
scarcity, 232–37, 271
scenius, 267
Schmidt, Peter, 130–31
Sciamma, Céline, 167
science, 7–10, 13, 18
   discoveries in, 151
Scorpio Rising, 145
Scriabin, Alexander, 173
Scriptnotes (podcast), 229
séances, 114, 115
seasons, 272–73
Second City, 260
Secret Dakini Oracle, 129
Seitzinger, Elisa, 128
Selassie, Haile, 76

INDEX

Self, 314
self-doubt, 222–24
Selig, Paul, 110
Seligmann, Kurt, xviii, 36–37, 121
Sendak, Maurice, 60
Serpent Power, The (Avalon), 75
Seuss, Dr., 83
Seven Strategies for Wealth and Happiness (Rohn), 314
sex, 50, 167
Sex Magic (Hale), 205–6
Sex Pistols, 267
Shakespeare, William, 180–81
shamans, 86–87, 175
Shams al-Ma'arif, 195
Shangri-La (music studio), 47
shape-shifting/name-taking, 85–98
Shekinah, 59, 224
Shelley, Mary, 236
Shepherd, Cybill, 315–16
sheydim, 217, 218
shinrin-yoku, 56
Shinto, 48, 87, 280
shoutput, 302
Sia, 86
Siddhartha, 31, 220
Siegel, Adam, 124–25
sigils, 188–91
signs, interpretation of (augury), 144–49, 277
Sill, Judee, 169–70
Silly Putty, 259
Silva, Frank, 259
Silver Spring (Freeman), 209–10
Sitney, P. Adams, 145
Slate, 263–64
Sleater-Kinney, 174
Slinger, Penny, 129
Slutist (blog), 232
Smith, Fred "Sonic," 207
Smith, Harry, 191, 285
Smith, Kiki, 3
Smith, Pamela Colman, 20, 28–30, 126–27
Smith, Patti, 207–8, 239–40, 267
Smith, Zadie, 226–27
smoke, 51
smudging, 51
snakes, 151–52
Snyder, Gary, 137
soap, 52

Sollée, Kristen J., 232–34, 237
Solomonic texts, 188–91, 218
Soloway, Joey, 315
soufflage, 125
sound baths, 173
Soupault, Philippe, 120
Source, 14, 295
Southwark Mysteries, The (Constable), 278
Spare, Austin Osman, 63, 190, 191
speaking in tongues, 111
SPELLLING, 127
spells, 155–57, 164
   energy in, 165–68
   hexes, 160
   intentions in, 159–64
   love, 201
   nine knot (witch's ladder), 179–80
   words in, 178–85
Spells (Finch), 179
Spicer, Jack, 102, 280
Spiral Dance, The (Starhawk), 35
Spirit, 14–15, 38, 43, 104, 113, 155, 165, 197, 213, 229, 231, 240, 253, 288, 289, 290, 294, 295, 303, 318, 321
   breath and, 49
   communicating with, 123, 131, 144, 152, 200
   giving thanks to, 315–16, 320
   judgment and, 247–50
   magic circle and, 58
   place and, 277
   play and, 257, 263
   release and, 302, 307, 310, 311–12
   trust and, 45
spirit photographers, 115
spirits, 48
   of deceased, *see* deceased
   local, 280
   requesting assistance from, 67–69
spiritual advisors, 113–18
Spiritualist movement, 20, 115, 116
spontaneity, 259
squares, magic, 194–95, 312
Starhawk, 35, 155
starlight vision, 35
Starr, Ringo, 269
stars, 156, 157, 161
Star Wars, 254
Steinbeck, John, 277
Steiner, Rudolf, 197–98

INDEX

Stevens, Matthew Levi, 140
Stevens, Wallace, 117
Stewart, Potter, 14
Stipe, Michael, 230
Stone, Moira, 285
Stonehenge, 58
Strayed, Cheryl, 277
stream-of-consciousness writing, 119–22
strife, 58
struggling artist cliché, xvii
Stucky, Janaka, xxii, 69, 132, 185
Studio 60 on the Sunset Strip, 236
submersion, 52–53
suffering, 242–45, 293
Sufi dervishes, 31–32
Sun, The, 116
Sun of Knowledge, The, 195
Sun Ra, 93
Surrealist Manifesto (Breton), 120–21
Surrealists, xviii, 5, 17, 22–23, 36–37, 89, 94, 120–21, 125, 128, 129, 270
Suspiria, 169
Suzuki, D. T., 138
Swedenborg, Emanuel, 120
Swift, Taylor, 193
Symbolists, 173
symbols, 188, 191
  correspondences and, 200–206
  sigils, 188–91
sympathetic magic, 200–206
synchronicity, 145–46
synthesis, 33

T magazine, 145
  Australia, 84
talismans, 83, 84, 254
  drawn or written, 187–88
  numbers as, 193, 194
Talk Easy (podcast), 112
Talmud, 95, 218
Tange, Kenzō, 208
Tantrism, 75, 166, 199
Taoism, 197
tarot, 23, 29, 30, 56, 60, 126–30, 140, 142
  Dalí, 37
  Dior and, 83–84
  Empress in, 128
  Hanged Man in, 187
  Magician in, *see* Magician

Rider-Waite-Smith, 20, 28–30, 126–27
Thoth, 20–21
Tarot Garden, The, 127–28
Tarot for Change (Dore), 16
Tarot of Perfection, The (Pollack), 130
tasseomancy, 123
Tea, Michelle, 130
tea leaves, 123
temenos, 73
Tempest, The (Shakespeare), 180
Terce (Christian), 167
Tetragrammaton, 95
Thalia, 67
theater, 86, 87
Theosophists, 21, 22, 75, 120, 170, 197
Think and Grow Rich (Hill), 268–69, 314
thin places, 63
Third Mind, The (Burroughs and Gysin), 139, 268
30 Rock, 236
Thoth tarot, 20–21
Thou, 69–70, 262
Thought-Forms (Besant and Leadbeater), 22
Three Books of Occult Philosophy (Agrippa), 195, 201
Tibetan monks, 181
time, 165, 287–88
  divine timing, 271–75
  eternity, 287–92, 303
Timeless Way of Building, The (Alexander), 107
Times, 244
Tin Can Forest, 230
Tlazoltéotl, 54–55
Tomberg, Valentin, 16
Tonight Show, The, 193
Torah, 95, 186
Total I Ching (Karcher), 136
trance states, 112
Transcendental Magic (Lévi), 16
Transcendental Meditation, 64–65, 244
Transparent, 315
travel, 277–78
Travels with Charley (Steinbeck), 277
trees, 56
Tricycle, 138
Truth in Comedy (Halpern, Close, and Johnson), 262, 267–68
Turner, Victor, 62–63
Twin Peaks, 259
Two-Headed Woman (Clifton), 118

INDEX

Tyler, Kathy, 128
Tzara, Tristan, 139

Unified Field, 65
uniforms, 77–78
Uriel, 59

Valiente, Doreen, 26–27, 179
Vancouver Sun, 76
van Gogh, Vincent, 242
Vanity Fair magazine, 68, 77
Varo, Remedios, xx, 3, 23, 36, 56, 94, 121, 291
Veal, Michael, 75–76
Vedic traditions, 59, 93, 170
Venus, 201
Venus Glass, 124
Verbasizer, 140, 141
Vertex, 137
Vietnam Veterans Memorial (Lin), 208
viriditas, 15
Virtue, Doreen, 194
Vision, A (Yeats), 120
Visionary Film (Sitney), 145
V Magazine, 92
vocalization, 69, 185
Vodou and Vodun, 111, 117, 188, 190
Voice of the Fire (Moore), 279
Void, 59

wabi-sabi, 238–39
Wachowski siblings, 269
Waite, A. E., 30, 126–27
Waking the Witch (Grossman), 53, 54, 148–49, 222–23, 235, 245, 312
Waldman, Anne, 177, 181–82
Wallis, Christopher D., 93
Walls Do Not Fall, The (H.D.), 290
Walz, Rebecca, 269
Wasson, R. Gordon and Valentina, 176
Waste Land, The (Eliot), 127
water, 58–59, 197
  as cleansing method, 51–54
  divination by wax in, 124–25
  magic circle and, 58, 61
Waters, John, 249
Watson, James, 269
wax in water, 124–25
"we are between worlds," 61–62
Weber, Max, 8

Weinberger, Eliot, 136
Weiner, Matthew, 130
Westcott, William Wynn, 202
Westwood, Vivienne, 267
What Is a Witch (Grossman and Tin Can Forest), 230
What I Talk About When I Talk About Running (Murakami), 230
Wheel of the Year, 272–73
Whitman, Walt, 98, 292
Wicca, 26, 25–27, 58, 79, 197, 202, 261, 262, 272
Wild (Strayed), 277
Wilhelm, Richard, 137
Willett, Cat, 285
Williams, Abigail, 124
Williams, J. H., III, 297
Williams, Robin, 243
Wilson, John, 145–46
Wind, 59
Winfrey, Oprah, 88
Wirth, Oswald, 30, 126
Witchcraft for Tomorrow (Valiente), 26–27
Witch Crafting (Curott), 50
Witchcraft Today (Gardner), 16, 26, 262
Witches, Sluts, Feminists (Sollée), 234
witches, witchcraft, 8, 25–27
  author and, xviii, 4, 5–6, 25, 43, 56, 155, 160, 168
  Beltane and, 50
  clothing and hats of, 78–81
  dancing and, 165–66
  Drawing Down the Moon ritual of, 32
  feminism and, 233–35
  Salem trials of, 124
witch's ladder spell, 179–80
Witch Wave, The (podcast), xxii, 16, 49, 66, 78, 92, 130, 134, 148–49, 150, 204–5, 270, 284
Wizard of Oz, The (film), 254
Wolfe, Chelsea, 78
Wonderful Wizard of Oz, The (Baum), 21–22
wood, 59, 197
words, 178–85
work, xvi, 8
Working It Out (podcast), 229, 262
World Literature Today, 279–80
World Tree, 187
wrestling, 85, 98
Wright, James, 259
writing, 187–88

351

INDEX

writing (*cont.*)
   automatic, 119–22
   by hand, 285
   see also language
WTF (podcast), 146
Wu Xing diagrams, 197
WWE, 85

Yang, Bowen, 269
Yeats, William Butler, 20, 117, 119–20, 292

"yes and," 260
Yggdrasil, 187
Yorke, Thom, 141, 169
Your Illustrated Guide to Becoming One with the Universe (Sakugawa), 219–20

Zakroff, Laura Tempest, 191
Zen Buddhism, 138, 198
Zürau Aphorisms (Kafka), 281

About the Author

Pam Grossman is a writer, curator, and teacher of magical practice and history. She is the host of *The Witch Wave* podcast and the author of *Waking the Witch: Reflections on Women, Magic, and Power* and *What Is A Witch*. She is also co-editor and co-author of the *WITCHCRAFT* volume of Taschen's Library of Esoterica series.

Pam's writing has appeared in numerous mediums, including *The New York Times*, *The Atlantic*, TIME.com, *Ms. Magazine*, *Electric Literature*, *Film Comment*, and various press publications. She has maintained *Phantasmaphile*, a blog that specializes in art with an esoteric or fantastical bent, since 2005.

Pam's workshops on spellcraft, creativity, and occult history have been attended by thousands of students around the world. She is a featured expert in such documentaries as *All of Them Witches* (AMC), *Suranne Jones: Investigating Witch Trials* (Channel 4), and *WITCH* (BBC). As a guest on myriad radio shows and podcasts, Pam has discussed the role of witchcraft and magic in contemporary life. She has also consulted for such brands as Charlotte Tilbury, House of Hackney, and Treadwell's Books, as well as for film and television.

Pam is a graduate of New York University, where she studied cultural anthropology, art history, and comparative religion. She divides her time between Brooklyn and the Western Catskills alongside her husband, the playwright Matthew Freeman, and their two feline familiars.

pamgrossman.com   **@phantasmaphile**

We hope you enjoyed this Hay House book. If you'd like to receive our online catalogue featuring additional information on Hay House books and products, please contact:

Hay House UK Ltd
1st Floor, Crawford Corner,
91–93 Baker Street, London W1U 6QQ
Tel: +44 (0)20 3927 7290; www.hayhouse.co.uk

Published in the United States of America by:
Hay House LLC
PO Box 5100, Carlsbad, CA 92018-5100
Tel: (760) 431-7695 or (800) 654-5126
www.hayhouse.com

Published in Australia by:
Hay House Australia Publishing Pty Ltd
18/36 Ralph St., Alexandria NSW 2015
Tel: +61 (02) 9669 4299
www.hayhouse.com.au

Published in India by:
Hay House Publishers (India) Pvt Ltd
Muskaan Complex, Plot No. 3,
B-2, Vasant Kunj, New Delhi 110 070
Tel: +91 11 41761620
www.hayhouse.co.in

Let Your Soul Grow

Experience life-changing transformation – one video at a time – with guidance from the world's leading experts.

www.healyourlifeplus.com

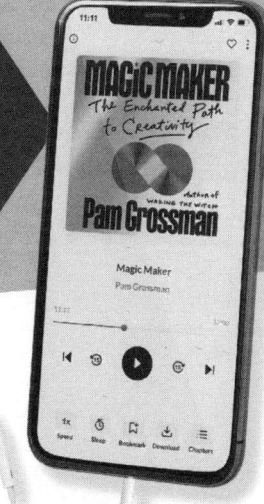

CONNECT WITH
HAY HOUSE
ONLINE

🌐 hayhouse.co.uk   @hayhouse

 @hayhouseuk   @hayhouseuk.bsky.social

 @hayhouseuk   @HayHousePresents

Find out all about our latest books & card decks • Be the first to know about exclusive discounts • Interact with our authors in live broadcasts • Celebrate the cycle of the seasons with us • Watch free videos from your favourite authors • Connect with like-minded souls

'The gateways to wisdom and knowledge are always open.'

Louise Hay